Living Under The Patriot Act: Educating A Society

Paul A. Ibbetson

Bloomington, IN  Milton Keynes, UK

AuthorHouse™
1663 Liberty Drive, Suite 200
Bloomington, IN 47403
www.authorhouse.com
Phone: 1-800-839-8640

AuthorHouse™ UK Ltd.
500 Avebury Boulevard
Central Milton Keynes, MK9 2BE
www.authorhouse.co.uk
Phone: 08001974150

This book is a work of non-fiction. Unless otherwise noted, the author and the publisher make no explicit guarantees as to the accuracy of the information contained in this book and in some cases, names of people and places have been altered to protect their privacy.

© 2007 Paul A. Ibbetson. All rights reserved.

No part of this book may be reproduced, stored in a retrieval system, or transmitted by any means without the written permission of the author.

First published by AuthorHouse 3/9/2007

ISBN: 978-1-4259-8391-8 (sc)

Library of Congress Control Number: 2006911204

Printed in the United States of America
Bloomington, Indiana

This book is printed on acid-free paper.

Table of Contents

Acknowledgments		vii
Part I	The Patriot Act	1
Chapter 1	Why Study the Patriot Act?	3
Chapter 2	Understanding the Challenge	7
Chapter 3	The Patriot Act: One Piece at a Time	14
Chapter 4	The Quiet Giants	36
Chapter 5	Giving Perspective on Detention Issues	55
Chapter 6	Support for the Patriot Act	75
Chapter 7	Opposition to the Patriot Act	91
Chapter 8	Evaluating History	107
Chapter 9	What Writers Write: A Content Analysis	123
Chapter 10	A Sociological Perspective of the Patriot Act	146
Chapter 11	Polling the Patriot Act	159
Part II	The Road to Patriot Act II	177
Chapter 12	The Little Law That Wasn't	179
Chapter 13	Viewing the Political Landscape	187
Chapter 14	The House of Representatives	199
Chapter 15	The Senate	211
Chapter 16	The Creation of the "Coalition of Opposition"	218
Chapter 17	The Second Extension of the Patriot Act	240
Chapter 18	The Renewal of the Patriot Act	250
Chapter 19	Conclusion	268
Bibliography		271
Index		315

ACKNOWLEDGMENTS

WHEN REFLECTING ON THE GROUP effort that went into making this book possible, there is no way to adequately acknowledge everyone who had some input during the long but rewarding process of bringing the knowledge of the Patriot Act to the public. However, while it will inevitably be incomplete, it is my honor to say thanks to those who are foremost in my mind. I would like to thank my editor, friend, and often source of support, Janice Stong. This book, as well as so many other Patriot Act projects, would not have reached the high level of quality without your help. I am intellectually indebted to Alison Brown J.D. for several months of group reflection on the Patriot Act. I think that period of study forced me to look at this legislation from more angles than I would have on my own. Dr. Michael Birzer, thank you for so many collaborations on Patriot Act projects. It has been a pleasure working with you. Dr. Michael Palmiotto, thank you for taking the time to give your mentorship, I will never forget it. Special thanks go to my mom and dad who have been a source of support my whole life; I have been truly blessed to be your child. Finally, I would like to say thank you to my wife and love of my life, Naynie. Thank you for all the hours you let me spend with my face in a book or behind a computer screen. We did it!

Part I

The Patriot Act

CHAPTER 1

Why Study the Patriot Act?

YOU MAY BE ASKING YOURSELF how one law could possibly warrant so much attention, let alone the construction of a comprehensive book. First, let it be said that this book is more like a manual. A how-to manual if you will. How to what? You may find some other how-tos before you reach the back cover, but the bottom line is that this book covers how to understand the process to bring a law to reality. More specifically, you will come to understand the unique environment in the country bringing about the Patriot Act's birth. You will learn how to look critically at many of the most controversial sections of the Patriot Act, utilizing simplistic but comprehensive section descriptions. In a departure from most Patriot Act literature, you will receive unique perspectives on important sections that have not garnered media attention. These unique perspectives will make you more rounded in your Patriot Act knowledge and better able to think out of the box, something that has been lacking in the country prior to this book.

There are many challenges to learning about the Patriot Act. To avoid adding yet another challenge, this book is put together in a simple learner-friendly manner. The book has two major parts. Chapters 1 and 2 are set up to give readers a background on some of the challenges to Patriot Act research, and also answer some of the questions that frustrated researchers often ask themselves when trying to learn this law. Chapters 3 through 11 cover a myriad of topics ranging from section descriptions to unique analysis on many aspects of the Patriot Act. Chapters 3 through 11 also look at the Patriot Act before the renewal period, with Chapters 6 and 7 covering many of the specific arguments, both in support and opposition, to the law. Chapters 6 and 7 also prepare readers for many of the arguments that would make the renewal period of the Patriot Act as exciting and unpredictable as any cinematic motion picture. Chapters 12 through 19 represent Part II of the book and focus on the renewal of the Patriot Act. Through these chapters, readers will get to know many of the major politicians, individuals, and events that shaped the renewal period.

While all this information should be helpful to understand what's in this book, the question still stands: Why study the Patriot Act? The answer to this question will vary to some degree depending on whether you are an academic, a layperson, a serious researcher, or someone just hung up on one single aspect of the Patriot Act. It may also vary depending on whether you are looking for information to support or oppose the law. Regardless of your situation or motivation for turning the pages of this book, a vast reservoir of information awaits you.

What cannot be denied is that the Patriot Act is a landmark document. Simply put, the Patriot Act is one of the most powerful laws of modern day and has powerful ramifications for the future. The Patriot Act DOES affect you, whether you are a U.S. citizen or just a visitor in the country. The ramifications of the Patriot Act may be farther reaching than any modern legislation to date. These ramifications include important issues like civil liberties, the war on terror, and issues that will affect you and your children.

One of the problems with most of the mainstream outlets for news is that they offer a limited amount of information. Specifically, most news organizations only give the viewer a snapshot, that is, a single limited picture of a topic. The response of most viewers who become interested in a news item is to watch enough limited segments from differing news sources in the hopes of receiving a full and comprehensive understanding of the subject. That rarely happens. Why? First, news is composed of reports taken from individuals, groups, or entities who have beliefs and ideals that are specific to themselves and rarely advance all possible sides of the issue. Secondly, most media outlets tend to cover the same information. Thirdly, it is important to note that media outlets, just like people on the street, have their own biases and beliefs that may hinder the dissemination of truly educational information to the public. Is it being forwarded that the news is not a viable form of information? No, not at all. News, by its own construction, is a limited form of information and should not be the only source utilized by inquisitive people to get answers to important questions. It would be intellectually dishonest to say that the author's views will not inevitably encroach into some aspects of the information presented in this book. What is promised is that this important factor is recognized at the onset of this project, and that all possible actions were taken to give you, the reader, unbiased information.

The Internet, historically speaking, is a relatively new tool that is often used to answer questions. Without a doubt the Internet has revolutionized the speed and depth in which information can be collected. There is a plethora of information that can be collected on the Patriot Act from the Internet, and it is recommended that a person utilize the various Internet search engines for research. The Internet has one distinct advantage over news services alone in that the researcher can type in "keywords" that will more closely direct them to the specific answers they seek about the Patriot Act. This can be accomplished because the Internet contains information beyond the cloned current "hot topic" reports covered by the news services. These sources of information include, but are not limited to, congressional hearings, white papers, political speeches, scholarly journals, civil liberty Web sites, among others. The years of research that were undertaken to complete this book included, among other things, many hours perusing the Internet. During the extensive Internet review conducted for this book, over 300 Web sites were visited. Compared to the literal plethora of cites that were visited, only a precious few were used for the book. It would be only fair to give a word of warning about the Internet at this point. As the Internet can be a valuable source for information, it can also lead you to a lot of junk. What is junk? Junk is un-sourced, unsubstantiated, or flat out crazy information that is too often displayed as the truth by individuals and organizations. What *Living Under the Patriot Act: Educating a Society* has done is to painstakingly traverse hundreds of potential landmines that are contained on the Internet, and withdraw factual information that can be directly linked back to credible sources.

In separating yourself from the ignorant masses you may be wondering the value of having a full copy of the Patriot Act text. The full text of the Patriot Act, which is over 300 pages in hard copy, may be of use in certain situations. However, the situations that come to mind pertain more to the seldom found need for a good paperweight or doorstop than actually assisting a person who wishes to win an argument or educate a friend. More than likely, if you were resourceful enough to buy this book, you have probably searched the Internet using keywords and retrieved a full-text copy of the Patriot Act. If you haven't done so, the Patriot Act in its entirety can be accessed at www.epic.com, as well as from many others Web sites.

Having viewed the Patriot Act for many long hours, it becomes clear why a book like this is necessary. Simply put, the Patriot Act is a complex, vague, confusing, monstrosity if studied by itself. Chapter 2 goes into far more detail analyzing why the Patriot Act studied alone scares and overwhelms most people but, for now, just accept it as the truth.

It may seem to many that to really understand something a person must reach for more than one source. However, to fully understand the Patriot Act, a person must concede to the fact that they must step beyond the mighty media machine and random Internet searches. This is a mountain that many are unable to climb. However, it can be done. Remember, all mountains are conquered one step at a time. Because the sole purpose of this book is to educate, and not advocate, supporters, detractors, and those generally confused about the Patriot Act will all come out winners. Congratulate yourself, you're climbing the mountain and progressing wonderfully.

CHAPTER 2

Understanding the Challenge

MOST PEOPLE HAVE A VERY limited knowledge, or worse, a completely false knowledge of the Patriot Act. Let's make sure we are all on the same page about knowledge and personal opinion. It is important to separate being uninformed from being informed and disagreeing with others. It is expected that readers will finish this book with very different opinions on whether we need a Patriot Act or not. The success of this book will be attained if readers leave with more knowledge than they had upon arrival. It's as simple as that.

As alluded to in the first chapter, many people rely solely on the media or haphazard Internet searches to educate themselves on this landmark piece of legislation. This chapter will address what happens to those who find the official Patriot Act text. This should be the Holy Grail for accurate information, right? That is, it would be reasonable to believe that after reading the sections of the Patriot Act, a person should know all the ins-and-outs of how the Patriot Act works. In short, the answer is it does not work that way. If you have a copy of the Patriot Act, maybe the one time it will be of use, even if only momentarily to verify the last statement. Not only does the Patriot Act not explain its function, the more you read the more confused and upset you will become.

The Patriot Act, or H.R. 3162, is a physically daunting document due to the enormous amount of pages that must be waded through by the interested researcher. Within the Patriot Act 350 subject areas are covered, which involve 40 different federal agencies (Collins, 2002). The Patriot Act consists of 156 separate sections under 10 titles (Kollar, 2004). Even if the

Patriot Act were constructed in a reader friendly format, it would be a literal "monster" of complexity. The true challenge for any reader is to accept that the Patriot Act is not a single coherent law (Kerr, 2003). The difficulty that many find in understanding exactly what the Patriot Act does is not solely due to the immense amount of reading required to cover the entire law. The problem in understanding what is happening in each section is often due to the fact that the Patriot Act, for the most part, is a large conglomeration of word and phrase changes from past laws. That is, previous laws have been selected, and by the use of word and phrase changes, omissions, and alterations, the laws have been greatly altered with only small changes actually being made to the specific law. The Patriot Act shows the changes that have been made to these prior laws. However, without being able to see how the word or phrase change fits into and affects the meaning of the original law, the changes themselves really don't offer much information by which to make any kind of determination.

Does this sound a little confusing? Welcome to Patriot Act research. Here is an example using one of the 16 most controversial pre-renewal sunset sections from Title II of the Patriot Act, Section 206. To create the greatest amount of illumination on Section 206 of the Patriot Act, a historic analysis must be conducted to explain the original law, the Foreign Intelligence Surveillance Act, from which Section 206 of the Patriot Act was adopted. This is something that is altogether absent if you read an official copy of the Patriot Act. Within this historical perspective, the substantial changes in regard to roving wiretaps will be made evident. A comprehensive evaluation of the proponents and dissenters to this section of legislation is provided to give a perspective of the current thinking on Section 206 by different groups. Section 206 was not selected as an example by chance. As readers will see as the Patriot Act story is unfolded, Section 206 will remain one of the more contentious sections through both the original legislation and the dynamic renewal period of this law. The current amount of government usage of Section 206 will be forwarded, along with a summary section, which will attempt to look at what the future will bring for this section of the Patriot Act.

> Section 206 of the Patriot Act states the following:
> Section 105(c)(2)(B) of the Foreign Intelligence Surveillance Act of 1978 (50 U.S.C. 1805(c)(2)(B)) is amended by inserting ", or in circumstances where the Court finds that the actions of the target of the application may

have the effect of thwarting the identification of a specified person, such other persons," after "specified person." (EPIC, 2001)

The enormity of the impact of this phrase addition to this section of law is vague, at best, because the Patriot Act does not give the context of the original law being modified. To understand what is going on a reader needs what? More information, right? Well the Patriot Act won't give that to you, but I will. Here is the background information on what is happening with Section 206 of the Patriot Act.

The Patriot Act addition is found within Title 50 - War and National Defense of the U.S. Code, at Chapter 36, titled Foreign Intelligence Surveillance, under Subchapter I - Electronic Surveillance. The body of text prior to the Patriot Act addition covers the issuing of ex parte orders by a judge for electronic surveillance. Within this section of the Foreign Intelligence Surveillance Act (FISA), the lineage of authority, and the stipulation requirements for the submission of electronic surveillance applications, are forwarded. A federal officer investigating, with probable cause to believe an individual is a foreign power or an agent of a foreign power, can forward an application for surveillance to the attorney general who has the authority to approve the order. The attorney general receives his or her power to approve the surveillance order by the President of the United States. Special attention is made that an individual of the United States cannot be considered a foreign power or agent based solely on activities protected by the First Amendment of the Constitution. Applications for surveillance must include the areas or facilities that are being used, or about to be used, by a foreign power or agent of a foreign power. The necessity for all applications to be thoroughly completed is stressed. The chapter includes information to explain the factors that a judge may take into account when considering whether probable cause exists in an electronic surveillance application. Further explanation is given that all approved electronic surveillance applications will specify the following: the identity of the subject, location where surveillance is to take place, type of information sought, activities subject to surveillance, how surveillance will be implemented, how long the surveillance will last, and how many surveillance devices will be used (Foreign Intelligence Surveillance Act, 1978).

At this juncture of the text, § 1805(c)(2)(B), during a description of the minimization procedures, Section 206 of the Patriot Act is inserted. The original section read as follows:

> (B) that, upon the request of the applicant, a specified communication or other common carrier, landlord, custodian, or other specified person furnish the applicant forthwith all information, facilities, or technical assistance necessary to accomplish the electronic surveillance in such a manner as will protect its secrecy and produce a minimum of interference with the services that such carrier, landlord, custodian, or other person is providing that target of electronic surveillance; (Foreign Intelligence Surveillance Act, 2005)

With a little background it is much easier to understand what subject matter was being dealt with in the original legislation. Now, let's look at how the addition of Section 206 of the Patriot Act alters the content and meaning of the original section. Notice the bold italicized print-representing Patriot Act wording as it is added to the original text. The adapted version reads as follows:

> (B) that, upon the request of the applicant, a specified communication or other common carrier, landlord, custodian, or other specified person, ***or in circumstances where the Court finds that the actions of the target of the application may have the effect of thwarting the identification of a specified person, such other persons*** [italics added], furnish the applicant forthwith all information, facilities, or technical assistance necessary to accomplish the electronic surveillance in such a manner as will protect its secrecy and produce a minimum of interference with the services that such carrier, landlord, custodian, or other person is providing that target of electronic surveillance; (Foreign Intelligence Surveillance Act, 2005)

This small addition has several implications. While there may be many views on how each word addition affects the entire chapter, a definite observance is made to a target's actions that may be articulated as attempting to thwart the identification of that person. If it is proven that a target regularly changes his communications methods, possibly thwarting the investigation, Section 206 allows for surveillance wiretaps of multiple means of communications. The authorities do not have to prove that the target is actually using a specific means of communications before initiating the wiretap (Gross, 2004; Lyden, 2003). Potentially, this may allow situations where innocent individuals are monitored (Gross, 2004).

In his article, "The USA PATRIOT Act: A New Way of Thinking, an Old Way of Reacting, Higher Education Responds," David Lombard Harrison (2004) speaks to the purpose of Section 206 by saying, "This section is an attempt to thwart the use of disposable cell phones, changing e-mail accounts, and the use of multiple phone locations" (p. 195). Jennifer M. Hannigan (2004) talks specifically to this expansion of surveillance authority by the government in her article entitled, "Playing Patriot Games: National Security Challenges Civil Liberties," when she suggests that,

> The Fourth Amendment of the Constitution protects Americans from unreasonable searches and seizures. However, several provisions of the Patriot Act authorize federal law enforcement to skirt the line of reasonableness. For example, section 206 of the Patriot Act 'amends FISA and eases restrictions involving domestic intelligence gathering by allowing a single wiretap to legally "roam" from device to device, to tap the person rather than the phone.' (p. 1382)

While it is known that under Section 206 there may be multiple wiretaps crossing the country under one warrant (Becker, 2003; Kendrick, 2004; Sekhon, 2003; Thomas, 2003), there is a growing concern over specific locations that this wiretap authority may attach itself. Susan Nevelow Mart (2004) speaks about this in her article, "Protecting the Lady from Toledo: Post-USA Patriot Act Electronic Surveillance at the Library." Speaking on issues related to the Patriot Act's expansions of government authority, Mart stated, "section 206 made this FISA wiretap a roving wiretap, to be attached to any computer a suspect uses, including a library computer" (p. 451). It is the expansion of the wiretap authority, with the lack of probable cause standards, which is the crux of the opponents' concern, not the wiretap procedure itself per se. As Lauri Thomas Lee (2003) explains in her article, "The USA Patriot Act and Telecommunications: Privacy Under Attack," she observes that "roving wiretaps are not new. In fact, since 1986, the ECPA has allowed law enforcement to follow a suspected criminal purposefully switching from one phone to another in an attempt to thwart a tap, without getting a new warrant" (pp. 396-397). Lee continues:

> Now, section 206 of the Patriot Act expands this authority to FISA court orders, extending the use of roving wiretaps from criminal investigations to terrorist probes and eliminating the probable cause requirement.
> Allowing roving wiretaps under FISA creates Fourth Amendment concerns and the potential for abuse. (p. 397)

This is just one example of how contentious the sections are within the Patriot Act. The huge impact of small alterations, combined with the extremely vague presentation of those changes within the Patriot Act, has to account for at least some of the mistrust and opposition to the Act. The vastness in the scope of the differing powers given to the government by the Patriot Act also accounts for why groups like the ACLU and the Gun Owners of America, each on obvious different sides of the spectrum, have at times taken issue with the law. These groups and their platforms for and against the Patriot Act will be analyzed later but, for now, just understand that the Patriot Act is simply a tough nut to crack. So buckle up, you're about to see the Patriot Act like never before.

References

Becker, S. W. (2003). "Mirror, mirror on the wall...": Assessing the aftermath of September 11th. *Valparaiso Law Review, 37*, 563-626.

Collins, J. M. (2002). And the walls came tumbling down: Sharing grand jury information with the intelligence community under the USA Patriot Act. *American Criminal Law Review, 39*, 1261-1286.

Electronic Privacy Information Center [EPIC]. (2001). *HR 3162 RDS: 107th Congress.* Retrieved September 25, 2004, from http://www.epic.org/privacy/terrorism/hr3162.html

Foreign Intelligence Surveillance Act of 1978, 50 U.S.C. § 1805 (1978).

Foreign Intelligence Surveillance Act of 1978, 50 U.S.C. § 1805 (2005).

Gross, E. (2004). The struggle of a democracy against terrorism—protection of human rights: The right to privacy versus the national interest—the proper balance. *Cornell International Law Journal, 37*, 27-93.

Hannigan, J. M. (2004). Playing patriot games: National security challenges civil liberties. *Houston Law Review, 41*, 1371-1406.

Harrison, D. L. (2004). The USA Patriot Act: A new way of thinking, an old way of reacting, higher education responds. *North Carolina Journal of Law & Technology, 5*, 177-211.

Kendrick, L. N. (2004). Alienable rights and unalienable wrongs: Fighting the "war on terror" through the Fourth Amendment. *Howard Law Journal, 47*, 989-1035.

Kerr, O. S. (2003). Internet surveillance law after the USA Patriot Act: The big brother that isn't. *Northwestern University Law Review, 97*, 707-673.

Kollar, J. F. (2004). USA Patriot Act, the Fourth Amendment, and paranoia: Can they read this while I'm typing? *Journal of High Technology Law, 3*, 67-93.

Lee, L. T. (2003). The USA Patriot Act and telecommunications: Privacy under attack. *Rutgers Computer and Technology Law Journal, 29*, 371-403.

Lyden, G. A. (2003). The International Money Laundering Abatement and Anti-terrorist Financing Act of 2001: Congress wears a blindfold while giving money laundering legislation a facelift. *Fordham Journal of Corporate & Financial Law, 8*, 201-243.

Mart, S. N. (2004). Protecting the lady from Toledo: Post-USA Patriot Act electronic surveillance at the library. *Law Library Journal, 96*, 449-473.

Sekhon, V. (2003). The civil rights of "others": Antiterrorism, the Patriot Act, and Arab and South Asian American rights in post-9/11 American society. *Texas Forum on Civil Liberties & Civil Rights, 8*, 117-148.

Thomas, P. A. (2003). Emergency and anti-terrorist power: 9/11: USA and UK. *Fordham International Law Journal, 26*, 1193-1229.

CHAPTER 3

The Patriot Act: One Piece at a Time

TO FULLY UNDERSTAND THE MYSTERIES of the Patriot Act a person needs to learn how the Patriot Act was born. The crux of many arguments that center around the Patriot Act are based on the belief that the Patriot Act is the result of a hasty rush to legislate following the terrorist attacks of 9-11.

Charles Doyle (2002), Senior Specialist for the American Law Division of the Congressional Research Service, documents the creational period of the Patriot Act in the Introduction of his report entitled, *The USA Patriot Act: A Legal Analysis*, by submitting:

> The Act originated as H.R.2975 (the PATRIOT Act) in the House and S.1510 in the Senate (the USA Act). S.1510 passed the Senate on October 11, 2001, 147 *Cong.Rec.* S10604 (daily ed.). The House Judiciary Committee reported out an amended version of H.R. 2975 on the same day, H.R.Rep.No. 107-236. The House passed H.R. 2975 the following day after substituting the text of H.R. 3108, 147 *Cong.Rec.* H6775-776 (daily ed. Oct. 12, 2001). The House-passed version incorporated most of the money laundering provisions found in the earlier House bill, H.R. 3004, many of which had counterparts in S.1510 as approved by the Senate. The House subsequently passed a clean bill, H.R. 3162 (under suspension of the rules), which resolved the differences between H.R. 2975 and S.1510, 147 *Cong.Rec.* H7224 (daily ed. Oct. 24, 2001). The Senate agreed, 147 *Cong.Rec.* S10969 (daily ed. Oct. 24, 2001), and H.R. 3162 was sent to the President who signed it on October 26, 2001. (p. CRS-1)

The terrorist attacks that took place on September 11, 2001, within the United States placed all government officials with legislative capabilities under a unique pressure to take legislative action. The need to respond in some form was seen as a general bipartisan agreement. The joint resolution denouncing the attacks on September 12, 2001, and the joint resolution authorizing the use of force on September 21, 2001, are examples of a general consensus that some form of unified response was justified (Howell, 2004). The fact that H.R. 2500 had been previously created, had been passed by the House of Representatives, and was currently before the Senate prior to the September 11, 2001, attacks was evidence that the topic of terrorism in general had been seen as a viable subject for debate and deliberation (Howell, 2004). While H.R. 2500 had 17 titles and addressed several terrorist related subjects, it was foreseeable that the specific events of the terrorist attacks of September 11, 2001, would create several special concerns that would need to be addressed by new legislation (Howell, 2004).

Chronology of Events that Lead to the Patriot Act

1. 09-11-01--Terrorist attack.

2. 09-12-01--First joint resolution condemning attacks.

3. 09-13-01--Proposed amendment to CJS appropriations bill (had 17 amendments, including Hatch-Feinstein amendment, passed the same day, known as H.R. 2500).

4. 09-14-01--2nd resolution passed authorizing military force.

5. 09-17-01--Attorney General John Ashcroft requests that the Congress pass the Administration's yet unfinished bill by the end of the week.

6. 09-19-01--Attorney general meets with both Houses and presents legislative proposal.

7. 09-19-01--Senator Leahy submits a 165-page draft entitled "Uniting & Strengthening America Act" (USA ACT).

8. 09-21-01--Senator Leahy gives update report (which praises the efforts of the president and attorney general).

9. 09-24-01--Attorney general gives 30 minute briefing before House Judiciary Committee and stresses urgency to pass legislation. (Democrats in House Judiciary voice complaints.)

10. 09-25-01--Attorney general testifies before Senate Judiciary Committee (for 2 hours) again stressing urgency for legislative action.

11. 09-25 or 09-26-01--Vice President Dick Cheney meets with Republican members of the Senate at Capitol and sets deadline for passage of anti-terrorism legislation for October 5, 2001.

12. 09-30-01--Attorney general publicly reinforces possible terrorist threats in the United States and applies pressure on Congress to act.

13. 09-30-01--Republican Senator Orrin Hatch publicly endorses Vice President Dick Cheney's legislative deadline.

14. 10-02-01--House Judicial Committee reaches agreement on language and introduces bill.

15. 10-02-01--Senate unable to produce its own bill yet.

16. 10-02-01--Attorney General publicly attacks Democrats for slowness to action in creating a Senate bill.

17. 10-03-01--Senator Feingold, among others, holds committee meetings on civil liberties issues involving surveillance powers.

18. 10-04-01--Senate bill S. 1510 introduced (contains 9 titles).

19. 10-08-01--Attorney general gives public updates on terrorist attack investigation (reinforces need for new legislation).

20. 10-09-01--USA ACT 2001 is bypassed through the normal procedures of a mark up committee to speed it through the Senate (with objections from Senator Feingold).

21. 10-10-01--Senate bill debated. Senator Russ Feingold has 4 government power limiting amendments that are tabled or put down to keep the bill going forward. Managers amendment added for technical corrections.

22. 10-10-01--Senate passed S. 1510 in the late evening.

23. 10-11-01--House of Representatives pass H.R. 2975.

24. 10-12-01--H.R. 3108 passed. Modeled liked the USA ACT with 5-year sunset provision (administration liked the Senate bill better with no sunset provisions).

25. 10-12-01--H.R. 2975 and H.R. 3108 are put together which had large pieces taken from S. 1510. Republican House leaders elect not to request a conference for merging S. 1510 and H.R. 2975/H.R. 3108.

26. 10-15-01--Anthrax scare to government facilities puts additional pressure on Senate.

27. 10-17-01--House of Representatives shuts down offices to test for anthrax

28. 10-17-01--Sunset provisions for surveillance were changed from 5 years to 4 years (negotiations continue).

29. 10-23-01--Negotiations end. Chairman of House Judiciary Committee urges that the bill be passed the next day.

30. 10-24-01-H.R. 3162 passes House 357 to 66 (this puts pressure on the Senate to pass bill).

31. 10-25-01--Senate passes H.R. 3162, 98 to 1 (Senator Russ Feingold is lone dissenter).

32. 10-26-01--President George W. Bush signs H.R. 3162, also known as the USA Patriot Act, into law (Howell, 2004).

When looking at the chronology of the events that led to enactment of the Patriot Act, it is important to remember that the Patriot Act was just one component of a myriad of events that were transpiring in the supercharged environment following the terrorist attacks. The following timeline will place the Patriot Act within the greater context of world events following 9-11.

Chronology of Events Surrounding Construction of the Patriot Act

1. 09-11-01--Terrorists strike America.

2. 09-11-01--Flag sales are reported by Wal-Mart to increase 1,800 percent; ammunition sales are reported to increase by 100 percent.

3. 09-12-01--President Bush delivers national address.

4. 09-14-01--Televisions around the world document President Bush's visit to ground zero in New York.

5. 09-17-01--President Bush announces that the U.S. will be fighting a "new kind of evil."

6. 09-20-01--Cabinet-level position of Homeland Security created.

7. 09-20-01--A non-congressional declaration of war on terrorism is declared by President Bush.

8. 09-21-01--Congress attempts to assist the U.S. airline industry with a $15 billion in federal aid.

9. 09-21-01--Hollywood celebrities raise money for victims of 9/11 by sponsoring *America: A Tribute to Heroes* fundraiser.

10. 09-27-01--National Guard is allocated for airport security.

11. 09-27-01--The first information on the terrorist hijackers is released to the public.

12. 10-05-01--The first of several anthrax deaths is reported.

13. 10-07-01--Air assault by U.S. coalition forces begins in Afghanistan.

14. 10-13-01--Anthrax scare receives full national coverage.

15. 10-19-01--Ground combat begins in Afghanistan.

16. 10-26-01--Patriot Act is passed into law.

17. 10-28-01--The first implementation of the Patriot Act begins.

18. 10-30-01--FBI alerts citizens that new terrorist attacks are possible.

19. 11-07-01--Afghanistan war hits one month mark.

20. 11-28-01--American forces in Afghanistan suffer first casualty.

21. 12-08-01--Ground war in Afghanistan draws to a close (Denzin & Lincoln, 2003).

Basic Structure of the Patriot Act

Title I - Enhancing Domestic Security Against Terrorism
- Counterterrorism fund
- Condemns discrimination against Arabs & Muslims
- Increased funding to Technical Support
- Expansion of National Electronic Crime Task Force
- Explanations of Presidential Authority

Title II - Enhanced Surveillance Procedures
- Authority to intercept wire, oral, and electronic communications
- Inter-agency information sharing
- Employment of language translators
- Roving surveillance
- Voice-mail seizures
- Scope of subpoenas for records
- Delayed notice of search warrants
- Pen register traps
- Access of records & items under FISA

Title III - International Money Laundering Abatement Anti-Terrorist Financing Act of 2001
- Four year congressional review
- Cooperative effort to deter money laundering
- Anti-terrorist forfeiture protection
- Long-arm jurisdiction over foreign money launderers, money laundering and foreign banks
- Reporting of suspicious activities
- Anti-money laundering strategy
- Civil and criminal penalties

Title IV - Protecting the Border
- Personnel on the northern border
- Authority to pay overtime
- Definitions related to terrorism
- Mandatory detention of suspected terrorists
- Foreign student monitoring
- Special immigration status
- No benefits to terrorists' family members
- Machine readable passports

Title V - Removing Obstacles to Investigating Terrorism
- Attorney general's ability to pay rewards
- DNA identification of terrorists
- Extension of secret service jurisdiction
- Disclosure of educational records
- NCES surveys

Title VI - Providing For Victims of Terrorism, Public Safety Officers, and Their Families
- Payments for public safety officers
- Public safety officer benefit program
- Crime victim fund
- Crime victim compensation
- Crime victim assistance

Title VII - Increased Information Sharing for Critical Infrastructure Protection
- Expansion of regional information sharing system to facilitate Federal-State-Local law enforcement response to terrorist related attacks

Title VIII - Strengthening the Criminal Laws Against Terrorism
- Terrorist attacks against mass transit systems
- Definition of domestic terrorism
- Prohibition against harboring terrorists
- Assets of terrorists organizations
- Revisions to international definition of terrorism

Title IX - Improved Intelligence
- Responsibilities of the Director of the Central Intelligence Agency
- International terrorist activities under FISA Act of 1947
- Sense of Congress on the establishment of intelligence relationships to acquire information on terrorists

Title X Miscellaneous
- Sense of Congress to condemning acts of violence or discrimination against any American First Responders Assistance Act
- Creates amendments to Crimes Against Charitable Americans Act of 2001

The Most Prominent Sections of the Patriot Act

The following sections of the Patriot Act are considered by many to be some of the more prominent sections. They include, but are not limited to, the following:

Section 101 creates a new counterterrorism fund. This fund has no fiscal year limitations, the amount of money to be placed in this fund is unnamed, and the fund is to be operated by the Justice Department (Foerstel, 2004).

Section 102 conveys the sense of congress that the civil rights and civil liberties of Americans, Muslin, Arab, and South Asian Americans not withstanding, should continue to be protected from violence and discrimination (Doyle, 2001).

Section 103 serves to assist in the restructuring of the Justice Department's Technical Support Center. This section allocates $200 million for the years 2002 through 2004 for technical support services (Foerstel, 2004).

Section 104 amends previous statutory exception, 18 U.S.C. 2332e to the Posse Comitatus Act and its administrative auxiliaries, 18 U.S.C. 1385, 10 U.S.C. 375, that allowed armed forces explicit temporary authority to give civilian agencies assistance during emergencies involving weapons of mass destruction. Prior to this section, the exception only included emergencies involving biological or nuclear weapons (Doyle, 2001).

Section 105 allows the Secret Service to construct a "national network of electronic crimes task force" across the United States to assist in preventing and investigating electronic related crimes (Doyle, 2001; Foerstel, 2004).

Section 106 changes provisions pertaining to the International Emergency Powers Act. This section gives the president the authority, in times of national armed conflict, to confiscate property of a foreign person, organization, or country that is believed to have planned, authorized, or aided in the hostilities (EPIC, 2001). It is important to note that the president also has similar confiscation powers under the same grounds in Section 806 (Doyle, 2001).

Section 201 adds several crimes to the list for which federal courts may authorize wiretapping of people's communications under federal statute 18 U.S.C. § 2516 (EPIC, 2001). These crimes include the following additions: chemical weapons offenses, 18 U.S.C. 229, crimes involving weapons of mass destruction, 18 U.S.C. 2332a, violent crimes that cross national borders, 18 U.S.C. 2332b, financial transactions with countries that have been designated as supporting terrorism, 18 U.S.C. 2332d, giving material support to terrorists, 18 U.S.C. 2332A, and giving material support to designated terrorist organizations, 18 U.S.C. 2339B (Doyle, 2001).

Section 202 deals with the authority to intercept wire, oral, and electronic communications relating to computer fraud and abuse offenses. This is an amendment of Section 2516(1)(c) which strikes the words "mail fraud," and adds the words "mail fraud, computer fraud and abuses" (EPIC, 2001).

Section 203 requires the sharing of intelligence information between federal agencies in cases involving national defense, national security, and foreign affairs. (Foerstel, 2004). Before the enactment of Section 203, federal law enforcement officers who uncovered information involving activities that included terrorist organizations could not forward the information to federal intelligence officers (Doyle, 2001).

Section 203b allows the FBI to disseminate wiretap information to other federal officials, including "law enforcement, intelligence, protective, immigration, national defense [and] national security" officials. To legally share the information, it must contain "foreign intelligence," "counterintelligence," or "foreign intelligence information," and its disclosure must be "appropriate to the proper performance of the official duties of the officer making or receiving the disclosure" (EPIC, 2001).

Section 203d allows for the disclosure of any foreign intelligence or counterintelligence information, no matter the means of collection, to other law enforcement branches unless this disclosure is in direct violation of existing law. This section also provides for disclosure of threat information obtained during criminal investigations to "appropriate" federal, state, local, or foreign government officials for the purpose of responding to the threat. Such information can include threat of attack, other "grave hostile acts," sabotage, terrorism, or clandestine intelligence gathering activities (EPIC, 2001).

Section 204 strikes limitations for the use of pen register and trap trace devices which capture "sender and recipient" addressing information. In short, the standard for collecting legal court directed orders for stored voice-mail communication has been lowered from the stringent wiretap orders to the less challenging search warrant (EPIC, 2001).

Section 205 reduces legal red tape in the hiring process of translators for the purpose of assisting the FBI in counterintelligence operations and investigations. Under this section the director of the FBI is responsible for all the necessary security requirements for such hires. The attorney general is responsible to report to the Committee on the Judiciary of the total numbers of new translators employed by the FBI and the Department of Justice (Doyle, 2001).

Section 206 deals with roving surveillance authority. This is an amendment of Section 105(c)(2)(B) of the Foreign Intelligence Surveillance Act of 1978 (FISA). This amendment allows authorities to petition the court in a jurisdiction for a surveillance warrant on multiple sources of communication. This can be done when it is articulated to, and accepted by the court that to do several warrant applications in different jurisdictions would hamper an investigation (EPIC, 2001). Section 206 amends FISA to allow for a general command for assistance from third parties, such as common carriers, custodians, and landlords, among others, in cases where the target of the application has or may have taken action that will have an effect of thwarting the investigation. An example of this would be the act of terrorists changing their location and modes of communication right before implementing a critical stage of an operation (Doyle, 2001).

Section 207 increases the time limit on FISA surveillance warrants from 90 to 120 days. This 120-day warrant extension is also extended to physical searches that had previously been limited to 45 days, (50 U.S.C. 1805(e), 1824(d) (2000 ed.). Under Section 207, FISA wiretap warrants and physical search warrants can stay in effect for up to 120 days. Extension periods have been extended from 90-day increments to one year increments (Doyle, 2001; EPIC, 2001; Foerstel, 2004).

Section 208 increases the number of FISA judges and the time limit on FISA warrants (Foerstel, 2004). Prior to this section, the FISA court consisted of 7 judges scattered through the country. Section 208 increases the FISA court to a total of 12 judges with 3 of those judges required to live no more than 20 miles from the District of Columbia, 50 U.S.C. 1803(a) (Doyle, 2001).

Section 209 addresses the seizure of voice-mail messages pursuant to warrants. This is an amendment of U.S.C. Title 18, specific to Section 2510, which adds the phrase "wire and electronic" to the warrant application that previously stated "electronic communications" only. This section eliminates the voice monitoring of vocal mail messages from the application of Title III and also lowers the standard that must be satisfied to monitor them (EPIC, 2001). For all intents and purposes voice mail is now treated the same as e-mail (Doyle, 2001).

Section 210 broadens the categories of subscriber records that can be obtained by a subpoena. This is an amendment of Section 2703(c)(2) of U.S.C. Title 18, re-designated by Section 212 (EPIC, 2001). The argument for this section is that terrorists often use false names when registering on the Internet and the ability to seize information by subpoena, on records such as credit card information, may assist law enforcement officers with identifying terrorists' true identities (Doyle, 2001).

Section 211 allows certain disclosures of government entities. This section is an amendment of the Communications Act of 1934 (EPIC, 2001). By amending 47 U.S.C. 551 of the Communications Act of 1934, cable companies that offer communication services are subject to the provisions of Title III and Chapters 121 and 206 of Title 18 of the U.S. Code (Doyle, 2001).

Section 212 allows electronic communication providers to give authorities information that pertains to their subscribers. This section lowers the standards for law enforcement requests for disclosure of customer communication records from "reasonable belief," to a "good faith belief" (EPIC, 2001).

Section 213 gives authority for delaying notice of the execution of a warrant. This is an amendment of Section 3103a of U.S.C. Title 18. This amendment allows the delaying of notification of a search warrant execution in cases were property may be analyzed or confiscated within the guidelines of Chapter 121 (EPIC, 2001). Further extensions of search and seizure guidelines include, but are not limited to, the following: entry into a home either physically or electronically, physical searching, visual observance, taking measurements, taking photographs and downloading or mailing computer files (Doyle, 2001). These cases are limited to instances where immediate notification may have an adverse effect on an investigation. This section has been coined by some as the "sneak and peek" amendment (EPIC, 2001).

Section 214 greatly expands the situations in which a pen trap can be used. This is an amendment of Section 402 of the Foreign Intelligence Surveillance Act of 1978 (EPIC, 2001).

Section 215 addresses accessing records and other items under the Foreign Intelligence Surveillance Act. This is an amendment of Title V of the Foreign Intelligence Surveillance Act of 1978. This amendment grants the proper personnel the ability to petition the court for books, records, papers, documents, and other items belonging to a United States citizen, as long as the investigation is not completely based on activities protected by First Amendment freedoms (EPIC, 2001). As well, the court order may only be requested in an investigation that is for the purpose of protecting the United States from international terrorism or other clandestine intelligence activities (Doyle, 2001). The court order will not be listed as based on an investigation to fight terrorism, and an individual who produces items collected pursuant to this court order will not be liable in future proceedings (EPIC, 2001).

Section 216 addresses expansion of the definitions on communications for the purposes of trap and trace devices. Originally these devices applied primarily to telephones; however, this is no longer the case. This section removes the "probable cause" standard for trap and trace orders to a standard of "relevancy to an ongoing investigation." Also, the agent of a foreign power requirement was removed from the requirements for an application for a trap and trace device (EPIC, 2001).

Section 217 deals with the interception of computer trespasser communications. This is an amendment of Chapter 119 of U.S.C. Title 18. This amendment means that a person who accesses a protected computer has no expectation of privacy and any transmission or communication is not protected under law. This section states that it will not be unlawful for officers of the court to intercept communications from a computer when they have the permission by the legal owner, during the course of an investigation, pertaining to communications that are deemed relevant to the investigation, and are limited to those communications only (Doyle, 2001; EPIC, 2001).

Section 218 expands the investigations that can apply to the secret FISA court by lowering the intelligence gathering requirements from "sole purpose" to "a significant purpose." This is an amendment of Section 104(a)(7)(B) and Section 303(a)(7)(B), 50 U.S.C. 1804(a)(7)(B) and 1823(a)(7)(B), of the Foreign Intelligence Surveillance Act of 1978 (EPIC, 2001).

Section 219 establishes the authority for a judge in the district of a terrorism investigation, either domestic or international in nature, to issue a single district search warrant that may be served within or outside that district. That is, the search warrant may be used in investigations that cover several states as well as possible international warrant service (Doyle, 2001; Foerstel, 2004).

Section 220 allows for nationwide warrants and court orders for electronic communications and customer records without having to apply for a warrant in the jurisdictional location where the information is stored. Now any federal court can issue the warrant or court order for different geographic locations (EPIC, 2001).

Section 221 extends trade sanctions to the territory of Afghanistan for the purpose of blocking products that might be used in the production of chemical, biological, or other weapons of mass destruction. This is an amendment of the Trade Sanctions Reform and Exports Enhancement Act of 2000 (Doyle, 2001; EPIC, 2001).

Section 223 extends both civil liability and administrative discipline to federal officers and employees who unlawfully violate prohibitions against disclosure of information gathered under this act (EPIC, 2001).

Section 224 states that the following sections will expire if not renewed by Congress by December 31, 2005: Section 201, Section 202, Section 203(b), Section 203(d), Section 204, Section 206, Section 207, Section 209, Section 212, Section 214, Section 215, Section 217, Section 218, Section 220, Section 223, Section 225 (Doyle, 2001; EPIC, 2001).

Section 225 deals with immunity for compliance with FISA wiretap. This section states that no civil action can be taken against any provider of a wire or electronic communication service, landlord, custodian, or other person. This includes any law enforcement officer, employee, or agent that furnishes any information or technical assistance in accordance with a court order or request for emergency assistance under the Patriot Act (EPIC, 2001).

Section 311 allows investigators for the federal government to impose "special investigators" upon financial institutions for the purpose of collecting documents pertaining to terrorist activities. Institutions are compelled under this section to respond to federal inquiries within a 120 hour time period (Foerstel, 2004).

Section 312 requires the creation of due diligence mechanisms to detect and report money laundering transactions (EPIC, 2001).

Section 313 disallows U.S. correspondent accounts with foreign shell banks (EPIC, 2001).

Section 319 deals with forfeiture of funds in the United States from interbank accounts. This is an amendment of Section 981, U.S.C. Title 18, for the purpose of forfeitures under this section, or under the Control Substance Act (21 U.S.C. 81 et seq.). If funds are deposited in a foreign bank, and that bank has an interbank account, then it is considered the same as if the money was being deposited in the United States. When the account is deemed to be controlled by a terrorist group or individual, the funds may be seized or frozen. It is not a requirement that all the funds be traced to see where every dollar came from in the account. The bank or financial institution that freezes or releases the funds to the government is protected from liability to the original account holder (EPIC,2001).

Section 323 authorizes federal application for restraining orders to preserve the availability of property subject to a foreign forfeiture or confiscation judgment (EPIC, 2001).

Section 326 obligates the secretary of the treasury to create uniform standards for financial institutions (banks, credit unions, security dealers, etc.) for identifying their customers (EPIC, 2001). The object of this section is to deter illegal money funneling by terrorist organizations, identity theft, and other forms of fraud similar to what has been historically seen in white collar crimes. Banks now give written disclosure of Section 326 of the Patriot Act within documents pertaining to financial accounts. These documents include, but are not limited to, credit card applications and the requests to alter existing credit card accounts. Individuals opening checking accounts also fall under Section 326 requirements. Information currently being collected by institutions include name, date of birth, address, social security number, and driver's license. Institutions of banking may request additional information from account applicants if so desired. These customer identification requirements fall within general guidelines prescribed by Section 326 mandates which were created by the Treasury Department, Treasury's Financial Crimes Enforcement Network, Board of Governors of the Federal Reserve System, the Commodity Futures Trading Commission, the Federal Deposit Insurance Corporation, the National Credit Union Administration, the Office of the Comptroller of the Currency, the Office of Thrift Supervision, and the Securities and Exchange Commission.

Under this section, financial institutions are required to implement the following procedures: (1) verify the identity of any person opening an account; (2) maintain records of the information used to verify the person's identity; and (3) determine whether the person appears on any list of known or suspected terrorists or terrorist organizations. In some places these provisions have been called the "know your customer rules" (Merrimack, 2006).

Section 327 amends the Bank Holding Company Act of 1956 and the Federal Deposit Insurance Act to require consideration of the effectiveness of a company or companies' bank shares acquisitions or mergers (EPIC, 2001).

Section 328 instructs the treasury secretary to take actions encouraging foreign governments to require the inclusion of the name of the originator in wire transfer instructions sent to the United States and other countries, with the information to remain with the transfer from its origination until the point of disbursement (EPIC, 2001).

Section 329 designates criminal penalties for federal officials or employees who seek to accept bribes in connection with administration of this title (EPIC, 2001).

Section 352 gives authority to the treasury secretary to exempt from minimum standards for anti-money laundering programs any financial institution not subject to certain regulations governing financial recordkeeping and reporting of currency and foreign transactions (EPIC, 2001).

Section 355 amends the Federal Deposit Insurance Act to allow written employment references to contain suspicions of involvement in illegal activity (Doyle, 2001).

Section 358 is an amendment of Section 5311 of Title 31 of the United States Code. Section 358 allows the secretary of the treasury to refer certain cases to U.S. intelligence agencies for the purpose of conducting intelligence or counterintelligence activities to protect the country against international terrorism (Doyle, 2001).

Section 361 officially places the Financial Crimes Enforcement Network in the Department of the Treasury (EPIC, 2001).

Section 363 makes changes to the maximum penalties for money laundering crimes. The civil fine, previously $10,000, is now raised to $1 million as a maximum fine. Criminally, the fines are raised from $250,000 to $1 million (EPIC, 2001).

Section 365 amends federal law to require reports relating to coins and currency exceeding $10,000 received in a non-financial trade or business (EPIC, 2001).

Section 371 is an amendment of Subchapter II of Chapter 53 of the currency reporting requirements of Title 31 of the United States Code. Initially created to deal with drug related money smugglers, this section has been amended to allow the government to seize the currency of any individual who attempts to smuggle more than $10,000 in currency into or out of the United States (EPIC, 2001).

Section 375 dramatically increases the penalties for crimes involving counterfeiting foreign currency and obligations. For instance, the penalty for uttering counterfeit foreign obligations is raised from 3 years to 20 years. Possessing plates or stones for counterfeiting foreign securities is raised from 5 to 20 years. The penalty for possessing counterfeit foreign bank notes is raised from 2 to 20 years imprisonment (Doyle, 2001).

Section 402 authorizes the tripling of border patrol officers, customs service, and INS personnel. This section also authorizes additional funding for support facilities to assist in the function of protecting the northern border (EPIC, 2001).

Section 403 requires a new information system to assist the State Department with accessing criminal files currently kept by the FBI alone. Also included within this section is a mandate for new standards related to visas and border checkpoints (Foerstel, 2004).

Section 404 amends the Department of Justice Appropriations Act of 2001 which previously held restrictions and limitation of INS overtime compensation (EPIC, 2001). Prior to Section 404, the Justice Department had placed a limit of $30,000 that could be paid to one INS officer. Section 404 repealed the pay cap for fiscal year 2001 (Doyle, 2001).

Section 405 charges the attorney general to oversee the study, and the creation of a report, on the feasibility of improving the FBI's Integrated Automated Fingerprint Identification System (IAFIS) for better screening at border entry points as well as other locations. Section 405 allocates $2 million dollars for this project (Doyle, 2001).

Section 411 greatly expands the vulnerability of a non-citizen to being forcibly removed from the country. The vulnerability lies in an extensive definition of the following terms: terrorist activity, engagement in terrorist activity, and terrorist organization. This is an amendment of the grounds of inadmissibility set out in Section 212(a)(3) of the Immigration and Nationality Act, 8 U.S.C. 1182(a)(3)(iv), which adds three more categories including: espousing terrorist activity, being the spouse or child of an inadmissible alien, and having association with a terrorist organization with the intent to place the safety and welfare of the United States in danger or peril (Doyle, 2001; EPIC, 2001).

Section 412 allows the attorney general to detain a non-citizen without a hearing or a showing that the non-citizen poses a threat to national security for up to seven days. The standard for detaining non-citizens is that there are "reasonable grounds" to believe that the non-citizen is part of a terrorist activity. This is an amendment of 8 U.S.C. 1101 et seq. of the Immigration and Nationality Act (EPIC, 2001).

Section 413 allows the visa application records collected by the State Department to be shared with other countries by the secretary of state in cases that include the following: terrorism, drug trafficking, gun running, smuggling of immigrants, or other criminal related cases (Doyle, 2001).

Sections 414-417 create new standards for border entry points. Also within these sections are the mandates for increased foreign student monitoring programs (Doyle, 2001; Foerstel, 2004).

Section 427 states that no benefits under Subtitle B shall be given to anyone found guilty of the September 11, 2001, terrorist attacks. As well, any family members of anyone found guilty of the September 11, 2001, terrorist attacks will not qualify for any benefits under Subtitle B (Doyle, 2001).

Section 501 deals with the government's authority to pay informers for information valuable in the war on terrorism. Rewards exceeding $250,000 must be personally approved by the attorney general or the President of the United States (EPIC, 2001).

Section 503 increases the DNA information bank for the purpose of tracking and identifying criminals (Foerstel, 2004). Specifically, Section 503 expands federal law, 42 U.S.C. 14135a(d)(2), to allow the attorney general to collect DNA samples from people who have been convicted of the federal crime of terrorism (Doyle, 2001).

Section 504 states that federal intelligence officers conducting electronic surveillance, as well as searches under FISA court orders, may coordinate with law enforcement officers in cases involving international terrorism or hostile attack by a foreign power, agent of a foreign power, or secret foreign intelligence activities (Doyle, 2001).

Section 505 deals with telephone transactions. This is an amendment of Section 2709(b) of U.S.C. Title 18. In this amendment, the FBI can create and send an administrative subpoena, without court review (Electronic Frontier Foundation, 2005), to information providers, by way of a National Security Letter, requesting release of information on an individual's telephone communication records, IP addresses, length of service, and toll billing records that are considered relevant to an authorized investigation to protect against international terrorism, or clandestine intelligence activities. This can be done, provided that such an investigation of a United States citizen is not conducted solely on the basis of activities protected by the First Amendment to the Constitution of the United States (EPIC, 2001). Authorities are not required to make a notification that they have made an information collection on an individual (Electronic Frontier Foundation, 2005). There are currently three types of National Security Letters: (1) telephone and electronic NSLs pursuant to the Electronic Privacy Act; (2) financial record NSLs pursuant to the Right to Financial Privacy Act; and (3) information from credit bureau NSLs pursuant to the Fair Credit Reporting Act. Section 505 of the Patriot Act changes the predication for all three types of NSLs to a uniform set of requirements (Lormel, 2002). If a recipient of an NSL refuses to comply with an NSL, the FBI cannot force them to do so. Only a federal court has that authority (Brand & Pistole, n.d.). Section 505 lowers the standard by which the NSL may be applicable for request by the FBI from the previous standard, by which information sought had to be related to a foreign power, foreign agent, or international terrorist, to information certified by the FBI that is relevant to an authorized foreign counterintelligence investigation (Doyle, 2001). In effect, the standard for the intelligence subpoena has been lowered to that of the criminal subpoena.

Section 506 extends the secret service's jurisdiction to involve crimes involving "access device fraud, false identification documents, *and any fraud or other criminal or unlawful activity in or against any federally insured financial institution*" (Doyle, 2001). This is an expansion of 3056(b)(3) which stated that the secret service's jurisdiction included only crimes involving "credit and debit card frauds, and false identification documents and devices" (Doyle, 2001).

Section 507 deals with the disclosure of educational records. This is an amendment of Section 44 of the General Education Provisions Act. This added provision allows designated authorities to petition the court for an order to require educational agencies to provide educational records on suspected terrorists. The amendment also limits civil liability to the educational facility for releasing the information (EPIC, 2001).

Section 701 creates an initiative for a "secure information sharing system" to assist in investigating and prosecuting terrorist activities in multi-jurisdictions (Foerstel, 2004).

Section 802 deals with the new designation of "domestic terrorism" which entails a new comprehensive list of definitions pertaining to this crime (Foerstel, 2004).

Section 803 increases the number of crimes for harboring, concealing, and providing material support for those categorized as terrorists (Foerstel, 2004).

Section 806 deals with asset forfeitures by terrorist organizations. This is an amendment of Section 981(a) of U.S.C. Title 18. The amendment includes the forfeiture of all assets, foreign and domestic, of any individual, entity, or organization engaged in any planning or perpetration of any foreign or domestic terrorism (EPIC, 2001).

Section 808 increases the number of federal crimes that relate to terrorism (Foerstel, 2004).

Section 809 allows higher penalties for various terrorist related crimes with no statute of limitations (Foerstel, 2004).

Section 903 gives authorization to all officers and employees of the intelligence service to investigate terrorism (Foerstel, 2004).

Section 905 requires the attorney general, as well as any head of a federal department or agency with law enforcement responsibilities, to properly disclose to the Director of Central Intelligence any and all foreign intelligence acquired in the course of a criminal investigation (EPIC, 2001).

Section 908 creates a cross agency training program for enhanced training for state and local agencies to improve law enforcement's ability to handle foreign intelligence information and investigations (Foerstel, 2004).

Section 1005 releases funds for the purpose of training state and local fire and emergency agencies. These funds are to be released in the form of grants (Foerstel, 2004).

Section 1016 is to deal with increasing the protection to important infrastructures. (Foerstel, 2004).

While it would be reasonable to say that for every section of the Patriot Act there is probably someone who takes issue with it, these sections have, by far, received more attention in the media. While you read this book you will see some of these sections repeated in the form of arguments, debates, and analysis. Don't feel confused if others define these sections slightly different. This does not particularly mean that either definition is wrong. It does mean that different people may look at the same section of the Patriot Act and presume different meanings from the information based upon personal ideologies, life experiences, and so on. It is also not unique for confrontational topics to garner different support in different locations as people in particular areas have their own unique concerns and fears. It may be possible that the massive movements for and against the Patriot Act are just a conglomeration of many similar niches of thinking coming together within the U.S.

Former House Speaker Tip O'Neill aptly stated, "All politics is local" (Kettl, 2004, p. 57). Endorsing this line of thinking, it is very probable that many aspects of Homeland Security break down to what average people think they need for their specific location (Kettl, 2004). These varying perspectives should be intellectually nutritious for those avidly searching for superior Patriot Act knowledge, because a major human component of the Patriot Act is the differing perspectives in a critical time period of U.S. history.

A reader may wonder if there are any under-reported sections of the Patriot Act. The answer is yes. Some of the most powerful sections of the Patriot Act currently sit quietly outside the mainstream of debate. It's time to analyze, for our purposes, what we will call the "Quiet Giants" of the Patriot Act.

References

Brand, R. & Pistole, J. (n.d.). *The use and purpose of National Security Letters (NSLs)*. Retrieved July 7, 2005, from http://www.fbi.gov/page2/natsecurityletters.htm

Denzin, N. K., & Lincoln, Y. S. (2003). Appendix A. In N. K. Denzin & Y. S. Lincoln (Eds.), *9/11 in American culture* (pp. 277-279). Lanham, MD: AltaMira Press.

Doyle, C. (2001, December 10). *Terrorism: Section by section analysis of the USA Patriot Act*. The Library of Congress, Congressional Research Service. Retrieved April 15, 2005, from http://www.epic.org/privacy/terrorism/usapatriot/RL31200.pdf

Doyle, C. (2002, April 15). *The USA Patriot Act: a legal analysis*. The Library of Congress, Congressional Research Service. Retrieved November 16, 2004, from http://www.fas.org /irp/crs/RL31377.pdf

Electronic Frontier Foundation (2005). *Let the sun set on Patriot Section 505 - National Security Letters (NSLs)*. Retrieved October 5, 2006, from http://www.eff.org/patriot/sunset/ 505.php

Electronic Privacy Information Center [EPIC]. (2001). *HR 3162 RDS: 107th Congress*. Retrieved September 25, 2004, from http://www.epic.org/privacy/terrorism/hr3162.html

Foerstel, H. N. (2004). *Refuge of a scoundrel: The Patriot Act in libraries*. Westport, CT: Libraries Unlimited.

Howell, B. A. (2004). The future of Internet surveillance law: A symposium to discuss Internet surveillance, privacy & the USA Patriot Act: Surveillance law: Reshaping the framework: Seven weeks: The making of the USA Patriot Act. *George Washington Law Review, 72*, 1145-1207.

Kettl, D. F. (2004). *System under stress: Homeland security and American politics*. Washington, DC: CQ Press.

Lormel, D. (2002, October 9). *Testimony of Dennis Lormel, chief, terrorist financing operations section, counterterrorism division, FBI before the Senate Judiciary Committee, Subcommittee on Technology, Terrorism, and Government Information*. Retrieved January 1, 2005, from http://www.fbi.gov/congress/congress02/lormel100902.htm

Merrimack Mortgage Company, Inc. (2006). *USA Patriot Act of 2001, Section 326 Customer identification program (CIP) policy*. Retrieved October 5, 2006, from http://www.merrimackmortgage.com/Patriot_Act.asp

CHAPTER 4

The Quiet Giants

WITHIN THE SCHOLARLY COMMUNITY AND the general public, the Patriot Act has been the focus of intense debate. However, this debate has failed to scrutinize the Patriot Act from very many angles. The majority of study has been centered on the Title II provisions which cover aspects of surveillance. Recent issues involving detention have sparked additional study on Title IV provisions.

The goal of this chapter is to analyze Title VIII provisions of the Patriot Act. By approaching this seldom publicized part of the legislation, a unique and interesting domino effect will be seen in how the Patriot Act's reconstructed terrorism definitions, among others, have had on the entire law and its purpose in the war on terror. Furthermore, ramifications from, and changes to, Title VIII provisions will be viewed on a myriad of important issues ranging from insurance to sex offenders. It is believed that Title VIII has been understated and under analyzed, making its provisions the quiet giants of the Patriot Act. What follows is an article I previously wrote, published in Vol. 5, No. 4, of the *Illinois Law Enforcement Executive Forum*, July 2005, entitled "The Patriot Act: Title VIII: Analyzing the Quiet Giants."

While the Patriot Act was constructed to give the Department of Justice more power to investigate terrorism (Barbour, 2004), the foundation of Title VIII provisions are centered on the definitions of terrorism.

Patriot Act Section 802

Section 802 defines domestic terrorism. This definition is an amendment of the United States Code (U.S.C.) Title 18, Section 2331, which expands the descriptors of offenses to include "mass destruction." Furthermore, violating acts occurring primarily within the jurisdiction of the United States must be a violation of criminal law (EPIC, 2001). The only addition to the first federal definition found in the 1978 Foreign Intelligence Surveillance Act is the term *mass destruction* (Perry, 2004). Section 802 effectively takes a previous international definition and modifies the last section by placing the words *mass destruction* alongside the terms *assassination* or *kidnapping* (Doyle, 2001).

Patriot Act Section 808

Section 802 works in conjunction with Section 808 to encompass two major forms of terrorism. Section 808 defines the federal crime of terrorism and is a result of a transformation of U.S.C. Title 18, Section 2332b.

Originally, Section 2332b was drawn up containing two sections of prohibited acts. These prohibited acts were pertinent to individual acts exceeding U.S. boundaries and included the following: killing, kidnapping, maiming, assault with bodily injury, and assault with a weapon within the United States [18 U.S.C. § 2332b(a)(A) (2000)]. Additional offenses included creating a risk of bodily injury, as well as damaging property and structures within the United States [18 U.S.C. § 2332b(a)(B) (2000)]. The circumstances under which offenses are stated to be germane are as follows: when the mail or a mail facility is used; the offense obstructs interstate or foreign commerce; the victim of the offense is a U.S. official; the destroyed property is owned or controlled by the United States; the offense is committed in or on the sea, air, or islands of the United States; and the offense is committed within the maritime and territorial jurisdiction of the United States [18 U.S.C. § 2332b(b)(1)(A)-(F) (2000)]. A special section details the jurisdictional guidelines that exist for individuals to be liable as conspirators and accessories [18 U.S.C. § 2332b(b)(2) (2000)].

Section 2332b has an extensive penalties section, which includes penalties ranging from 10 years in prison to the death penalty. Violators are not allowed probation or sentences that run concurrently [18 U.S.C. § 2332b(c)(2) (2000)]. The final sections include a breakdown of government investigative authority and a definitional section.

Because the framers of the Patriot Act reviewed Section 2332b, "Acts of Terrorism Transcending National Boundaries," and amended certain sections, the law is greatly expanded. Specifically, in subsection (1) (f), the following violations were added: "351(e), 844(e), 844(f)(1), 956(b), 1361, 1366(b), 1366(c), 1751(e), 2152, or 2156" (EPIC, 2001). These new section additions, pulled from Title 18 and placed into Section 808 of the Patriot Act, contain the following:

- Section 351(e) is a section covering assassinating, kidnapping, and assaulting congressional, cabinet, and Supreme Court members [18 U.S.C. § 351 (2004)].

- Section 844(e) deals with the use of mail, telephone, and telegraph services, both foreign and domestic, in an attempt to kill or injure individuals or to damage a building [18 U.S.C. § 844(e) (2004)].

- Section 844(f) places guidelines and penalties for violations of 844(e) [18 U.S.C. § 844(f) (2004)].

- Section 956(b) deals with conspiracies within the United States to destroy foreign property [18 U.S.C. § 956(b) (2004)].

- Section 1361 covers aspects of malicious mischief, especially the destruction or attempted destruction of United States property. Penalties for violation of this section are also included [18 U.S.C. § 1361 (2004)].

- Section 1366(b) deals with fines and punishments for the destruction of energy facilities [18 U.S.C. § 1366(b) (2004)].

- Section 1366(c) is a definition for the term *energy facility*, which is taken from Section 60101 of Title 49 [18 U.S.C. § 1366(c) (2004)].

- Section 2152 comes from the chapter on sabotage and covers the guidelines and penalties for the trespassing and destroying of Harbor defenses and ocean defense systems or violating regulations by the president in concern to maritime vessels [18 U.S.C. § 2152 (2004)].

- Section 2156 also comes from the chapter on sabotage and deals with the destruction of national defense utilities [18 U.S.C. § 2156 (2004)].

Originally, Section 2332b(1)(f), entitled "Investigative Authority," spoke about the attorney general being responsible for investigating federal crimes of terrorism with the assistance of the Secretary of the Treasury. This section also stated that the secret service maintained its original investigative authority [18 U.S.C. § 2332b(1)(f) (2000)]. In effect, additional violations are added to the specific investigative authority of the Attorney General.

The last change in Section 808 of the Patriot Act is the striking and re-insertion of subsection (g)(5)(B), which contains a plethora of violations that pertain to federal crimes of terrorism. The Patriot Act version of subsection (g)(5)(B) is definitely expanded; however, the revised section is similar to the old version. There are 5 section deletions and 18 new additions as Section 2332b(g)(5)(B) is assimilated into Section 808.

Section 2332b, as modified in Section 808, dropped some of the more minor crimes, like simple assault, bomb scares, and malicious mischief, from the definition (Doyle, 2001). These terms were dropped with the caveat that they would still fall within the investigative jurisdiction of the Department of Justice (Doyle, 2001). Conversely, more serious crimes were added to Section 108: Harboring terrorists, crimes related to chemical weapons, crimes involving nuclear materials and explosives, crimes pertaining to computer protection, presidential and presidential staff assassination and kidnapping crimes, endangering life with an aircraft, homicide or attempted homicide using an aircraft (EPIC, 2001). From a constructional standpoint, Sections 802 and 808 would be considered deductive definitions. Both definitions contain a substantive element and include prohibited conduct; both contain a motivational requirement; and, finally, both contain a jurisdictional element (Perry, 2004). From an applicable standpoint, both definitions serve as the first falling dominos to affect Sections 809, 812, and 813 at a minimum (Smith, Seifert, McLoughlin, & Moteff, 2002). The struggle to formulate simplified and unified definitions of terrorism has been an ongoing challenge within the United States (Perry, 2004) and the international community (Orlova & Moore, 2005).

Are You Insured?

One of the most overlooked ramifications of the Patriot Act is how the implications of war and terrorism are portrayed to insurance carriers. The September 11, 2001, terrorist attacks on the World Trade Center brought forth insurance revelations that had implications almost as disastrous as the attacks themselves. From a financial perspective, the commercial property loss of the terrorist attacks was approximately $8.5 to $25 billion. The aviation industry was also significantly impacted (around $6 billion for passenger deaths and $434 million for aircraft destruction). Vehicle destruction around Ground Zero was nearly $90 million, while life insurance losses were estimated between $900 million to $6 billion. Later, workers' compensation would be estimated between $2.4 billion and $5 billion (Dhooge, 2003). While the losses could be efficiently tallied by the insurance carriers, what if no one qualified to collect?

Insurance carriers are not required to cover for any contingency that is not specifically stated within insurance policies. Unknown to most individuals, "acts of war" have long been exempt from coverage in various policies. In fact, the most comprehensive war exclusions were developed by the Insurance Services Office, Inc., and included the following: damages resulting from war that is declared, undeclared, or civil; losses coming from warlike action of a military force, including actions that hinder or defend against attack from any government, sovereign, or other authority using military personnel or other agents; and losses resulting from insurrection, rebellion, revolution, usurped power, or actions taken by the government to thwart any of these actions (Dhooge, 2003). After the events of September 11, 2001, the government coined the terrorist attacks as both "war" and "acts of terrorism." This provided a loophole for nonpayment of insurance claims that were exploited by more than one major insurance carrier.

Fearing that consumer confidence would be destroyed by an insurance catastrophe, the Committee on Financial Services of the U.S. House of Representatives, in cooperation with the National Association of Insurance Commissioners, took action to cover claims. One result of a cooperated effort to strengthen the viability of the insurance industry is seen in the Terrorism Risk Insurance Act of 2002. This Act allows for federal assistance to private insurers when a four-part definition of terrorism is met (Dhooge, 2003). The definitions of terrorism provided by the Patriot Act, in some ways, serve as a guideline for future insurance claims resulting from terrorist activities. The lack of such timely definitions, along with other legislation, could have been instrumental in a major breakdown in public confidence.

Patriot Act Section 809

Section 809 of the Patriot Act amends Section 3286 of U.S.C. Title 18. In comparison with the original Section 3286, there are several structural advances in the Patriot Act. As opposed to the original text, which was a short, compressed set of guidelines providing extensions for the statute of limitation [18 U.S.C. § 3286 (2000)], the Patriot Act has three specific sections: (1) an 8-year limitation section, (2) a no limitation section, and (3) an application section (EPIC, 2001). Prior to the Patriot Act, there were no limitations for prosecutions on charges of murder. This did not change with the Patriot Act; however, federal crimes commensurate with terrorism carried an 8-year statute of limitations. Some offenses involving explosives and destruction of federal property had a statute of limitation of 10 years. Barring these exceptions, most federal crimes had a statute of limitations of 5 years (Doyle, 2001). Section 809 eliminates the statute of limitations for federal offenses that meet the requirement that the offense risks or results in a death or serious bodily injury (Doyle, 2001; EPIC, 2001). Included within this category are modern-day technological computer crimes (Smith et al., 2002). Those offenses that do not meet the requirement have a statute of limitations of 8 years (Doyle, 2001; EPIC, 2001). This section is considered a more tapered form of the version originally requested by the administration (Leahy, 2001).

Terrorists and Sex Offenders

On March 11, 2003, during Congressional Testimony on H.R. 1161, a new sexual offender bill, politicians referenced extensions to the statute of limitations found within the Patriot Act as a precedent for requested extensions for the prosecution of sex offenders (*Child Abduction Prevention*, 2003). Ironically, while Section 809 of the Patriot Act is being referenced to support easing limitations on new legislation, a case from California, originating in 1993, threatens to strike down Section 809.

The case in question, *Stogner v. California*, stems from a piece of legislation known as Penal Code 803(g), enacted in 1993, to combat sexual offenders (Ashran, 2004; Frei, 2004). The *Stogner* case involved a 70-year-old man who was prosecuted for sexually abusing his daughters as early as 1955. After an initial conviction, the case was appealed to the Supreme Court. It was found that the California law that allowed for the prosecution of sexual crimes past the standard statute of limitations violated the *ex post facto* clause of the Constitution (Frei, 2004). The ramifications for California will be enormous as approximately 800 cases involving California Penal Code 803(g) are under review (Ashran, 2004). There is little doubt that the *Stogner* case will affect Section 809, but to what degree is not fully known. In a twisted example of historical satire, terrorists may have sexual predators to thank for prosecution limitations.

Patriot Act Section 810

Section 810 starts with an amendment of U.S.C. Title 18, at Section 81, entitled "Arson Within Special Maritime and Territorial Jurisdiction." This section covers individuals who set fire or burn buildings, naval stores, and materials, and/or navigational property within U.S. maritime territory. This section previously included punishments that were not to exceed 25 years [18 U.S.C. § 81 (2000)]. The Patriot Act strengthens the punishment section by inserting "for any term of years or for life" (EPIC, 2001).

The Patriot Act amends U.S.C. Title 18, at Section 1366, entitled "Destruction of an Energy Facility." This section deals with individuals who commit over $100,000 of damage to an energy facility [18 U.S.C. § 1366 (2004)]. The punishments are doubled in the Patriot Act from 10 years [18 U.S.C. § 1366 (2000)] to 20 years (EPIC, 2001). Furthermore, if arson results in the death of any person, there is no limit to the prison sentence an individual can serve (EPIC, 2001).

The Patriot Act also amends U.S.C. Title 18, at Section 2339A(a), entitled "Providing Material Support to Terrorists." This section involves offenses committed by supporting, assisting, or concealing terrorists. This illegal assistance is found to have occurred when an offender assists individuals who have committed one or more of the following acts:

- Destroyed aircraft or an airport
- Committed violence in an international airport
- Committed arson within a special maritime jurisdiction
- Produced or possessed biological weapons
- Possessed illegal chemical weapons

- Kidnapped or killed a congressional, cabinet, or supreme court member
- Illegally produced or possessed nuclear material
- Possessed illegal explosives
- Possessed a firearm in a federal facility
- Committed conspiracy to kill
- Killed or attempted to kill employees of the United States
- Murdered or manslaughtered foreign officials
- Purposely took hostages
- Destroyed government property
- Destroyed communications lines and systems
- Destroyed an energy facility
- Killed or kidnapped a U.S. president or presidential staff member
- Disabled or derailed a train
- Attacked a mass transportation system
- Destroyed a national defense facility
- Committed violence against maritime navigation
- Used a weapon of mass destruction against the United States
- Committed a bombing within the United States
- Committed sabotage on a nuclear facility
- Committed aircraft piracy

Among the punishments for these numerous acts of terrorism, the Patriot Act raises the standard penalty from 10 years [18 U.S.C. § 2339A(a) (2000)] to 15 years (EPIC, 2001). If a death results from one of these actions, the Patriot Act adds a penalty of "any term of years or for life" (EPIC, 2001).

U.S.C. Title 18, Section 2339B(a)(1) also addresses giving material support to terrorists but focuses on the banking industry. Particularly, when banking institutions become aware that they are holding funds or assets of a terrorist organization, they must maintain control of the funds and contact government officials [18 U.S.C. § 2339B(a)(2)(A) (2004); 18 U.S.C. § 2339B(a)(2)(B) (2004)]. The Patriot Act applies the same penalty amendments from 10 years [18 U.S.C. § 2339B(a)(1) (2000)] to 15 years (EPIC, 2001), notwithstanding actions that result in death that are amended to any term of years or life (EPIC, 2001).

The sentencing in U.S.C. Title 18, Section 2155(a), is doubled from 10 years to 20 years (EPIC, 2001). In cases of death, penalties include prison for any term of years or life. U.S.C. Title 18, at Section 2155(a), "Destruction of National-Defense Materials, National-Defense Premises, or National-Defense Utilities," deals with the destruction or contamination of national defense materials, premises, or utilities with the intent to obstruct the national defense of the United States [18 U.S.C. § 2155(a) (2000)].

The Patriot Act adopts, after an amendment, Section 236(a) of the Atomic Energy Act of 1954; U.S.C. Title 49, at Section 46505(c), "Carrying a Weapon or Explosive on an Aircraft: Criminal Penalty Involving Disregard for Human Life," and U.S.C. Title 49, at Section 60123(b), which concerns the damage or destruction of an interstate gas or hazardous liquid pipeline facility. All three sections have prison terms extended to 20 years if the crimes committed do not cause death. If a death occurs in the course of a violation, an individual may be imprisoned for any number of years including life (EPIC, 2001).

Originally, the Justice Department suggested implementing an alternative life sentence punishment for all terrorist-related crimes; however, the original proposal did not have an adequate mechanism to designate lower level acts of terrorism from the heinous versions. Section 810 of the Patriot Act allowed for an upgraded punishment, based on a standard definition, which included the loss of human life in the commission of a designated terrorist crime (Doyle, 2001).

Patriot Act Section 811

Section 811 of the Patriot Act, "Penalties for Terrorist Conspiracies," is an expansive section involving lengthy amendments of seven sections of U.S.C. Title 18, one section of U.S.C. Title 42, and three sections of U.S.C. Title 49 (EPIC, 2001).

The first section amended by the Patriot Act is U.S.C. Title 18, Section 81, "Arson Within Special Maritime and Territorial Jurisdiction." Section 81 originally did not have a conspiracy element in the definition [18 U.S.C. § 81 (2000)]. Furthermore, attempted arson is replaced in conjunction with conspiracy to commit arson (EPIC, 2001).

The next section amended by the Patriot Act is U.S.C. Title 18, Section 930(c). This section, "Possession of Firearms and Dangerous Weapons in Federal Facilities," as in the previous section, originally had no conspiracy element [18 U.S.C. § 930(c)(2000)] until after the Patriot Act. Additionally, U.S.C. Title 18, Section 1113, which identifies attempted murder, is struck and then reintroduced with an additional section, 1117, which identifies conspiracy to commit murder.

U.S.C. Title 18, Section 1362, "Communication Lines, Stations, or Systems," is also affected. This section deals with the destruction of various communications in the numerous ways in which they are installed and implemented. As with the previous section, Section 1362 has wording for a criminal "attempt," but nothing for a conspiracy [18 U.S.C. § 1362 (2000)]. In the Patriot Act, the word *attempt* is struck and replaced with the word *conspires* (EPIC, 2001). U.S.C. Title 18, Section 1363, "Buildings or Property within Special Maritime and Territorial Jurisdiction," is amended in the same fashion. As before, U.S.C. Title 18, Section 2339A, "Providing Material Support to Terrorists," changes verbatim to the last four sections.

It is important to note not only the *conspiracy* addition within these sections, but the placement of the term within the text. In all described sections, the insertion of the term *attempt*, grouped with the term *conspiracy*, is specifically placed at the end of the descriptions of possible victimizations. This is important as it maximizes the effect of the addition by making it applicable to the entire section.

Prior to the Patriot Act, Section 2340A, "Torture," which covers torture committed outside the United States, had only two subsections, (a) and (b) (2000). The Patriot Act added a third subsection, (c), which is a definitional subsection that states, "A person who conspires to commit an offense under this section shall be subject to the same penalties (other than the penalty of death) as the penalties prescribed for the offense, the commission of which was the object of the conspiracy" [EPIC, 2001, Section 808; 18 U.S.C. § 2340A(c) (2004)]. This definitional change mirrors U.S.C. Title 18, Section 1992. This section, "Wrecking Trains," has the exact definitional addition as Section 2340A(c).

Section 236 of the Atomic Energy Act of 1954, is entitled "Sabotage of Nuclear Facilities or Fuel." This section is amended in the same way as in pervious sections, with the striking and relocating of *attempting* with *conspires* (EPIC, 2001). The same changes are made to U.S.C. Title 49, Section 46504, "Interference with Flight Crew Members and Attendants," as well as Section 60123(b), "Penalty for Damaging or Destroying Facility."

Osama Bin Laden and Al Capone: Gangster Prevention Strategies

Osama Bin Laden is now less likely to be identified as the leader of a military force and more likely to be categorized as part of a criminal organization. If that is so, can strategies used to deter criminal organizations in the United States be implemented on groups such as Al-Qaeda? For many Americans, Al Capone embodies the description of the powerful gangster. In the 1930s, Al Capone was the kingpin of Chicago. Having violated the Volstead Act at will, Capone's violations of bribery, bootlegging, and murder made him an extreme challenge for law enforcement (Richman & Stuntz, 2005). Authorities, after failing on several attempts to bring down the powerful connected mob leader, resorted to pretextual charging (Richman & Stuntz, 2005). Instead of charging the mob leader with the higher offense of murder, other lower offenses (in this case tax evasion) were brought forward to end Capone's reign of terror on Chicago.

If Osama Bin Laden, and his equivalents, do fit the description of a modern-day Capone, then creative criminal charging may be a timely consideration. It very well may be that Section 808, along with other sections of the Patriot Act, are modern examples of how the government is expanding the pretext for charges in the war on terror. There is little doubt that the government has only two options to deal with terrorism: (1) criminal action or (2) military action. Some believe that the idea of dismissed cases or acquitted defendants requires a military approach to terrorism; however, there also remains a school of thought that holds that the military response is more likely to create martyrs instead of lowly criminals (Travalio & Altenburg, 2003). While other options, such as the forcible abduction of terrorist leaders (Calica, 2004), have been considered, the government has been straddling the fence between military and criminal procedures.

Patriot Act Section 812

Section 812, "Post-Release Supervision of Terrorists," is an amendment of U.S.C. Title 18, Section 3583. This section of the United States Code, originally titled "Inclusion of a Term of Supervised Release After Imprisonment," gave the guidelines for supervised release of both felony and misdemeanor offenders [18 U.S.C. § 3583 (2000)]. The original Section 3583 did not have a subsection (j) predicated especially for supervised release of terrorist violators. Within the amended Section 3583(j), "Supervised

Release Terms for Terrorism Predicates," offenders being released for violations of 2332b(g)(B), that resulted in risk or injury to life, are subject to any number of years of supervision after release, including life post-release supervision (EPIC, 2001). Supervised release is a different concept than parole. Supervised release is imposed in addition to the original prison term, while parole is enacted instead of enforcing the full prison term (Doyle, 2001). Prior federal law generally rendered post-release sentences for released felons at approximately 3- to 5-year periods. Before the Patriot Act, there was no standard system in place for post-release supervision for terrorists (Department of Justice, n.d., *Myth v. Reality*).

Supervising True-Believers

Under the Patriot Act, the ramifications of post-release supervision are yet to be realized. Some in the field feel that post-release supervision has merits and encourage the addition of specialized conditions to bills that have similarities to the Patriot Act (Chesney, 2005). Others believe that Section 808 of the Patriot Act is overly intrusive and serves as an illegitimate excuse by the government to exert unjust social control over segments of the populace, all in the name of the war on terror (Saito, 2004). The question of post-release supervision is not a new concept. Sexual predators have been subject to post-release supervision due to a high recidivism rate. It is a perception by some that policymakers have not adequately addressed the expanded role that postrelease supervision should play within this unique population (Demleitner, 2004; La Fond, 2003). Juvenile offenders exiting boot-camp programs have been subject to post-release supervision to evaluate their re-education within the criminal justice system (Ravenell, 2002). Whether the perceived persistent or lifelong ideologies of convicted terrorists (Saito, 2004) justify post-release supervision, which could possibly last the rest of an individual's lifetime, is fair or not, is unknown. What is apparent is that the government has put in place a post-release system that has the ability to fluctuate with the evolving philosophies of supervision.

Patriot Act Section 813

Section 813 of the Patriot Act is almost a full adoption of U.S.C. Title 18, Section 1961. The only changes are an amendment that strikes "or (F)" and inserts "(F)," and inserts in the place of a semi-colon "or (G) any act that is indictable under any provision listed in section 2332b(g)(5)(B)" (EPIC, 2001).

While the Patriot Act incorporates Section 1961 of U.S.C. Title 18 almost verbatim, the adoption of the racketeering provisions into the war on terror has many interesting implications. Within Section 1961(1)(A), there is a complete definition on the meaning of racketeering. Subsection (1)(B) contains the substantive act portion of the racketeering law, which borrows portions of other Title 18 sections. Prohibited actions within this section include the following: bribery, Section 201; sports bribery, Section 224; counterfeiting, Sections 471, 472, and 473; theft from interstate shipments, Section 659; embezzlement from pension funds, Section 664; extortion of credit transactions, Sections 891-894; fraud of identification documents, Section 1028; fraud relating to access devices, Section 1029; transmission of gambling information, Section 1084; mail fraud, Section 1341; wire fraud, Section 1343; financial institution fraud, Section 1344; unlawful obtainment of citizenship, Section 1425; illegal production of naturalization papers, Section 1426; illegal sales of naturalization papers, Section 1427; obscene matter, Sections 1461-1465; obstruction of justice, Section 1503; obstruction of criminal investigations, Section 1510; obstruction of local or state law enforcement, Section 1511; tampering with a witness, victim, or informant, Section 1512; retaliation against a witness, Section 1513; giving a false statement involving the application of a passport, Section 1542; forgery or false use of a passport, Section 1543; misuse of a passport, Section 1544; fraud and misuse of a visa or other permits, Section 1546; peonage or slavery, Sections 1581-1588; interference with commerce, robbery, and extortion, Section 1951; items related to racketeering, Section 1952; items related to interstate transportation of wagering materials, Section 1953; illegal welfare payments, Section 1954; money laundering, Section 1956; use of interstate commerce for the purpose of murder-for-hire, Section 1958; sexual exploitation of children, Sections 2251, 2251A, 2252, and 2260; interstate transportation of motor vehicles, Sections 2312 and 2313; interstate transportation of stolen property, Sections 2314 and 2315; trafficking false labels for phonorecords, computer programs, videos, etc., Section 2318; criminal infringement of a copyright, Section 2319; unauthorized sale of sound recordings, Section 2319A; trafficking of goods bearing a false mark,

Section 2320; trafficking certain motor vehicles and parts, Section 2321; the illegal sales of cigarettes, Sections 2341-2346; and violations pertaining to white slave traffic, Sections 2421-2424 [EPIC, 2001; U.S.C. § 1961(1)(B)(2000)].

U.S.C. Title 18, Section 1961(1)(C), incorporates sections from U.S.C. Title 29 and deals with restrictions on loans and payments, Section 186; embezzlement of funds, Section 501; and offenses involving cases under Title 11. Further violations taken from Title 29 are fraud in sales and securities and felonious manufacture, importation, receipt, concealment, purchase, sale, or other involvement with controlled substances defined in Section 102 of the Controlled Substance Act [EPIC, 2001; U.S.C. § 1961(1)(C)(2000)]. U.S.C. Title 18, Section 1961(1)(E), includes any and all acts indictable under the Currency and Foreign Transaction Reporting Act, while subsection (1)(F) includes all indictable acts covered in the Immigration and Nationality Act [U.S.C. § 1961(1)(E) (2000); U.S.C. § 1961(1)(F) (2000)]. The violations and descriptions within Section 1961 stay the same in the 2000 version of Title 18 as they do in the 2001 version of the Patriot Act. Changes other than the "or F" to "F" change are found in addition to the previously nonexistent section "G."

U.S.C. Title 18, Section 1961(1)(G), includes any act that is indictable under any provision listed in Section 2332b(g)(5)(B). This section deals with the following: destruction of aircraft and aircraft facilities; biological weapons; arson within maritime and other jurisdictions; chemical weapons; assassination of government officials; bombing of government property; deaths during an attack on a federal facility; conspiracy to murder, kidnap, or maim persons abroad; items relating to computer protection; killing or attempting to kill officers of the United States; murder or manslaughter of foreign officials; destruction of communication lines; destruction of energy facilities; wrecking trains; terrorist attacks on mass transportation systems; violence against maritime fixed platforms; maritime communications; the bombing of public places; Harboring terrorists; providing material to support terrorists; financing terrorism; sabotage of nuclear facilities; assaults on flight crews with a dangerous weapon; and destruction of an interstate gas or hazardous liquid pipeline facility [EPIC, 2001; U.S.C. §2332b(g)(5)(B) (2000)].

U.S.C. Title 18, Section 1961, subsections (2), (3), (4), (5), (6)(A), (6)(B), (7), (8), (9), and (10), deal with definitions of words and concepts including the following: *state, person, enterprise, pattern of racketeering activity, unlawful debt, racketeering investigator, racketeering investigation, documentary material,* and *attorney general.*

War, Crime, and Terrorism: Revisiting the Capone Connection

The United States has always strived to draw a line between crime and war. In World Wars I and II, the distinction was kept clear. The problem comes when crime takes on the appearance of war, and vice versa, when war comes packaged in the guise of crime (Osler, 2003). After taking over Chicago rackets from Johnny Torrio in 1925, Al Capone made crime look like war. The same year, Capone took control of a literal army of criminals, and the city of Chicago suffered over 100 bombings. Capone's walking army, in combination with his economic pull through the use of legal and illegal business, gave it the appearance of a working government, which slowed his demise by 6 long years (Osler, 2003).

The government, in response to the inability to deal properly with individuals like Capone, devised special laws, in the form of the Racketeer Influenced and Corrupt Act (RICO), to deter Capone-like monopolies. RICO was enacted as Title IX of the Organized Crime Control Act of 1970. RICO has a conspiracy provision that does not require an overt act by the defendant. Congress intended for RICO to be utilized in a wide variety of criminal situations. In short, Congress enacted RICO to be a powerful and comprehensive tool to combat organized crime (Berg & Kelly, 2004).

Some might say that the Osama Bin Laden example is just the opposite of the Capone illustration. Senator Orrin Hatch speaks to this trickery in the international law and religion symposium entitled, *Religious Pluralism, Difference and Social Stability* by saying . . .

> I believe that the 19 hijackers who killed almost 3,000 civilians on September 11 also hijacked a religion... Today, Bin Laden has issued a call for fighters to come to the aid of Saddam Hussein, a well-known secular Arab... Saddam Hussein's desperate terror tactics—of car bombs and assassinations—are not the tactics of an ideologue or a man of faith. They are the tactics of a gangster, and Bin Laden has revealed his true colors by joining forces with this gangster. (Hatch, 2004, p. 319)

This historical proposition by Senator Hatch is very interesting as it establishes links between Osama Bin Laden and Saddam Hussein as "gangsters of a similar feather." Whether either of the analogies forwarded are accurate, the Patriot Act has the coverall answer in Section 813. Serving as a robust version of the original RICO laws, the Patriot Act can attack the financial dynasties of Bin Laden, Al Qaeda, or other equivalent terrorist organizations. This ability to attack the financial structural supports, like those found within the Capone empire, place terrorist groups abroad on a level playing field, no matter what persona is being projected. Within the United States, the effects are being felt.

University of South Florida professor Sami al-Arian, is one of the first domestic cases involving the Patriot Act. Sami al-Arian, along with seven other individuals, are charged in a 50-count indictment, which includes charges of racketeering and money laundering (Chachere, 2004; Lebowitz, 2003). Whether foreign or domestic, a criminal element contingency plan is being implemented in the war on terror.

Conclusion

When reflecting on the implications of Title VIII sections of the Patriot Act, it is paramount to avoid underestimating the implications of the terrorism definitions. Both the definitions of domestic and federal terrorism set the stage for all the preceding sections. Once qualifying under Sections 802 or 808, an individual is open to a plethora of sanctions by the government. In fact, the Patriot Act in its entirety is a reflection, to some extent, of what the government can and will do to an individual who has reached a certain designation.

The Title VIII sections have sat in the shadow of more controversial sections, such as Title II and Title IV. This may be due to the overt nature of other sections or the degree to which some sections have drawn the concern of civil liberties groups. In time, possibly as the debate over the Patriot Act II comes to a theatrical crescendo, these important and fundamental sections found in Title VIII will be recognized for what they truly are, the quiet giants.

References

Ashran, J. (2004). *Stogner v. California*: A collision between the *ex post facto* clause and California's interest in protecting child sex abuse victims. *Journal of Criminal Law and Criminology, 94*, 723-760.

Barbour, A. (2004). Ready…aim…foia! A survey of the Freedom of Information Act in the post-9/11 United States. *Boston Public Interest Law Journal, 13,* 203-226.

Berg, N., & Kelly, C. (2004). Racketeer-influenced and corrupt organizations. *American Criminal Law Review, 41,* 1027-1078.

Calica, A. J. (2004). Self-help is the best kind: The efficient breach justification for forcible abduction of terrorists. *Cornell International Law Journal, 37,* 389-492.

Chachere, V. (2004, January 25). Florida case puts Patriot Act to test, investigators use the law to convert years of surveillance into a criminal case, and defense attorneys attack the government's arguments [Electronic version]. *The Grand Rapids Press,* p. C5. Retrieved April 24, 2005, from the Infotrac Web database.

Chesney, R. M. (2005). The sleeper scenario: Terrorism-support laws and the demands of prevention. *Harvard Journal on Legislation, 42,* 1-89.

Child Abduction Prevention Act and the Child Obscenity and Pornography Prevention Act of 2003: Hearing before the Subcommittee on Crime, Terrorism, and Homeland Security of the Committee of the Judiciary of the House of Representatives, House of Representatives, 108th Cong., 1 (2003).

Demleitner, N. V. (2004). Risk assessment: Methodologies and application: Editor's observations: Risk assessment: Promises and pitfalls. *Federal Sentencing Reporter, 16,* 161-177.

Department of Justice. (n.d.). *Myth v. reality.* Retrieved April 24, 2005, from http:// www.lifeandliberty.gov/subs/add_myths.htm

Dhooge, L. J. (2003). A previously unimaginable risk potential: September 11 and the insurance industry. *American Business Law Journal, 40,* 687-778.

Doyle, C. (2001, December 10). *Terrorism: Section by section analysis of the USA Patriot Act.* The Library of Congress, Congressional Research Service. Retrieved April 15, 2005, from http://www.epic.org/privacy/terrorism/usapatriot/RL31200.pdf

Electronic Privacy Information Center [EPIC]. (2001). *HR 3162 RDS: 107th Congress.* Retrieved September 25, 2004, from http://www.epic.org/privacy/terrorism/hr3162.html

Frei, R. D. (2004). Does time eclipse time? *Stogner v. California* and the court's determination of the *ex post facto* limitations on retroactive justice. *University of Richmond Law Review, 38*, 1001-1045.

Hatch, O. G. (2004). Religious pluralism, difference, and social stability. *Brigham Young University Law Review, 2*, 317-323.

La Fond, J. Q. (2003, March/June). Preventive outpatient commitment for persons with serious mental illness: Outpatient commitment's next frontier: Sexual predators. *Psychology, Public Policy and Law, 9*, 159-182.

Leahy, P. (2001). *The Uniting and Strengthening America by Providing Appropriate Tools Required to Intercept and Obstruct Terrorism (USA Patriot) Act of 2001, H.R. 3162 section-by-section analysis.* Retrieved April 17, 2005, from http://leahy.senate.gov/press/200110/102401a.html

Lebowitz, L. (2003, February 25). Federal case against Florida professor treads new ground under Patriot Act [Electronic version]. *The Miami Herald (Knight Ridder/Tribune News Service),* p. K2478. Retrieved April 24, 2005, from the Infotrac Web database.

Orlova, A. V., & Moore, J. W. (2005). "Umbrellas" or "building blocks"?: Defining international terrorism and transnational organized crime in international law. *Houston Journal of International Law, 27*, 267-310.

Osler, M. (2003). Capone and Bin Laden: The failure of government at the cusp of war and crime. *Baylor Law Review, 55,* 603-615.

Perry, N. J. (2004). The numerous federal legal definitions of terrorism: The problem of too many grails. *Journal of Legislation, 30,* 249-274.

Ravenell, T. E. (2002). Left, left, left, right left: The search for rights and remedies in juvenile boot camps. *Columbia University School of Law, 35,* 347-370.

Richman, D. C., & Stuntz, W. J. (2005). Al Capone's revenge: An essay on the political economy of pretextual prosecution. *Columbia Law Review, 105,* 583-639.

Saito, N. T. (2004). For "our" security: Who is an "American" and what is protected by enhanced law enforcement and intelligence powers? *Seattle Journal for Social Justice, 2,* 23-62.

Smith, S. S., Seifert, J. W., McLoughlin, G. J., & Moteff, J. D. (2002, March 4). *The Internet and the USA Patriot Act: Potential implications for electronic privacy, security, commerce, and government.* The Library of Congress, Congressional Research Service. Retrieved April 16, 2005, from http://www.epic.org/privacy/terrorism/usa-patriot/RL31289.pdf

Travalio, G., & Altenburg, J. (2003). State responsibility for sponsorship of terrorist and insurgent groups: Terrorism, state responsibility, and the use of military force. *Chicago Journal of International Law, 4,* 97-119.

United States Code. (2001). Washington, DC: U.S. Government Printing Office.

United States Code. (2004). Retrieved April 24, 2005, from Cornell University Law School, Legal Information Institute Web site: http://straylight.law.cornell.edu/uscode

CHAPTER 5

Giving Perspective on Detention Issues

JUST AS WE ANALYZED SOME of the Patriot Act sections that remain somewhat quiet within the frenzy of current Patriot Act controversies, it is also important to put some of the most loudly fought media battles of the Patriot Act into perspective. The issue of detention has been in the forefront of the public in many forms. You have probably heard of individuals who have been detained as terrorists or terrorist sympathizers and within the mix is the Patriot Act. Few in American society have missed the tidal wave of news reports that have to do with the detainees at Guantanamo Bay. The common scene repeated in every form of media is that the civil rights organizations are against the detentions and the government is basically for it. The civil rights groups commonly portray the Patriot Act, specifically Sections 411 and 412, as the current tool the government is using to curtail civil rights.

Technically, Sections 411 and 412 give a great amount of power to the government to detain individuals. Section 411 increases the guilt of association to terrorist groups whereby non-citizens can find themselves being removed on terrorist grounds (Keith, 2004). Section 412, which receives even more publicity, is opposed by many as a law that allows the attorney general the power to detain non-citizens who are thought to be involved in terrorist activities (Keith, 2004).

As was explained at the outset of this book, the ultimate goal is not to shape the reader's mind to supporting or opposing the Patriot Act. The goal continues to be to give the reader the most expansive education on as many facets of the Patriot Act as possible. This goal remains the same on this highly contentious issue of detention. However, in giving you the facts, it will be very important to address a lot of preconceived notions that prevail as absolute truth involving the Patriot Act. One foundational notion is that the Patriot Act was a hastily crafted document that was constructed in a near panic following the September 11, 2001, terrorist attacks. For many, the thought of speed and legislation immediately placed the new law in the category of "faulty." As has been documented in Chapter 3, while the Patriot Act was constructed within a 7-week period, a multitude of deliberations were undertaken involving some of the sharpest legislative minds in the country (Doyle, 2002). In fairness, the idea that the Patriot Act was not given adequate reflection should at the least be re-evaluated. Other voices will be heard later in the book about this issue, including some of the most prominent crafters of the Patriot Act.

As far as detention, and more importantly indefinite detention, some preconceived notions should be addressed about the Patriot Act. Subtitle B of the Patriot Act, entitled "Enhanced Immigration Provisions," contains expansions of terms and laws pertaining to non-citizens and detention. However, some may not be aware that controversial Section 412 of the Patriot Act, in which Congress authorizes the detention of "terrorist aliens," has never been used (Cole, 2004). You may be wondering, why is Section 412 being challenged so much if it is not being used? What law or laws are being used to detain all these people seen on the television? These are valid questions and ones that most people never get to, why? Because most people never get these facts about the Patriot Act. Another major component is that the Patriot Act is just so darned controversial. Groups that advocate against the Patriot Act see a section that does not square with their philosophy and they run with it.

As I prepare to illuminate the detention issue, I should take a moment to put another misconception to rest. This misconception is often given by omission, and that is that only in America is there a law like the Patriot Act. That is just inaccurate. Great Britain has their own Patriot Act, entitled the "Anti-Terrorism, Crime and Security Act 2001" (ATCSA). As with the Patriot Act, ATCSA was the British response for purposes of national security due to the 9-11 attacks (Keith, 2004). While the Patriot Act's detention provisions, when contrasted against Great Britain's version, are evaluated as measured and restrained (Keith, 2004), this logic is lost on many who never knew that the information existed. Due to the fact that the Patriot

Act has been the focus of massive, sensitized debates, the true nature of its impact, and that of other immigration laws, has been distorted.

Regardless of the misconceptions over the Patriot Act, the argument over the legality of indefinite detention does not change. Without a doubt, the subject of "preventative detention" (Legomsky, 2005) and the more arbitrary term of "suspicionless preventative detention" (Cole, 2004), are being evaluated.

In many ways, the issue of the legality of indefinite detention goes far beyond the Patriot Act. That's correct, the majority of detention issues that affect most of the detainees in the war on terror pertain more to administrational policy than to the Patriot Act. However, understanding where the Patriot Act stops and other laws take over is just as important as knowing what issue of detention the Patriot Act is affecting.

If a debate is to take place over the government's authority to legally hold an individual in indefinite detention, it is only logical to start at the source. It is commonly understood that before a person can be at risk of being held forever without release, he or she must first be detained. Historically speaking, the government standard on civil liberties for noncitizens has been lowered in times of perceived national crisis (Engle, 2004; Thomas, 2003). History often reflects on how Executive Order 9066 (Sekhon, 2003), signed by President Roosevelt, precipitated the detention of approximately 110,000 Americans of Japanese decent (Block, 2005; Lilly, 2003; Sekhon 2003; Thomas 2003). The detentions began on December 7, 1941, and lasted for more than 12 months. The primary reason for the internments was a fear that Japanese within the country would sabotage the war effort (Block, 2005). During the Korean conflict, the Emergency Detention Act again gave authorities the power to construct internment camps for the purpose of holding individuals thought to be disloyal to the country (Block, 2005).

To answer the question of why the Patriot Act is not using Section 412 we have to move closer to present day. By the 1990s, illegal immigration concerns were in the forefront of U.S. debate. A growing number of people were concerned over the fact that U.S. resources were being consumed by undocumented workers, as well as a fear over the possibility of an influx of criminal aliens into the United States (McKenzie, 2004; Miller, 2005). This issue continues to rage at present. In response to the growing concerns over illegal immigration came a myriad of immigration laws. It is not only the number of laws, but how these laws worked together with the idea of "criminalizing immigration" (Miller, 2005), that is of great importance.

Fueling the issue of immigration reform even more were terrorism related incidents such as the 1995 Oklahoma bombing (Marshall, 2002). Two of the most pivotal laws that were enacted during this period were the Anti-Terrorism and Effective Death Penalty Act (AEDPA) and the Illegal Immigration Reform and Immigrant Responsibility Act (IIRIRA). The Anti-Terrorism and Effective Death Penalty Act effectively imposed a plethora of limitations for habeas corpus requests by detainees (Marshall, 2002), while giving authority to the secretary of state to designate foreign entities as terrorist organizations (Broxmeyer, 2004). In effect, the Anti-Terrorism and Effective Death Penalty Act worked to: expand the grounds for non-citizen deportation, restricted relief while requiring detention for most criminal offenders, and created harsher categories for deportable aggravated felonies (Miller, 2005; Vandenberg, 2004). The Illegal Immigration Reform and Immigrant Responsibility Act followed less than 6 months later and was considered an attempt to soften restrictions placed on non-citizens by the AEDPA. The IIRIRA had the opposite effect and actually widened the scope for deporting immigrants while expediting the process (Miller, 2005; Vandenberg, 2004).

In actuality, prior to the tragedy of September 11, 2001, before pen had ever been put to paper on the Patriot Act, immigration laws involving harsh new penalties in the areas pertaining to detention, among others, had been greatly amplified (Miller, 2005).

Just going this far into the history tells a person that the issue of indefinite detention is very complex. The fact is that the Patriot Act gets credit for some of the laws enacted in the 1990s. This fact, and those previously stated, do not in themselves prove the legality of indefinite detention, nor do they exonerate the Patriot Act of any deficiencies. What it does do is take you one step further to having a more rounded knowledge of where the Patriot Act starts and stops. Let's continue to evaluate more issues of detention by analyzing certain definitions and presidential responsibilities germane to the subject along with public cases seen in the media.

After the cataclysmic events of September 11, 2001, a rapid response to the terrorists' acts was seen in a virtual assembly line of new legislation. The Patriot Act, the Homeland Security Act, and the Enhanced Border Security and Visa Entry Reform Act were passed in succession with a common goal -- to protect the nation through the means of surveillance and detention of non-citizens who might threaten the national security of the country (Miller, 2005). Investigative detentions were also increased during the official Pentagon/Twin Towers Bombing Investigation. Arab Muslim males were the most prone to detention and questioning during this time period (Legomsky, 2005).

As the government began the process of detaining non-immigrants, a fine tuning process was being conducted in the designation process of terrorist countries. Legomsky (2005) stated, "On March 18, 2003, the Department of Homeland Security…announced an initiative called 'Operation Liberty Shield.' The initiative was accompanied by an administration list of thirty-four countries designated as harboring terrorists" (p. 164). Though the program was short-lived, it required detention of nationals seeking U.S. asylum who lacked proper documents (Legomsky, 2005). The groundwork had been laid by years of enhancing immigration laws to discourage threats that ranged from undocumented workers to tangible terrorist threats. A specific catalyst transpired in the September 11, 2001, attacks to stimulate even stronger national security legislation and the implementation of detention proceedings.

It is important to understand in what context the term "enemy combatant" is used. While there are many variations of its definition, a general description of "enemy combatant" would be -- an adversary who has taken up arms against the U.S. It is important to note that an enemy combatant can be a "lawful combatant," or an "unlawful combatant." A lawful combatant is one who complies with the laws of war, such as wearing a uniform, using hospitals for medical purposes only, etc. Lawful combatants are afforded the rights under the Geneva Convention (Ash, 2002). Unlawful combatants are individuals who also take up arms against the U.S. but do not adhere to the laws of war. These individuals may be tried for violating the laws of war. Enemy combatants, in general, are not detained because of probable cause like in the criminal courts. Instead, enemy combatants are detained due to their armed belligerent nature and the need to detain such individuals until they no longer pose a viable threat to the nation (Ash, 2002).

By the nature of some definitions of indefinite detention, it is presupposed that a termination point in detention will be reached at some point in time (Encarta, 2005). However, the term indefinite detention may also be defined as a detention that is "not clear" or "vague and uncertain" (Encarta, 2005). In clarifying the actual argument, whether or not the government has the legal authority to detain individuals for an unknown, rather than an unlimited, amount of time is the issue.

The term "enemy combatant" is inexorably tied to the concept of war. The responsibility for national security during times of war is a joint responsibility shared by Congress and the President of the United States (Block, 2005). The argument over the legality of indefinite detention and the war on terror often begins over the lack of a congressional declaration of war. The president is the commander in chief of the military, while Congress has the specific power to declare war. However, congressional declarations of war are infrequent. The last congressional declaration of war was obtained during the Franklin D. Roosevelt administration prior to World War II (Block, 2005). The more common accepted practice of warfare in recent history has been to bypass the congressional declaration of war and use the president's official constitutional powers as commander in chief of the military. However, while hostilities involving the U.S. and other belligerent entities have been verified as legal and constitutional, starting from the times of President Harry Truman in the Korean War, which launched the coinage of the term "police action" (Block, 2005), the non-congressional declaration of war has played a pivotal role in the ambiguity over the legitimacy of the current war against terror. In sifting through the complexities of enemy combatants and their civil liberties, one must not only understand the dynamic nature of difficult definitions, but also the definitional relationship in conjunction to the legality of warfare without a congressional declaration.

Historically, the case which brought forth the term "enemy combatant" was in *Ex Parte Quirin* (Jackola, 2004). In *Ex Parte Quirin*, (1942), eight German soldiers wearing military uniforms, carrying detonation equipment, exited a submarine near the coastline of New York and Florida. The soldiers removed their uniforms upon arriving, attempting to blend in for the purpose of committing sabotage on U.S. soil (Block 2005; Jackola, 2004; Kubler, 2004). After the soldiers were arrested they petitioned for habeas corpus. During the habeas corpus hearing the Supreme Court decided that the saboteurs could be tried by a military tribunal. Furthermore, the court created a new classification, enemy combatant, as the soldiers did not meet the definition of a traditional criminal or a prisoner of war (Jackola, 2004). The court in *Quirin* gave a working definition of an enemy combatant as: a belligerent who comes secretly across the lines, without a uniform, to wage war by destruction of life or property. In *Quirin* the courts also made it clear that U.S. citizens could be designated as enemy combatants (Jackola, 2004).

A very popular example of enemy combatant status is the case of Yaser Esam Hamdi. Yaser Esam Hamdi was born in Louisiana in 1980, and moved with his family to Saudi Arabia as a young boy. Hamdi started living in Afghanistan in 2001 (Kubler, 2004). During that year, it was reported that he was captured by the northern alliance in an active combat zone with members of the Taliban. Hamdi was reported to have been in possession of an assault rifle at the time of his capture (Committee on Federal Courts, 2004). Hamdi was originally taken to Guantanamo Bay, and then later transferred to a naval holding facility in Norfolk, Virginia (Kubler, 2004). The government classified Hamdi as an enemy combatant which, by its designation, allowed for his detention, without representation or formal charges being filed, indefinitely.

Hamdi's father filed a petition on his behalf stating that his son was in Afghanistan for the purpose of giving "relief aid" (Jackola, 2004). The petition argued that because Hamdi was an American citizen, that he should have all the rights delegated under the Constitution. The district court granted Hamdi counsel. The appeal court reversed the decision of the district court allowing counsel for Hamdi (Jackola, 2004). The Supreme Court heard the case and decided that under the congressional passage of the resolution Authorizing Use of Military Force (AUMF), the language, "necessary and appropriate force," provided for the authorization of Hamdi's detention and limited judicial inquiry (*Hamdi v. Rumsfeld*, 2004). That is, Hamdi's indefinite detention was not found illegal; however, he was allowed to challenge this detention through habeas corpus.

One interesting event that transpired during the *Hamdi v. Rumsfeld* case was the construction of a two prong test to determine the validity of an enemy combatant status. This test included the following: (a) the government must have legal authority to detain a prisoner as an enemy combatant, and (b) the government must supply basic facts to support its decision to detain the individual as an enemy combatant (Jackola, 2004). The creation of a viable standard by the court for the determination of an enemy combatant has important implications. First, by creating a standard, the courts are affirming the validity of the enemy combatant definition found in *Quirin*. Second, the courts are effectively forwarding the legitimacy of the presidential determination and detention of enemy combatants by attempting to standardize the process as opposed to eliminating the process. Third, the courts are guaranteeing the continued process of indefinite detention of enemy combatants by creating a legal precedent that is void in addressing any other legal issue but habeas corpus.

Currently, the United States is holding approximately 600 non-citizens at Guantanamo Bay (*Rasul v. Bush*, 2004). These individuals, other than John Walker Lindh whose case has already been decided in criminal court (Block, 2005), have been designated by the government as enemy combatants. Detained primarily for the purpose of interrogation (Welsh, 2004), prisoners at Guantanamo have not been allowed visitors, legal representation, or to petition for habeas corpus relief. The government has asserted that these alleged terrorists have been designated as enemy combatants in accordance with the president's commander in chief constitutional authority. The government further states that the Guantanamo Bay detentions are statutorily valid, leaning on the precedent found in *Johnson v. Eisentrager* (1950).

In *Johnson v. Eisentrager*, 21 German soldiers who were in China after World War II were captured by U.S. forces (Block, 2005). The soldiers were accused of continuing hostilities. After the soldiers submitted habeas corpus petitions, the courts ruled that they had no jurisdiction to intercede because the soldiers were captured and held on foreign soil (Block, 2005). The Guantanamo Bay detainees have been held primarily based on the precedent set in *Eisentrager* (Committee on Federal Courts, 2004).

In certain cases, the lower courts have denied Guantanamo detainees habeas corpus rights due to the precedent established in *Eisentrager* (*Gherebi v. Bush*, 2003); however, court decisions are subject to change. On June 28, 2004, the Supreme Court stated that detainees in Guantanamo Bay should be allowed habeas corpus proceedings. Some of the differences between the two cases were that in *Eisentrager* the detainees: were enemy combatants, had never been in the U.S., were tried for violations of laws of war, and held at all times outside of U.S. territory (*Rasul v. Bush*, 2004; Welsh, 2004). In contrast, the Guantanamo detainees fell into a different category which included the following characteristics: were not nationals of countries at war with U.S., they deny taking actions against the U.S., have not been tried or convicted, and were held on U.S. controlled territory (*Rasul v. Bush*, 2004; Welsh, 2004). While looking at these different issues, the courts centered on the jurisdictional issue of the United States' contract with Cuba and said that the detention facility was an "American territory," and would at the least afford detainees habeas corpus privileges (Committee on Federal Courts, 2004; *Rasul v. Bush*, 2004). Under the federal habeas corpus provision (28 USCA § 2241), the federal district court will review the legality of the detentions of the detainees at the Naval Base in Guantanamo Cuba (*Rasul v. Bush*, 2004).

The *Padilla* case, also known as *Padilla v. Bush* (2002), involves the arrest of Jose Padilla on May 8, 2002, at the Chicago O'Hare Airport. Padilla, an ex-Chicago gang member, changed his name to Adullah Al Muhajir after marrying a Muslim woman. Sometime after 1994, Muhajir (Padilla), moved to Egypt (Kubler, 2004). Padilla was originally arrested in Chicago as a material witness by the Southern District of New York (Block, 2005; Committee on Federal Courts, 2004). Padilla was given counsel and filed a writ of habeas corpus. After the motion had been filed, the government withdrew the grand jury subpoena and Padilla's classification was changed from a witness to an enemy combatant (Committee on Federal Courts, 2004). Thirty-one year old Jose Padilla would become the second American citizen to be labeled an enemy combatant in the war on terror (Kubler, 2004).

Under the classification as an enemy combatant, Padilla was alleged to have made contacts while in Afghanistan with the terrorist organization al Qaeda as well as taking up arms against U.S. forces. Padilla was alleged to have joined in a conspiracy to construct and detonate a "dirty bomb" within the United States. The government petitioned the district court to deny Padilla representation on the grounds of national security. However, different from the *Hamdi* detention that took place on foreign soil, the fact that Padilla had been detained on U.S. soil gave him a higher probability of the right to counsel guaranteed by the Constitution (Jackola, 2004). Issues involved in the *Padilla* case were the indefinite detention of Padilla without charges, as well as rights to counsel. The prosecution alleged the president had the authority to designate Padilla an enemy combatant based on the congressional passage of the Authorization of Military Force Law, No. 107-40, § 2(a), 115 Stat. 224, 2001 (*Padilla v. Bush*, 2002). Because Padilla had already been appointed counsel as a witness, the district judge stated that he would allow Padilla to retain representation. A government appeal of the judge's decision landed the case in the second circuit court which found the entire detention unconstitutional (Committee on Federal Courts, 2004; *Padilla v. Rumsfeld*, 2003). The case has been appealed to the Supreme Court for a definitive decision on questions such as whether or not indefinite detention is within the war power of the president. If the president was to have been found to not have this power of detention, then issues related to enemy combatant status, such as the holding of individuals incommunicado from the outside world without charges filed, and greatly restricted habeas corpus access, might have become non-issues (Committee on Federal Courts, 2004).

The *Padilla* case would be argued in front of the Supreme Court from April 28, 2004, to June 28, 2004 (The Oyez Project, n.d.). Unfortunately, the high court would make no decision on the matter. Instead, by a 5-4 decision, the court determined that the case had been improperly filed and sent the case back down for re-filing in South Carolina. The court stated the petition for habeas corpus had been inappropriately filed against Secretary of Defense Donald Rumsfeld instead of the brig commander, C.T. Hanft, who actually held Padilla (The Oyez Project, 2004). The case was re-filed in U.S. District Court in South Carolina where District Judge Henry Floyd sided with Padilla's defense team by saying that the government must bring about formal charges within 45 days or Padilla would be eligible for release (Hirschkorn, 2005). A complete turnabout was again seen in the 4th Circuit Court of Appeals where the court stated that the president had the right to detain Padilla as an enemy combatant (*Padilla v. C.T. Hanft*, 2005). Judge Luttig, who wrote the opinion for the court, stated:

> Given that Padilla qualifies as an enemy combatant under both the definition adopted by the Court in *Quirin* and the definition accepted by the controlling opinion in *Hamdi*, his military detention as an enemy combatant by the President is unquestionably authorized by the AUMF as a fundamental incident to the President's prosecution of the war against al Qaeda in Afghanistan. (*Padilla v. Hanft*, 2005, p. 11)

It is important to note that the appeals court took the time and effort to explain that the *Hamdi* case, as well as its ruling in *Padilla*, only gave the president the authority to detain Padilla for the duration of U.S. and al Qaeda hostilities in Afghanistan (*Padilla v. Hanft*, 2005). The appeals court decision was scheduled to go back before the Supreme Court when, on November 22, 2005, Padilla was indicted by a grand Jury in Miami, Florida. The grand jury indicted Padilla on charges that he conspired to "murder, kidnap, and maim" people overseas. Curiously, the dirty bomb conspiracy allegation that had followed Padilla for the length of his detention was not in the list of charges (Sherman, 2005; Arena, Frieden, & Hirschkorn, 2005).

This omission was not overlooked by the 4th Circuit Court of Appeals which admonished the administration (Markon, 2005).

On January 4, 2006, the Supreme Court allowed Padilla to be transferred by the military to Miami to face criminal charges (*Hanft v. Padilla,* 2006). The Padilla criminal case is still pending. Some say that the government's decision to go with a criminal indictment was to avoid further Supreme Court scrutiny (Arena et al., 2005; Sherman, 2005).

The *Padilla* case, while it continues to be battled in the courts has similar elements as the Civil War case, *Ex Parte Milligan* (1866). In *Milligan*, an American citizen was arrested for plotting to attack military installations. The Supreme Court ultimately allowed the accused American conspirator habeas corpus rights.

A similar case of a material witness later labeled an enemy combatant without the element of U.S. citizenship is seen in the case of al-Marri. Al-Marri, who was arrested on U.S. soil in Peoria, Illinois, filed a writ of habeas corpus after charges of credit card fraud were filed against him by the government. The habeas corpus petition was denied due to a jurisdictional problem with its submission (Committee on Federal Courts, 2004).

Center stage in the spotlight of the controversy over indefinite detention was the case of Zarcarias Moussaoui. Moussaoui provides a unique example for review as it deals with the issue of a non-citizen detained prior to September 11, 2001. Moussaoui, a 33-year-old French Moroccan, was arrested for a visa violation. Having been enrolled in flight school in Eagan, Minnesota, Moussaoui was alleged to have been unable to explain why he wanted to learn to fly a 747 (Novak, 2003). This mystery, in combination with testimony by captured al Qaeda members, implicated Moussaoui in the September 11, 2001, terrorist attacks (Jackola, 2004). The criminal court was quickly bogged down in several procedures that were not conducive to the prosecution's desires. Namely, while Moussaoui had not originally been designated as an enemy combatant; he had requested to call witnesses who were under that status. Citing concerns for national security, the government refused Moussaoui's request (Block, 2005). Later in the case, District Judge Leonie Brinkema advised prosecutors that the death penalty in the Moussaoui case would not be an option due to the fact that the defendant had not been given proper access to defense witnesses (Novak, 2003). The government then attempted to change Moussaoui's status to an enemy combatant and move him from the criminal courts to a military tribunal setting (Block, 2005; Jackola, 2004; Novak, 2003). This change of venue did not happen as Moussaoui pled guilty within the criminal court system. Many saw this as Moussaoui's effort to become an al Qaeda martyr as the death penalty had been reinstated as an option in the case. If this was Moussaoui's intent, to die a martyr's death, it would fail as a jury, by a one vote margin (Sniffen, 2006), sentenced the al Qaeda terrorist to life in prison, in what will most likely be the Supermax prison in Florence, Colorado, affectionately coined the "Alcatraz in the Rockies" (Hirschkorn, 2006). In Moussaoui's final court room outburst he exclaimed, "God curse America and save Osama bin Laden. You'll never get him" (Moussaoui, as cited in Hirschkorn, 2006). U.S. District Judge Leonie Brinkema reinforced the line of thinking that Moussaoui was being denied his own wishes by saying, "You came here to be a martyr and die in a great big bang, but to paraphrase the poet T.S. Eliot, instead you will die with a whimper" (Brinkema, as cited in Hirschkorn, 2006).

As with all the cases previously stated, double jeopardy figures into at least part of the issue at contention. The Moussaoui case, regardless of its final outcome, brought another very important legal element to bear on the enemy combatant and indefinite detention issue. This element is the concept of double jeopardy.

The U.S. Constitution addresses the subject of double jeopardy in the Fifth Amendment of the Constitution by saying:

> No person shall be held to answer for a capital, or otherwise infamous crime, unless on a presentment or indictment of a grand jury, except in cases arising in the land or naval forces, or in the militia, when in actual service in time of war or public danger; nor shall any person be subject for the same offense to be twice put in jeopardy of life or limb; nor shall be compelled in any criminal case to be a witness against himself, nor be deprived of life, liberty, or property, without due process of law; nor shall private property be taken for public use, without just compensation. (U.S. Constitution)

The double jeopardy attachments make the indefinite detention issue even more complex. For instance, double jeopardy can be asserted to apply at the point where a jury has been sworn in for active duty. In cases where there is no jury, double jeopardy can be asserted when the first witness in a trial swears in to give testimony (*Crist v. Bretz*, 1978). Double jeopardy does not attach when the defendant moves for a mistrial (*United States v. Dinitz*, 1976). If a case is dismissed before the trial takes place, there is no double jeopardy attachment. Double jeopardy may not apply after a jury has been sworn in if a dismissal by the prosecution involves a drafting error in the jurisdiction of the case that cannot be cured by an amendment (*Illinois v. Somerville*, 1973).

The concept of double jeopardy is a particularly complex subject within the context of the current war on terror. With both the criminal courts and military tribunals having the constitutional authority to try terrorists, and no adequate historical precedent to draw from (Jackola, 2004), what is the government to do? Even more common questions which have been recently forwarded are: Have double jeopardy violations already occurred; what will be the ramifications of the violations; and how can the controversy over this issue be alleviated within constitutional boundaries? The courts have to apply the Constitution to several different situations in the war on terror.

Rachel S. Martin (2003), when talking about the court's struggles in constitutional translation to Title II questions within the Patriot Act, made a unique observation of the duality of thinking within the courts on the Constitution today. The courts may interpret amendments literally with no flexibility, a strategy called "one-step originalism." In other situations, the courts may use a more broad approach where the original amendment's protections are translated into the current dynamic environment of today. This style is known as "translation theory" (Lessig, 1999, as cited in Martin, 2003).

While there have been parallels drawn between post 9-11 non-citizen detentions, which domestically number around 5,000, and historical incidents, such as the World War II Japanese internments and the Palmer Raids of the 1950s (Cole, 2004), these correlations may not paint an accurate picture of the facts. In actuality, the largest current impacts on immigration detention and deportation were seen pre-9-11 in the 1990s. In the 1990s, Congress made the deportation of criminal aliens a number one priority. It was in 1996 that a record number of immigrants were removed from the country. From 1993 to 1999 immigrant deportation went from a yearly average of approximately 42,000 to over 170,000 non-citizens (Johnson, 2003). It is interesting to note that the majority of these detained and deported non-citizens were not Arabs or Muslims, but Mexicans from the southern border (Johnson, 2003). While illuminating this point of history does not in itself prove the legality of indefinite detention, it portrays the blurred factual landscape in which this debate currently exists.

One of the most contentious points of indefinite detention is centered on the absence of a congressional declaration of war. The president retains the legal responsibility and constitutional authority as commander in chief of the military to defend the nation. This presidential responsibility, in combination with the Congress supported Joint Resolution 107-40 authorizing the use of military force (Block, 2005), makes many of the foundational arguments of the legality of indefinite detention in the war on terrorism moot. However, the added physiological legitimacy of a congressional declaration of war may have softened, or possibly eliminated, the cloud of suspicion and opposition that has followed the war on terror (Committee on Federal Courts, 2004), and the tools of that war, like the detention of enemy combatants, and the Patriot Act.

Exacerbating negative perceptions, the government has fallen into a trap of perceived illegality over the use of the criminal courts for the purpose of prosecuting enemy combatants. While the use of military tribunals, as well as criminal courts, are constitutionally allowable for the prosecution of enemy combatants (Jackola, 2004), the government found itself having trouble trying to deal with the dual jurisdiction. Specifically, the higher standards of the criminal courts served as a quagmire in the Moussaoui case (Jackola, 2004). While the evidence at this time supports the assertion that the attempt by the government to transfer Moussaoui from a criminal court to a military tribunal due to the prosecutor's jurisdictional error (*Illinois v. Somerville*, 1973), does not invoke a double jeopardy issue, rather it is a salient example of bad form. Once again, the government is caught looking terrible while actually standing on legal ground. The dual court system is a balancing act that is unnecessary and future complications may certainly be avoided by the majority of enemy combatant cases being prosecuted through military tribunals.

The Guantanamo Bay ruling is interesting as it will have an impact on many lives, but as importantly, it sets a precedent for future detention rulings. Legally, the decision by the Supreme Court made no judgment as to whether holding individuals as enemy combatants indefinitely, with none of the rights afforded in the U.S., is unconstitutional. In fact, the decision at Guantanamo speaks most strongly to the matter of location. If you are on U.S. soil or an equivalent, habeas corpus rights are more probable than for a similar detention on foreign soil, regardless of U.S. citizenship (Welsh, 2004). Even though legality of indefinite detention was not addressed in the Guantanamo case, it may signify that the courts are uncomfortable with the sharp contrasts between the U.S. military and U.S. criminal procedures for detainees.

The issue of enemy combatants and indefinite detention will continue to be a hotly contested issue. While there will always be the danger of legal punitive damages for illegal detention in times of war, such as the Japanese internments (Minami, Narasaki, Nimr, Chang, & Ting, 2004), the ramifications run deeper. Just as war itself pulls at the emotional fabric of human beings, dividing groups, and heating the blood, the impression of impropriety by the government feeds a forest fire of discontent. The government must understand that it truly is in a battle for the hearts and minds of not only friends and allies abroad, but the populace at home.

The future may see different and more expanded rulings by the courts on indefinite detention. At this time, it appears that if you are detained on U.S. soil you have a higher expectation of at least a habeas corpus hearing. If you are detained on foreign soil and are not a U.S. citizen, your habeas corpus rights will be highly questionable, as well as other standard rights and privileges, such as counsel and visitors. This wartime designation and implementation has not been struck down as unconstitutional. What the courts have done is show their uneasiness with the idea of military tribunals being conducted on Guantanamo Bay detainees in a war that has no congressional declaration. While the outcome of this current legal debate may move faster than the printers for this book, it is foreseen that that the current administration may have to make several accommodations to move forward with military tribunals in a climate which only becomes more sensitized with time.

Currently, Section 412 of the Patriot Act is sitting unused as the government implements enhanced detention laws from the 1990s. It could be debated, no matter what your perspective on detention is, whether the government should maintain sections in the Patriot Act that are not being used. Could viable alternatives be incorporated that would be more amenable and less contentious to civil rights in the court of public opinion? We will examine differing opinions on several aspects of the Patriot Act, and the groups that proffer them, in the next two chapters.

References

Arena, K., Frieden, T., & Hirschkorn, P. (2005, November 22). *Terror suspect Padilla charged*. Retrieved August 10, 2006, from http://www.cnn.com/2005/LAW/11/22/padilla.case/ index.html

Ash, R. W. (2002, June 11). *American Center for Law & Justice memo - Lawfulness of incarceration of al-Qaeda "dirty bomb" suspect*. Retrieved March 9, 2005, from http://www.aclj.org/Issues/Resources/Document.aspx?ID=138

Block, F. (2005). Civil liberties during national emergencies: The interactions between the three branches of government in coping with past and current threats to the nation's security. *New York University School of Law Review of Law and Social Change, 29,* 459-524.

Broxmeyer, E. (2004). The problems of security and freedom: Procedural due process and the designation of foreign terrorist organizations under the Anti-terrorism and Effective Death Penalty Act. *Berkeley Journal of International Law, 22,* 439-488.

Cole, D. (2004). The priority of morality: The emergency constitution's blind spot. *Yale Law Journal, 113,* 1753-1800.

Committee on Federal Courts. (2004). The indefinite detention of "enemy combatants": Balancing due process and national security in the context of the war on terror. *The Record of the Association of The Bar of the City of New York, 59,* 41-161.

Crist v. Bretz, 437 U.S. 28, 98 S. Ct. 2156 (1978).

Doyle, C. (2002, April 15). *The USA Patriot Act: a legal analysis*. The Library of Congress, Congressional Research Service. Retrieved November 16, 2004, from http://www.fas.org /irp/crs/RL31377.pdf

Encarta World English Dictionary [North American Edition]. (2005). [Electronic Version]. Retrieved April 1, 2005, from http://Encarta.msn.com/dictionary_/indefinite.html

Engle, K. (2004). Constructing good aliens and good citizens: Legitimizing the war on terror(ism). *University of Colorado Law Review, 75*, 59-114.

Ex Parte Milligan, 71 U.S. 2 (4 Wall.); 18 L. Ed. 281 (1866).

Ex Parte Quirin, 317 U.S. 1; 63 S. Ct. 2; 87 L. Ed. 3 (1942).

Gherebi v. Bush, 352 F.3d 1278 (9th Cir. 2003).

Hamdi v. Rumsfeld, 542 U.S. 507; 124 S. Ct. 2633; 159 L. Ed. 2d 578 (2004).

Hanft v. Padilla, 546 U.S. ____ (2006). January 4, 2006 Order in Pending Case. Retrieved August 10, 2006, from http://www.supremecourtus.gov/orders/courtorders/ 010406pzr.pdf

Hirschkorn, P. (2005, March 1). *Federal judge: Charge Padilla or release him.* Retrieved August 10, 2006, from http://www.cnn.com/2005/LAW/03/01/padilla.ruling/

Hirschkorn, P. (2006, May 5). *Moussaoui curses America but judge gets final word.* Retrieved August 10, 2006, from http://www.cnn.com/2006/LAW/05/04/moussaoui.verdict/ index.html

Illinois v. Somerville, 410 U.S. 458, 93 S. Ct. 1066; 35 L. Ed. 2d 425 (1973).

Jackola, A. T. (2004). A second bite at the apple: How the government's use of the doctrine of enemy combatants in the case of Zacarias Moussaoui threatens to upset the future of the criminal justice system. *Hamline Law Review, 27*, 101-132.

Johnson v. Eisentrager, 339 U.S. 763; 70 S. Ct. 936; 94 L. Ed. 1255 (1950).

Johnson, K. R. (2003). Beyond belonging: Challenging the boundaries of nationality: September 11 and Mexican immigrants: Collateral damage comes home. *DePaul Law Review, 52,* 849-870.

Keith, D. (2004). In the name of national security or insecurity? The potential indefinite detention of noncitizen certified terrorists in the United States and the United Kingdom in the aftermath of September 11, 2001. *Florida Journal of International Law, 16,* 405-481.

Kubler, J. (2004). U.S. citizens as enemy combatants; indication of a rollback of civil liberties or a sign of our jurisprudential evolution? *St. John's Journal of Legal Commentary, 18,* 631-673.

Legomsky, S. H. (2005). Immigration law and human rights: Legal line drawing post-September 11: Symposium article: The ethnic and religious profiling of noncitizens: National security and international human rights. *Boston College Third World Law Journal, 25,* 161-196.

Lilly, J. R. (2003). National security at what price?: A look into civil liberty concerns in the information age under the USA Patriot Act of 2001 and a proposed constitutional test for future legislation. *Cornell Journal of Law and Public Policy, 12,* 447-471.

Markon, J. (2005, December 1). Appeals court balks at Padilla transfer. [Electronic Version]. *The Washington Post,* p. A02. Retrieved August 10, 2006, from http://www.washingtonpost.com

Marshall, K. M. (2002). Finding time for federal habeas corpus: *Carey v. Saffold. Akron Law Review, 37,* 549-587.

Martin, R. S. (2003). Watch what you type: As the FBI records your keystrokes, the Fourth Amendment develops carpal tunnel syndrome. *American Criminal Law Review, 40,* 1271-1300.

McKenzie, A. (2004). A nation of immigrants or a nation of suspects? State and local enforcement of federal immigration laws since 9-11. *Alabama Law Review, 55,* 1149-1165.

Miller, T. (2005). Immigration law and human rights: Legal line drawing post-September 11: Symposium article: Blurring the boundaries between immigration and crime control after September 11th. *Boston College Third World Law Journal, 25,* 81-123.

Minami, D., Narasaki, K., Nimr, H., Chang, J., Ting, P. (2004). Sixty years after the internment: Civil rights, identity politics, and racial profiling. *Asian Law Journal, 11,* 151-176.

Novak, V. (2003, October 27). How the Moussaoui crumbled. [Electronic Version]. *Time, 162*(17).

The Oyez Project. (n.d.). *Rumsfeld v. Padilla, 542 U.S. 426 (2004).* Retrieved August 10, 2006, from http://www.oyez.org/oyez/resource/case/1730/

Padilla v. Bush, 233 F. Supp.2d 564 (S.D.N.Y. 2002).

Padilla v. Hanft, No. 05-6396 (4th Cir., Sept. 9, 2005). Retrieved August 10, 2006, from http://pacer.ca4.uscourts.gov/opinion.pdf/056396.P.pdf

Padilla v. Rumsfeld, 352 F.3d 695 (2d Cir. 2003).

Rasul v. Bush, 542 U.S. 466; 124 S. Ct. 2686; 159 L. Ed. 2d 548 (2004).

Sekhon, V. (2003). The civil rights of "others": Antiterrorism, the Patriot Act, and Arab and South Asian American rights in post-9/11 American society. *Texas Forum on Civil Liberties & Civil Rights, 8,* 117-148.

Sherman, M. (2005, November 22). *Dirty bomb suspect Padilla indicted.* Retrieved August 10, 2006, from http://www.sfgate.com/cgi-bin/article.cgi?f=/n/a/2005/11/22/national/ w080854S36.DTL

Sniffen, M. J. (2006, May 12). Moussaoui appeals judgment and sentence. [Electronic Version]. *The Washington Post.* Retrieved May 14, 2006, from http://www.washingtonpost.com/wp-dyn/content/article/ 2006/05/12/AR2006051200367.html

Thomas, P. A. (2003). Emergency and anti-terrorist power: 9/11: USA and UK. *Fordham International Law Journal, 26*, 1193-1229.

United States v. Dinitz, 424 U.S. 600, 96 S. Ct. 1075; 47 L. Ed. 2d 267 (1976).

U.S. Constitution, Amendment V.

Vandenberg, Q. H. (2004). How can the United States rectify its post-9/11 stance on noncitizens' rights? *Notre Dame Journal of Law, Ethics & Public Policy, 18,* 605-645.

Welsh, S. C. (2004, June 30). *Law watch - detainees: Supreme Court Guantanamo decision.* Washington, DC: The Center for Defense Information. Retrieved March 11, 2005, from
http://www.ciaonet.org/wps/wes07/

CHAPTER 6

Support for the Patriot Act

THE PURPOSE OF THIS CHAPTER and the one to follow is to give readers a glimpse of the differing views and positions on the Patriot Act. The views that will be forwarded by individuals and various groups may not encompass their entire argument on the subject. Furthermore, source information may be used to provide a context by which certain stances are often taken on the Patriot Act without embodying the personal feelings of individuals or groups on this subject. Positions for supporting the Patriot Act may or may not contain a counter argument in the following chapter. If a counter argument is not present, it is not meant to imply that such an argument does not exist. It is important to note that certain events that may be seen as either supporting or detracting from the Patriot Act argument transpired specifically during the renewal process and readers should not despair if they do not see certain events documented in this specific section. As importantly, readers may or may not find their own views on the Patriot Act within these two chapters. It is most possible that the reader's view may be somewhere in between. The goal of the following chapters is **not** to try to sway readers to a certain ideology on the Patriot Act but to open minds to the various opinions that already exist.

The events of 9-11 shook the world. This was in part because the U.S., compared to many nations of the world, had been more or less unblemished by the horrors of terrorism. This naiveté was probably shared by the greatest majority of Americans who lived their lives with terrorism as a far removed concept that was quietly delegated to third world countries on the other side of the globe. On February 16, 2005, speaking for the

Regional Community Policing Training Institute at Wichita State University, Wichita, Kansas, terrorism expert Dr. David Carter spoke about the western mindset prior to 9-11. During the educational lecture, entitled *Terrorism and Criminal Extremism: A Perspective for Community Members*, Carter summed up the unique way that Americans think by saying, "We in America look at terrorism with a western logic" (Carter, *Wichita State University Lecture*, 2005).

Richard Crockatt talks about the United States' harsh re-awakening to the cold realities of terrorism in his book, *America Embattled: September 11, Anti-Americanism and The Global Order* by saying,

> The attacks were a 'wake-up call for Americans.' They constituted the 'end of American innocence,' a final blow to America's privileged position of detachment from the messy and violent conflicts that blighted less favored countries. America had now once and for all entered the 'real world' of international politics, its 'illusion of invulnerability' finally shattered. (2003, p. 7)

To many, this shocking and dark period of public fear would require a leader with the strength and determination of the like not seen since Franklin Roosevelt and Harry Truman. For many, President George W. Bush was the right president at the right time. One individual who saw strong character qualities in President Bush is *New York Times* best selling author Ronald Kessler. Kessler, author of the book, *A Matter of Character: Inside the White House of George W. Bush,* documents the reported differences in White House staff perceptions between the Clintons and the man from Midland, Texas, who would be in the middle of one of the most controversial pieces of legislation of modern times. In contrast to the Clintons, who were described by a former secret service agent as "...arrogant, standoffish, and paranoid" (Kessler, 2004, p. 9), George Bush was described by staff as being punctual, polite, and focused. The nation would most definitely require a focused leader following the catastrophe of September 11, 2001.

While some have voiced concern over President Bush's public religious references and cowboy talk, in combination with White House staff prayer sessions, there has been little doubt that he aggressively follows his personal vision for the country. In 2003, a Gallup Poll indicated that 80% of the public reported that their opinion was that the president "is a strong and decisive leader." For this polled question, President Bush received the highest poll numbers in the organization's history (Domke, 2004). There is little doubt that the Patriot Act and the Bush administration are inexorably tied together. Those who support the war on terror are more likely to support the tools by which that war is fought. For those who support the war on terror, one of their most endearing platitudes toward the president was his ability to exude confidence and clarity as to what needed to be done in retaliation after 9-11 and his "sturdiness" to stay the course in the face of opposition. Writer Ronald Kessler speaks to the events of 9-11 as a terrorist strategy to spread anarchy in the United States. In his opinion, President Bush's support for the Patriot Act was a prudent action that was often lost in partisan politics. Kessler (2004) cites a salient example as follows:

> Ironically, the same liberals and pundits like Senator John F. Kerry and Maureen Dowd of the *New York Times* who assailed Bush for not stopping the attacks of 9/11 were the ones who railed against him for proposing the Patriot Act in an effort to prevent the next attack. *New York Times* columnist Paul Krugman attacked Bush for not putting more federal money into homeland security measures. In doing so, he failed to recognize that with no additional expenditure, the Patriot Act could do more to stop the next attack than billions of dollars spent on defensive security. Those who claimed, as Senator Edward M. Kennedy did, that Bush was leading the nation to a "perilous place" forgot that the country was in a perilous place when the attacks of 9/11 occurred. (p. 169)

Many who support the Patriot Act today are quick to reflect on the huge support the Patriot Act received in the House of Representatives and the Senate during the various voting stages of its birth. If the 9-11 attacks taught America anything, it was that there were fanatics who hated America and its way of life so much that they would train for years to come and give up their lives in the most unbelievable way (Crockatt, 2003). For many, it was believed that years of weak U.S. policy on terrorism had been a major factor in the catastrophe, and that bold action was needed to secure the nation.

When questioned, those who support the Patriot Act give explanations for practical and positive uses pertaining to some of the more controversial sections. Here are a few of the substantiations forwarded in support of the Patriot Act. Section 802 of the USA Patriot Act gives a carefully considered and comprehensive three-part definition of domestic terrorism. This is extremely important as the mislabeling of terrorism may not only negatively affect civil liberties, but may also make reducing terrorism ineffective (*The Federalist Patriot*, n.d.).

Utilizing Sections 203, 218, and 504 in various combinations, the government has had some noticeable success in the war on terror. These sections in particular deal with the sharing of information between intelligence agencies and law enforcement agencies. Prior to the Patriot Act, a great amount of ambiguity regarding the rules of information sharing between agencies hindered the government's effort to seek out and stop terrorist activity. Patrick Fitzgerald, U.S. Attorney for the Northern District of Illinois, gave testimony to this when he said,

> I was on a prosecution team in New York that began a criminal investigation of Usama Bin Laden in early 1996. The team – prosecutors and FBI agents assigned to the criminal case – had access to a number of sources. We could talk to citizens. We could talk to local police officers. We could talk to other U.S. Government agencies. We could talk to foreign police officers. Even foreign intelligence personnel. And foreign citizens. And we did all those things as often as we could. We could even talk to al Qaeda members – and we did. We actually called several members and associates of the al Qaeda to testify before a grand jury in New York. And we even debriefed al Qaeda members overseas who agreed to become cooperating witnesses.
>
> But there was one group of people we were not permitted to talk to. Who? The FBI agents across the street from us in lower Manhattan assigned to a parallel intelligence investigation of Usama Bin Laden and al Qaeda. We could not learn what information they had gathered. That was 'the wall'. (Statement of Patrick Fitzgerald before the Senate Committee on the Judiciary, October 21, 2003, as cited in Department of Justice, 2004, p. 4)

Sections 203, 218, and 504, remove the following barriers: perceived statutory impediments, formal administrative restrictions, and informal cultural restrictions on information sharing (Department of Justice, 2004).

This removal of restrictions on information sharing, known as "the wall," is highlighted as landmark construction in the enhancement of domestic security within the U.S. In a Heritage Special Report titled, *The Patriot Act Reader,* Paul Rosenzweig, Alane Kochems, and James Jay Carafano (2004) detail a startling aspect in the war on terror, immigration. As of 2002, over 500 million individuals are estimated to enter the U.S annually. Of this number, 330 million are not citizens of the U.S. (Rosenzweig et al.). While casting no aspersions on the entire group, many immigrants come from countries aligned with terrorist organizations or feared for possible allegiances (Rosenzweig et al.).

After detailing the host of statistics pertaining to immigrations, the authors stress the need for a law enforcement intelligence cooperative effort to combat terrorism. Specifically they stated,

> As should be clear from the outline of the scope of the problem, the suppression of terrorism will not be accomplished by military means alone. Rather, effective law enforcement and/or intelligence gathering activity are the key to avoiding new terrorist acts. Recent history supports this conclusion. In fact, police have arrested more terrorists than military operations have captured or killed. Police in more than 100 countries have arrested more than 3,000 al-Qaeda-linked suspects, while the military captured some 650 enemy combatants. Equally important, it is policing of a different form--preventative rather than reactive, since there is less value in punishing terrorists after the fact when, in some instances, they are willing to perish in the attack. (Rosenzweig et al., 2004, pp. 25-26).

Section 905 requires federal law enforcement agencies to share intelligence directly with the Director of Central Intelligence unless otherwise directed by the attorney general (Department of Justice, 2004). This mandate does not insure that all information will be forwarded properly; however, it does make federal agents responsible for their actions and clarifies their responsibilities.

Michael O'Hanlon, Peter Orszag, Ivo H. Daalder, I. M. Destler, David Gunter, James Lindsay, Robert Litan, and James Steinberg (2002) talk about the importance of the Patriot Act in the visa approval process in their book, *Protecting The American Homeland: One Year On*, when they said, "The Patriot Act directed the Federal Bureau of Investigation (FBI) to share the National Crime Center's Interstate Identification Index with both the State Department and the Immigration and Naturalization Service. This is an improvement on the old system..." (p. 28).

Section 373 of the USA Patriot Act amended the federal law on money transfers to terrorist organizations. Previously, federal law had in place an affirmative defense for those unlicensed money transferring businesses that might get caught committing this violation. Individuals could just say they did not know the applicable state licensing requirements. Now this loophole is gone (Department of Justice, 2004). Section 371 specifically forbids hiding more than $10,000 in money and bringing it out of, or into, the country. Before, people were required to report currency of this amount under the same situations; however, if caught trying to smuggle funds it was considered a reporting violation only (Department of Justice, 2004).

Section 219 allows a federal judge with jurisdiction over an offense to issue search warrants in other judicial districts (Department of Justice, 2004). Before the USA Patriot Act, investigators had to waste time trying to contact multiple judges in several jurisdictions to do the same thing.

The list and descriptions of sections within the Patriot Act cited above do not represent the Patriot Act in total. However, the list does include some of the most hotly debated sections to date. Daniel Krislov (2004) talks about the legal soundness of Title II provisions of the Patriot Act in the book, *The Politics of Terror: The U.S. Response to 9/11,* as follows:

> Despite the haste with which this bill was produced, it seems to be fairly well tailored to prevent it from being significantly overturned by the courts. I do not predict that there will be much judicial overruling of the provisions of Title 2 for several reasons. First, many of the provisions that deal with the sharing of information are attempts to revere the traditional divide between domestic and foreign intelligence. To some extent, this division reflects old political compromises needed to create foreign intelligence structure in the late 1940s--compromises that simply do not reflect the current political environment. (pp. 153-154)

Addressing the issue of haste in legislating the Patriot Act, an issue many civil liberty groups use as a foundation for Patriot Act admonishment, Former Assistant Attorney General and major Patriot Act constructionist Viet Dinh, in the white paper titled, "How the USA Patriot Act Defends Democracy," said,

> What is odd about the current debate over the Patriot Act and its surveillance provisions is that this legislation resulted from considerable informed debate. Contrary to popular myth, the Patriot Act was not rushed onto the statute books. During the six weeks of deliberations that led to the passage of the Act, the drafters heard from, and heeded the advice of, a coalition of concerned voices urging caution and care in crafting the blueprint for America's security. That discussion was productive and the Act benefited from these expressions of concern. (2004, p. 3)

Furthermore, Dinh puts in perspective questions of fear over the government security measures by saying,

> The fundamental question facing Americans today is not the false trade-off between security and liberty, but rather how we can use security to

protect liberty. Any debate over security and liberty must start with the recognition that the primary threat to American freedom comes from al-Qaeda and other groups that seek to kill Americans, not from the men and women of law enforcement agencies who protect them from that danger. (p. 2)

The following official accounts show results of the Patriot Act in action. Utilizing Sections 218 and 504, investigators were able to use surveillance on members of a terrorist cell in Portland, Oregon, who attempted to travel to Afghanistan in 2001 and 2002. At least one member of the cell was also formulating a plan to attack Jewish schools. The authority granted to the FBI under these sections enabled U.S. prosecutors to collect evidence for convictions on the entire group, later labeled the "Portland Seven" (Department of Justice, 2004). These same sections of the Patriot Act were also used to arrest weapons dealers who offered hundreds of pounds of heroin (Murdock, 2006) and up to five metric tons of hashish to undercover FBI agents in trade for Stinger missiles that would then be sold to al Qaeda and the Taliban (The White House, 2006). As well, Yemeni nationals Mohammed Al-Moayed and Mohammed Zayed, suspected fundraisers for al Qaeda and Hamas were arrested under Sections 218 and 504 of the Patriot Act (Sabin, 2004). Subsequently both individuals were convicted of giving material support to terrorism for funneling more than $20 million to the terrorist organizations (Murdock, 2006; The White House, 2006). Thanks to the Patriot Act, both men were sentenced to over 40 years in federal prison (The White House, 2006).

Barry Sabin, Chief of the Counterterrorism Section, Criminal Division, spoke to the value of Sections 218 and 504 of the Patriot Act in an official statement before the Committee on Financial Services, U.S. House of Representatives, on August 23, 2004. Mr. Sabin stated:

The Counterterrorism Section believes that Sections 218 and 504 of the USA PATRIOT Act, which has been vital to bringing these prosecutions, represent a key Congressional contribution to our counterterrorism efforts, and we are gratified that this view was shared by the National Terrorism Commission in its report. (2004, p. 7)

According to Nedra Pickler (2005), Sections 203 and 218 of the Patriot Act were used to assist in the arrest of terrorist conspirator Lyman Faris. Faris, a U.S. citizen who was born in Kashmir and went by the alias Mohammad Rauf was convicted for providing material support to al-Qaida as well as conspiring to provide the terrorist organization with information that could be used for future U.S. attacks (Department of Justice, 2003, October 28). Reported to have traveled to Afghanistan in 2000, where he was introduced to none other than Osama bin Laden, Faris began assisting the terrorist organization in preparation for future U.S. attacks which included a plot to destroy the Brooklyn Bridge in New York City (Department of Justice, 2003, October 28). Prior to being arrested, Faris would be in contact with the notorious Khalid Shaikh Mohammed in preparation for what authorities later suggested was a planned set of secondary terrorist attacks after September 11, 2001 (Pickler, 2005). Faris was convicted and sentenced to 20 years in prison (Department of Justice, 2003, October 28; Pickler, 2005).

In Florida, prosecutors used Section 373 to charge Libardo Florez-Gomez, a suspected money laundering agent for the Revolutionary Armed Forces of Columbia (FARC), a known terrorist group. Gomez was apprehended at the Miami International Airport with $182,000 in euros which he planned to transfer into secret unknown accounts. Gomez was convicted and sentenced to 18 months in prison (Department of Justice, 2004).

Under Section 371, Alaa Al-Sadawi, a New Jersey imam with connections to foreign terrorist groups, was caught attempting to smuggle $659,000 in cash to Egypt. Previously this would have only been a reporting offense (Department of Justice, 2004; Murdock, 2006).

Collectively, the Patriot Act has been instrumental in the following: the identification and disruption of over 150 terrorist cells and threats; two-thirds of al-Qaeda's known senior leadership being captured or killed; terrorist cells being dissolved in Buffalo, Seattle, Tampa, and Oregon; multiple arrests, including shoe-bomber Richard Reid and "American Taliban" John Walker Lindh; and over 515 individuals linked with the September 11th investigation being removed from the United States (Department of Justice, n.d., *DOJ Accomplishments*). According to Murdock (2006) and Bush (2005), the Patriot Act has been directly responsible for over 400 individuals being charged, with approximately half of those charges ending in conviction.

The Patriot Act has enjoyed the support of the majority of the polled populace. According to polling data, 55% of the nation's adults felt that the Bush administration had conducted itself "about right," 19% answered "not far enough," 21% answered "too far," and 5% had no opinion (*USA Today*/CNN/Gallup Poll, August 29, 2003, as cited in the Department of

Justice, n.d., *Support*). A poll of registered voters asked the question: Would you say the Patriot Act is a good thing or a bad thing for America? The responses were as follows: 55% responded "good," 27% "bad," 9% mixed, and 9% were not sure (FOX News/Opinion Dynamics Poll, July 31, 2003, as cited in Department of Justice n.d., *Support*). Within the same poll, the question was asked if the Patriot Act had affected their civil liberties. The responses were as follows: 91% responded "no," 4% responded "yes," and 5% were unsure (FOX News/Opinion Dynamics Poll, July 31, 2003, as cited in Department of Justice, n.d., *Support).*

There are several arguments cited by liberal groups who fear and detest the Patriot Act. One claim, advanced in an ACLU fundraising letter, is that ordinary political organizations, such as Greenpeace, could now be victims of surveillance, wiretapping, harassment, and criminal action under the Patriot Act (Department of Justice, n.d., *Dispelling*). However, the Patriot Act is limited to actions that break criminal law and endanger human life (Patriot Act, Section 802, as cited in Department of Justice, n.d., *Dispelling*). Another claim is that people should be warned that libraries are known targets of government surveillance, and that the "thought police" may target average citizens for what they read or research on the Internet (ACLU, July 22, 2003, as cited in Department of Justice, n.d., *Dispelling*). On September 15, 2003, at a National Restaurant Association meeting in Washington, D.C., Attorney General John Ashcroft addressed this allegation.

> If you were to listen to some in Washington, you might believe the hysteria behind this claim: 'Your local library has been surrounded by the FBI.' Agents are working round-the-clock. Like the X-Files, they are dressed in raincoats, dark suits, and sporting sunglasses. They stop patrons and librarians and interrogate everyone like Joe Friday. In a dull monotone they ask every person exiting the library, 'Why were you at the library? What were you reading? Did you see anything suspicious?'
>
> According to these breathless reports and baseless hysteria, some have convinced the American Library Association that under the bipartisan Patriot Act, the FBI is not fighting terrorism. Instead, agents are checking how far you have gotten on the latest Tom Clancy novel. (Department of Justice, 2003, September 15)

Ashcroft assured the audience that:

> The law enforcement community has no interest in your reading habits. Tracking reading habits would betray our high regard for the First Amendment. And even if someone in the government wanted to do so,

it would represent an impossible workload and a waste of law enforcement resources. (Department of Justice, 2003, September 15)

The reality is that the government, through the Patriot Act, protects the First Amendment rights and terrorist investigators have no interest in the library habits of ordinary Americans.

The ACLU says that the Patriot Act's provision about delayed notification of search warrants is a radical change in the way search warrants are handled in the United States (ACLU, October 23, 2001, as cited in Department of Justice, n.d., *Dispelling*). In fact, courts nationwide have upheld for decades the same delayed notification style of warrants for criminal cases. The Patriot Act has simply incorporated this style into terrorism cases (Department of Justice, n.d., *Dispelling*).

The Patriot Act is not, nor will it ever be, a magic wand or a silver bullet to eradicate terrorism. By its nature, terrorism will continue, to some degree, no matter what efforts are taken. Jeffrey D. Simon (2001) speaks to the nature of terrorism in his book, *The Terrorist Trap*.

> Terrorism persists because it takes so little to activate the terrorist machinery—a car bombing in one place, a hijacking in another, a kidnapping somewhere else—and yet there are so many potential payoffs awaiting the terrorist: publicity for their cause, freedom for imprisoned comrades, money or arms for future operations, personal satisfaction in seeking and gaining revenge, and general disruption and sabotage of specific developments or events. (p. 377)

However, it is just as important to understand that the Patriot Act is not a Pandora's box in which the most hideous of evils await to spring. The sunset conditions found in Section 224 of the Patriot Act required the reauthorization of several key elements of the law, which otherwise would expire on December 31, 2005 (EPIC, 2001). It appears that precautions, such as the sunset provision found in Section 224 of the Patriot Act, are salient examples of restraint and not recklessness.

When we cut through the fear and hype, we find that the Patriot Act is simply a tool. Like all the other laws on record it should be monitored to maintain its credibility within our society for its purpose of existence. The Patriot Act is operated under rigorous oversight. Currently, the Department of Justice has provided witness to over 115 hearings before Congress related to the Patriot Act and the war on terrorism, including providing over 100 pages of responses to House Judiciary Committee questions on its implementation (Department of Justice, n.d., *Responding*).

Any question as to the need for a Patriot Act can be answered with a quick review of the domestic and foreign terrorist attacks on the U.S. during the 1990s. These attacks include, but are not limited to, the following: 1993, the basement of the World Trade Center is bombed killing six (Glendinning, 2005; Kelly, n.d; Windrem, n.d.); 1995, Alfred P. Murrah building in Oklahoma City is bombed by domestic terrorist Timothy McVeigh. killing 168 (Kelly, n.d.); 1996, U.S. military housing complex near Dhahran, Saudi Arabia is bombed killing 19 (Glendinning, 2005; Windrem, n.d.); 1998, U.S. embassies in Kenya and Tanzania, Nairobi, and Dar es Salaam are bombed in combination killing over 220 (Glendinning, 2005; Kelly, n.d.; Windrem, n.d.); 2000, the U.S.S. Cole is bombed killing 17 (Glendinning, 2005; Kelly, n.d.; Windrem, n.d.); 2001, the bombing of the twin towers in New York and the Pentagon, along with deaths of passengers in four hijacked planes, totaled over 3,000 (Kelly, n.d.; Glendinning, 2005; Windrem, n.d.).

While the September 11, 2001, terrorist attack on the U.S. may be considered by some as the single contributing factor to initiating the birth of the Patriot Act, it is not completely so. September 11, 2001, served more as the final straw in a consistent string of occurring terrorist events. It is prudent to realize that the terrorist threat to America's citizens does not have to come from terrorist agents from abroad. The Murrah Building bombing in Oklahoma City is but one tragic example of U.S. home-grown terrorism. America has had, and will probably continue to have, its own home-grown terrorist organizations. The Patriot Act has been instrumental in dealing with these groups as well. For example, Section 201 of the Patriot Act was used in the arrest of David W. Hull, an Imperial Wizard of the White Knights of the Ku Klux Klan. Hull was sentenced to 12 years in prison after being convicted of attempting to blow up an abortion clinic (Murdock, 2006).

It would not be surprising if some of the arrests made under this contentious law are new to readers. In fact, it could be surmised that many of the good deeds of the Patriot Act go unheralded, at least in comparison to what would happen if terrorists were to be successful in attacking the country again. This is something that has not happened since the application of the Patriot Act.

The British scholar Paul Wilkinson eloquently commented on terrorism and public opinion when he said, "Fighting terrorism is like being a goal keeper. You can make a hundred brilliant saves but the only shot people remember is the one that gets past you" (Quotes, 2004). Taking this quote into the context of our current time environment, one must weigh the implications of terrorists and weapons of mass destruction as well as conventional weapons. On this subject, Nunn (2000) states the implications of the fall of the Soviet Union saying,

> While the fall of the Soviet Union has certainly diminished the risk of a major war between the United States and a would-be challenger, it has also created new risks which could have an impact on the U.S. Never before has an empire collapsed leaving some 30,000 nuclear weapons, hundreds of tons of fissile material, at least 40,000 tons of chemical weapons, advanced biological weapons, huge stores of sophisticated conventional weapons and thousands of scientists with the knowledge to make all of the above. (p. 36)

After explaining many of the misunderstood elements of the Patriot Act, a final disclaimer is offered. Even with the meticulous nature of the Patriot Act's construction, enacted for the purpose of protecting citizens during a time of war without violating constitutional rights, it is not a perfect document. However, that is true of all documents, laws, people, and concepts. As readers will see in Part II of this book, which looks at the renewal process, the Patriot Act was constructed to be evolvable for the future, either by its continuance or dissolution in accordance with law. Until then, it is possible that a rethinking should take place as to some civil rights, and their ability to evolve, to maintain the security of the society at large. Benjamin Netanyahu spoke of this when considering possible revision of rights by saying,

> Advocates of absolute civil liberties forget that legally protected freedoms are not ends in and of themselves; they are means to ensuring the health and well-being of the citizens. The United States Constitution, said Justice Robert Jackson, is not a suicide pact. And when a protected "right" in practice results in the encouragement and breeding of terrorist monstrosities ready to devour others members of society, then it is clear that such a right has ceased to serve its true end and must be either revised or reduced. (Benjamin Netanyahu, 1995, as cited in Freeh, 2000, p. 177)

Supporters would argue that the Patriot Act was one of many bold and timely responses to a national crisis. Interestingly enough, 9-11 was similar in many ways to another momentous event within the U.S. History, Pearl Harbor. As with the terrorist attacks, the Japanese used a surprise aerial attack and caught an ill-prepared United States vulnerable to attack. Though documenting differences, Richard Crockatt (2003) speaks to the similarities in the mental impact to the nation in both attacks.

> The element of surprise was common to both attacks, and the sudden resolve of the United States in both instances to respond immediately and massively was in part a function of the absence of warning. The sense of America's having been violated, resentment at the enemy for failing to play 'by the rules,' the underhanded nature of the attacks, and the naked exploitation of America's openness (its 'innocence') unified the country and all but silenced doubts about the need to respond vigorously. (p. 9)

While support can be found for the Patriot Act from scholars, politicians, and philosophers, the greater majority of information outlets and testimonials in this section are seen from government officials and law enforcement personnel. While it is reasonable to see this as the government and its law enforcement branches working more closely with the Patriot Act, it would be unfair to not recognize that these entities have the most to lose if the Patriot Act is perceived to be a failure. It would also be unrealistic to abstain acknowledgement that the Patriot Act has the potential to affect individuals other than terrorists. One example of the Patriot Act being applied in non-terrorism related situations would be the use of Section 212 of the Patriot Act. This section was instrumental in the rescue of a 13-year-old child who had been abducted from her own home by a 38-year-old child molester (Buchanan, 2006). Of course, while few would fail to applaud the safe return of a child, the usage of this law for civilian law enforcement purposes, as opposed to terrorism, is one aspect of the Patriot Act that is highly controversial. In presenting a complete and rounded view of the Patriot Act, you will now hear from the opposing voices to this landmark legislation.

References

Buchanan, M. B. (2006, January 3). *U.S. attorneys discuss Patriot Act meeting with the president.* Retrieved August 6, 2006, from http://www.whitehouse.gov/news/releases/2006/01/20060103-3.html

Bush, G. W. (2005, June 9). *Remarks by the president on the Patriot Act.* Retrieved August 6, 2006, from http://www.gop.com/NEWS/Read.aspx?ID=5533

Crockatt, R. (2003). *America embattled: September 11, anti-Americanism, and the global order.* New York: Routledge.

Department of Justice. (n.d.). *Dispelling the myths: preserving life and liberty.* Retrieved September 20, 2004, from http://www.lifeandliberty.gov/subs/u_myths.htm

Department of Justice. (n.d.). *DOJ accomplishments in the war on terror: preserving life and liberty.* Retrieved September 20, 2004, from http://www.lifeandliberty.gov/subs/ a_terr.htm

Department of Justice. (n.d.). *Responding to Congress: preserving life and liberty.* Retrieved September 20, 2004, from http://www.lifeandliberty.gov/subs/r_congress.htm

Department of Justice. (n.d.). *Support of the people: preserving life and liberty.* Retrieved September 20, 2004, from http://www.lifeandliberty.gov/subs/s_people.htm

Department of Justice. (2003, September 15). *Prepared remarks of Attorney General John Ashcroft: the proven tactics in the fight against crime.* Retrieved September 20, 2004, from http://www.usdoj.gov/archive/ag/speeches/2003/091503nationalrestaurant.htm

Department of Justice. (2003, October 28). *Iyman Faris sentenced for providing material support to Al Qaeda.* Retrieved August 6, 2006, from http://www.usdoj.gov/opa/pr/2003/ October/03_crm_589.htm

Department of Justice. (2004, July). *Report from the field: the USA Patriot Act at work.* Retrieved September 20, 2004, from http://www.lifeandliberty.gov/docs/071304_report_ from_the_field.pdf

Dinh, V. D. (2004, June 9). *How the USA Patriot Act defends democracy.* Retrieved August 25, 2004 from http://www.defenddemocracy.org/usr_doc/USA_Patriot_Act.pdf

Domke, D. (2004). *God willing? Political fundamentalism in the White House, the "war on terror," and the echoing press.* Ann Arbor, MI: Pluto Press.

Electronic Privacy Information Center [EPIC]. (2001). *HR 3162 RDS: 107th Congress.* Retrieved September 25, 2004, from http://www.epic.org/privacy/terrorism/ hr3162.html

The Federalist Patriot. (n.d.). The 2001 USA Patriot Act. Retrieved September 20, 2004, from http://patriotpost.us/papers/03-41_paper.asp

Freeh, L. J. (2000). Expanding the FBI's powers is a necessary response to terrorism. In L. K. Egendorf (Ed.), *Terrorism: opposing viewpoints* (pp. 173-178). San Diego, CA: Greenhaven Press.

Glendinning, M. (2005, July 7). *Timeline: Al Qaeda attacks on western targets.* Retrieved August 7, 2006, from http://www.npr.org/templates/story/story.php?storyId=4733944

Kelly, M. (n.d.). *Terrorism through America's history.* Retrieved August 23, 2004, from http://Americanhistory.about.com/library/fastfacts/blffterrorism.htm

Kessler, R. (2004). *A matter of character: Inside the white house of George W. Bush.*
New York: Penguin Group (USA) Inc.

Krislov, D. (2004). Civil liberties and the judiciary in the aftermath of 9/11. In W. Crotty (Ed.), *The politics of terror: The U.S. response to 9/11* (pp. 134-159). Boston: Northeastern University Press.

Murdock, D. (2006, February 1). *Let the numbers do the talking: Patriot Act successes.* Retrieved August 6, 2006, from http://www.nationalreview.com/murdock/ murdock200602011350.asp

Nunn, S. (2000). Weapons of mass destruction pose a terrorist threat. In L. K. Egendorf (Ed.), *Terrorism: Opposing viewpoints* (pp. 35-41). San Diego, CA: Greenhaven Press.

O'Hanlon, M. E., Orszag, P. R., Daalder, I. H., Destler, I. M., Gunter, D. L., Lindsay, J. M., et al. (2002). *Protecting the American homeland: one year on.* Washington, DC: Brookings Institution.

Pickler, N. (2005, June 9). *Bush: Patriot Act helped to nab terrorists.* Retrieved August 8, 2006, from http://www.sfgate.com/cgi-bin/article.cgi?f=/n/a/2005/06/09/national/ w092105D91.DTL

Quotes From Famous People. (2004). *Famous terrorism quotations.* Retrieved September 20, 2004, from http://home.att.net/~quotesexchange/terrorism.html

Rosenzweig, P., Kochems, A., & Carafano, J. J. (Eds.). (2004). *The Patriot Act: Understanding the law's role in the global war on terrorism.* Washington, DC: The Heritage Foundation.

Sabin, B. (2004). *Statement of Barry Sabin before the Committee on Financial Services, U.S. House of Representatives: August 23, 2004.* Retrieved August 6, 2006, from http://financialservices.house.gov/media/pdf/082304bs.pdf

Simon, J. D. (2001). *The terrorist trap: America's experience with terrorism* (2nd ed.). Bloomington, IN: Indiana University Press.

The White House. (2006, January 3). *U.S. attorneys discuss Patriot Act meeting with the president.* Retrieved August 6, 2006, from http://www.whitehouse.gov/news/releases/ 2006/01/20060103-3.html

Windrem, R. (n.d.). *Hunt for Al-Qaida: Al-Qaida timeline: Plots and attacks.* Retrieved August 7, 2006, from http://www.msnbc.msn.com/id/4677978/

CHAPTER 7

Opposition to the Patriot Act

WHEN LOOKING AT THE INDIVIDUALS and groups who oppose the Patriot Act, we find that they are diverse groups which, in some cases, have little to do with each other. Donald Kettl (2004) eloquently surmises this idea of the Patriot Act's ability to transcend political lines when he says,

> Rarely had any public policy issue united critics from both conservative and liberal ends of the political spectrum. On the right, condemnation came from those who had long worried that a strong government might hinder the exercise of individual freedom. On the left, opponents were concerned that innocent individuals would be swept up in the administration's zeal to fight terrorists. Critics from both sides quietly suggested that the administration was using the war against terrorism to promote new governmental powers that Congress had rejected in years past. (p. 106)

Take for instance the conservative, right-wing, pro-gun ownership group, "The Gun Owners of America." On February 27, 2004, Larry N. Pratt, the executive director of the organization, went on record to attack the Patriot Act. The point of objection was primarily based on the fact that the Patriot Act allows for individuals to be designated as domestic terrorists (Section 802). Pratt gave an example of farmers in Oregon who had previously protested a water issue with the government, asserting that these individuals could, under the Patriot Act, be labeled as terrorists. This concern was joined by an additional objection over the power of the sneak and peek provision (Section 213) which was considered to be a potential inroad to the future seizing of gun owners' weapons, not unlike some asserted incidents that took place under the Clinton administration prior to Patriot Act (Free Congress Foundation, 2004). Shortly after an interview in the "Coalition for Constitutional Liberties Weekly Update," where Pratt had voiced his concerns over the Patriot Act, the official Gun Owners of America Web site issued an e-mail alert to its 300,000 plus members criticizing the law. The Gun Owners of America e-mail alert contained the prior complaints on the Patriot Act, but also included additional concerns. These concerns included the following: searches of library records, surveillance of religious services, and detention without due process (Gun Owners of America, 2004). It was interesting to see that in this second complaint list, the right-wing group now found themselves on common ground with many left-wing groups who, politically speaking, are at each others' throats over gun freedom issues.

It would be remiss to fail to acknowledge at least a few of the individual conservatives who have voiced concerns over the Patriot Act. Before leaving office in 2002, House Majority Leader Dick Armey not only warned against the threat that the Patriot Act might place on personal liberties, but also insisted that some of the sunsetting provisions should be allowed to expire (Lochhead, 2002). Armey would keep close ties with the ACLU which also shared his concerns over the law (Rabinovitz, 2004). It was also reported that Armey was considering a job offer forwarded by the ACLU that might take place after he departed the House of Representatives (Lochhead, 2002). Timothy Lynch, director of the Cato Institute's Project on Criminal Justice, stated that the Patriot Act had succeeded only in reducing individual privacy (Lynch, 2003). Lynch would take issue with controversial Section 215 of the Patriot Act saying that specific wording within the section took away any true judicial checks on whether a judge could reject a records request application (Lynch, 2003). David A. Keene of the American Conservative Union would echo concerns over the Patriot Act, while also attacking Attorney General John Ashcroft's Patriot Act promotional tour as being disingenuous (Keene, 2003). Peyton Knight, Executive Director of the American Policy Center, condemned Sections 213, 215, and 802 as being unconstitutional (Knight, 2005). Knight's argument against these sections may have taken a slightly different position than some in opposition to the law. Specifically, Knight stated,

> Imagine if Bill Clinton's Justice Department had possessed these powers! Imagine these unprecedented powers in the hands of future presidents with Clinton-like 'morals.' The prospect is downright frightening. The

next Janet Reno will have a field day going after gun owners, pro-lifers, conservatives, and anyone deemed a 'political enemy.' (¶ 9)

Alan Caruba, prolific writer, booker reviewer, and founder of the National Anxiety Center, would also find himself at odds with the controversial law. Caruba would share his concerns over the Patriot Act in a review of Walter M. Brasch's book, *America's Unpatriotic Act: The Federal Government's Violation of Constitutional and Civil Rights*. While Caruba was quick to state that he was in most ways a polar opposite of Brasch, whom he described as a "liberal," he praised the book as highlighting what he agreed were conflicts that the Patriot Act produced with the First, Fourth, Sixth, and Eighth Amendments to the U.S. Constitution (Caruba, 2005). Regardless of the concerns surrounding the Patriot Act that have caught the attention of conservatives, there is little doubt that there are many who share views that are in opposition to the law.

While efforts have been made to recognize conservative individuals and groups which are often underreported as opposing this legislation, attention is now turned to where the bulk of opposition is found. The liberal groups that oppose the Patriot Act are legion and to construct an absolute chronicling of these groups is impossible. However, it is believed that an adequate view of the positions and concerns of these groups in general can be attained. With that said, no other organization has so detailed their opposition to the Patriot Act as the American Civil Liberties Union (ACLU). The ACLU was founded in 1920 by Roger Baldwin, Crystal Eastman, and Albert DeSilver. Founded by these civil liberty activists, the organization contains approximately 400,000 members and handles around 6,000 cases a year over the entire United States (ACLU, n.d., *About Us*).

In October 2002, the ACLU launched a $3.5 million national campaign to repeal portions of the Patriot Act (Madigan, 2002). In July 2003, the ACLU was the first to file a lawsuit against the Patriot Act. The lawsuit challenged Section 215. The suit was filed on behalf of six mostly Arab and Muslim-American groups (Bohn, 2003). On September 30, 2004, in a case brought forward by the ACLU, a federal judge struck down a provision of the Patriot Act dealing with authorities having the power to obtain private information. The ruling would not take effect for 90 days, allowing for an appeal of the judgment (Preston, 2004).

The differing levels of attack on the Patriot Act by the ACLU is staggering; however, it would be prudent to begin the foundational argument of disagreement that is reported to motivate this group. The ACLU takes issue with the Patriot Act primarily over what they believe are threats to constitutional rights. Theses rights would include, but are not limited to, the following: the First, Fourth, Fifth, Sixth, Eighth, and Fourteenth Amendments. The First Amendment of the Constitution insures freedom of religion, speech, assembly, and the freedom of the press. The Fourth Amendment encompasses issues related to search and seizure. The Fifth Amendment guarantees that no person can be deprived of life, liberty, or property without due process. The Sixth Amendment involves the right to a speedy trial, impartial jury, confronting witnesses, and assistance of council. The Fourteenth Amendment delegates that persons within the U.S. are entitled to due process and equal protection under the law (ACLU, n.d., *The USA*).

The ACLU (n.d., *FreedomWire*) takes issue with the following sections of the Patriot Act:

Section 802. The ACLU opposes this section as it expands the definition of domestic terrorism. Specifically, this is a concern as student groups and other activists are considered to be at risk of being labeled terrorists.

Section 505. The concern over this section revolves around the fear that the government will now begin to collect information on individual's credit histories, travel, insurance records, and other Internet transactions.

Section 507. This section is believed to be a threat to individuals, such as college students, as it gives the government the ability to get student records while eliminating civil liability to educational providers for the disclosure of these records to the authorities.

Section 213. This section, commonly known as the "sneak and peek" section, is opposed because the government does not have to give immediate notice of a search of a home or dwelling. Additionally, it is reported that authorities are using this section in cases that have nothing to do with the war on terror.

Section 215. This section is considered to give the government too much access to confidential records.

Ann Beeson and Jameel Jaffer, in a 2003 official ACLU publication entitled, "Unpatriotic Acts: The FBI's Power to Rifle Through Your Records and Personal Belongings Without Telling You," details the multiple concerns found in Section 215, by utilizing the addition of new Patriot Act script to the original Foreign Intelligence Surveillance Act (FISA) wording to illuminate how the Patriot Act changes the original intent on the law. This is how the original FISA section is changed by the Patriot Act Section 215:

Access to certain business records for foreign intelligence and international terrorism investigations

> (a) (1) The Director of the Federal Bureau of Investigation or a designee of the Director (whose rank shall be no lower than Assistant Special Agent in Charge) may make an application for an order requiring the production of **any tangible things** (including books, records, papers, documents, and other items) for an investigation to obtain foreign intelligence information not concerning a United States person or to protect against international terrorism or clandestine intelligence activities, **provided that such investigation of a United States person is not conducted solely upon the basis of activities protected by the first amendment to the Constitution.**
>
> (2) An investigation conducted under this section shall
>
>> (A) be conducted under the guidelines approved by the Attorney General under Executive Order 12333 (or a successor order); and
>>
>> (B) not be conducted of a United States person solely upon the basis of activities protected by the first amendment to the Constitution of the United States.
>
> (b) Each application under this section
>
> (1) shall be made to--
>
>> **(A) a judge of the court established by section 1803(a) of this title; or**
>>
>> (B) a United States Magistrate Judge under chapter 43 of Title 28, who is publicly designated by the Chief Justice of the United States to have the power to hear applications and grant orders for the production of tangible

things under this section on behalf of a judge of that court; and

(2) **Shall specify** that the records concerned **are sought for** an authorized investigation conducted in accordance with subsection (a)(2) of this section to obtain foreign intelligence information not concerning a United States person or to protect against international terrorism or clandestine intelligence activities.

(c) (1) Upon an application made pursuant to this section, the judge **shall enter** an ex parte order as requested, or as modified, approving the release of records if the judge finds that the application meets the requirements of this section.

(2) An order under this subsection shall not disclose that it is issued for the purpose of an investigation described in subsection (a).

(d) **No person shall disclose** to any other person (other than those persons necessary to produce the tangible things under this section) that the Federal Bureau of Investigation has sought or obtained tangible things under this section.

(e) A person who, in good faith, produces tangible things under an order pursuant to this section shall not be liable to any other person for such production. Such production shall not be deemed to constitute a waiver of any privilege in any other proceeding or context. (pp. 5-6)

Prior to the Patriot Act, the FBI was limited to the collection of records. Now, the FBI can get "any tangible thing" (Beeson & Jaffer, 2003). Things done, in part based on First Amendment rights, can now be investigated. These activities could possibly include letter writing or protests (Beeson & Jaffer, 2003). Section 215 orders are entertained by FISA judges who are limited in the authority to reject the applications. Furthermore, the FBI is not held to the "probable cause" standard and shielded from public disclosure for the petition of FISA applications for sensitive records (Beeson & Jaffer, 2003).

ACLU staff attorney Jameel Jaffer has also lent his services to attacking a government Web site that reports to give a "Myth and Reality" section that supports its view of the Patriot Act and diminishes ACLU claims (Jaffer, 2003).

It should be noted that there is far from a consensus on just how productive the Patriot Act has been in stopping terrorists. For example, as stated earlier in Chapter 6, the government's claim that the Patriot Act has been responsible for over 400 arrests, with half of those arrests ending in conviction, was put to the test by intensive analysis conducted by *The Washington Post* (Eggen & Tate, 2005). Questioning the government's portrayal of the conviction rate, the study found that only 39, not 200, individuals were actually arrested for crimes that could be said to be linked to terrorism (Eggen & Tate, 2005). The other 161 convictions were for lower crimes, such as giving false statements and immigration violations (Eggen & Tate, 2005). In what also might be a disheartening figure, the median sentence length for those convicted was only 11 months (Eggen & Tate, 2005). Sociologist and Patriot Act researcher Amitai Etzioni, who would not be classified as a Patriot Act abolitionist, has been outspoken for some time concerning the need for independent oversight involving the Patriot Act (Etzioni, 2003). Specifically, Etzioni would like to see a panel of citizens, comprised of people who have no employment ties to the government, form a "citizens board" which would release summary statements on the effectiveness, or lack thereof, of the Patriot Act to the public (Etzioni, 2003).

As there is controversy that surrounds the arrest statistics for this law, the ACLU joins others in a concern over detention policies implemented through the Patriot Act. This concern, which is still considered viable today, was originally brought about by the detention of 75 Arabs and South Asians who were detained, based on minor immigration violations, immediately following 9-11 (Weich, 2002). The ACLU has been very quick to give legal representation to individuals detained by the government in the war on terror. The ACLU has had, and continues to have, court petitions in many cases, including *Rumsfeld v. Padilla, Hamdi v. Rumsfeld, U.S. v. Awadallah,* and *Rasul v. Bush,* among others (ACLU, 2003).

Finally, the ACLU has enacted a country-wide petition drive to oppose the Patriot Act. Through October, 2006, resolutions have been passed by 401 communities in 43 states. Included in these numbers are 7 state-wide resolutions opposing the Patriot Act. It is reported that the communities in opposition to the Patriot Act represent 62 million individuals (ACLU, n.d., *List*).

Because the ACLU has served as the flagship in opposition to the Patriot Act does not mean that they are the only ship in the fleet. Brian Levin, of the Southern Poverty Law Center, talks about the dangers of civil liberty infringements during times of war in his article, "Freedom and Dissent: The Nation Struggles to Balance Civil Liberties and Police Power in the Aftermath of the September Horror." Within the article, Levin recalls injustices to civil liberties in the forms of the Palmer Raids of WWI and the Japanese internment during WWII. Special attention is given within the article to highlight the fact that while many of the civil rights violations were later corrected, irreversible damage to many individuals' lives were inevitably done (Levin, 2001). Some see the unrelenting aggressiveness during the first years of the Patriot Act, by then Attorney General Ashcroft, as disheartening and a possible step toward the mistakes of the past (Amster, 2003). Others focus less on the messenger and promoter, Attorney General John Ashcroft, and attack the complexity of the Patriot Act due to its haphazard construction by saying, "By any standard, the Patriot Act is a terrible piece of legislation. The bill was a cut-and-paste effort that resulted in an omnibus, catch-all piece of legislation" (Crotty, 2004, p. 199). Some see the seeds of trickery being sown in the construction of the title of the Patriot Act. Donald F. Kettl (2004) talks about this concept in his book, *System under Stress: Homeland Security and American Politics*. Kettl asserts:

> The legislation's authors formally labeled it the "Uniting and Strengthening America by Providing Appropriate Tools Required to Intercept and Obstruct Terrorism Act"—or the "USA Patriot Act," surely one of the most clever and symbolically powerful Washington acronyms of all time. It not only found the right words to spell out the title for the act, but it wrapped the legislation in the cloak of patriotism, which the drafters hoped no one could resist in the frightening days after September 11. (p. 96)

As opposed to civil liberties groups, libraries would appear to be a less likely group to be included in the list of active Patriot Act detractors. However, many library groups, including the American Library Association, are in the thick of the Patriot Act controversy. The reason for their concern has to do with the large patronage that libraries receive, and the large amount of information that is collected from, and stored at, libraries. This information includes, obviously, the books that are checked out, but also patron information that is stored in the library databanks. The specific areas of the Patriot Act which concerns the libraries include, but are not limited to, Sections 214-216. Section 215 has already been detailed, and Section 214 is very close in nature. Section 216 is a concern because it modifies the use of registers and trap and traces. This extends telephone monitoring to include e-mail services, and IP and URLs for Web pages. In short, the Patriot Act affects libraries not only in the books that are being checked out and the information of the patrons, but the growing technology so often utilized within today's libraries, the use of the Internet (Riba, 2002).

On March 6, 2003, U.S. Representative Bernie Sanders of Vermont introduced the Freedom to Read Protection Act (H.R. 1157). This act would exclude booksellers, as well as libraries, from being liable under Section 215 of the Patriot Act (Vermont Library Association, 2002). Currently, over 200 libraries and librarians within Vermont have signed on in support of the bill (Vermont Library Association, 2002). Additionally, Don Essex's article "Opposing the USA Patriot Act: The Best Alternative for American Librarians," details many alternatives to Section 215. These alternatives range from the acquisition of the Benjamin Franklin True Patriot Act (H.R. 3171), which would eliminate Section 215 after a 90-day review, and the Antiterrorism Enhancement Act of 2003 (H.R. 3037), which gives the attorney general the authority to subpoena witnesses and records during a federal investigation involving terrorism. Both propositions are considered superior to the current Section 215 (Essex, 2004).

As early as 2002, librarians have been discussing not only the requirements of the Patriot Act but how to resist it (Rice, 2002). Officially, the American Library Association (ALA) on January 23, 2002, released the "Resolution Reaffirming the Principles of Intellectual Freedom in the Aftermath of Terrorist Attacks," which documented their belief that a library patron's right to privacy was considered an inalienable human right (Rice, 2002). In an attempt to reduce the government's ability to seize sensitive patron information, the ALA has suggested that libraries reduce their records to only the fundamental records needed to operate. In addition, library staff have been advised as to specific procedures in dealing with law enforcement personnel (Riba, 2002).

What exactly has brought about so much resistance by librarians to the Patriot Act? The answer is at least twofold. The first reason has to do with a long standing antagonistic relationship shared by the FBI and libraries that started back in the 1980s. During the 1980s, the FBI enacted what was called the "FBI Awareness Program" or "Library Awareness Program," in which the library habits of suspicious individuals were monitored. It was during this time period that some FBI personnel are alleged to have asserted that they were not subject to statues that protect library records

(Minow, 2002; Rice, 2002). Attempting to shed light on this program, ALA Chairperson Judith Drescher contacted the FBI and received a response from Director Milt Ahlerich. Ahlerich stated,

> We have programs wherein we alert those in certain fields of the possibility of members of hostile countries or their agents attempting to gain access to information that could be potentially harmful to our national security. In this regard, our New York Office has contacted staff members of New York libraries to alert them to this potential danger and to request assistance... The FBI relies in great measure on the willingness and cooperation of the American people to assist us in fulfilling our responsibilities, and we have found programs of these types helpful. (Foerstel, 2004, p.3)

The ALA made it well known that they did not support the FBI program. Exacerbating the frustration of libraries with the FBI was the fact that the FBI continually gave confusing and contradicting information about the areas that the programs were being implemented in, and the full description of the program itself. This vagueness, at times, turned to denial of the program completely until 1988 when the FBI was forced to turn over documents pertaining to the "Library Awareness Program" due to the Freedom of Information Act (Foerstel, 2004).

The second issue which has been contentious with libraries is based on the mass removal of government information considered potentially sensitive to national security from Web sites following the 9-11 attacks. The libraries' stance is that this information is wanted and needed by everyday citizens, and that the removal of this previously public information is an infringement on citizens' rights (Rice, 2002).

Recognizing the frustration of libraries appears pale compared to the extreme disappointment felt by Senate Democrat Russ Feingold. Herbert N. Foerstel (2004) recounts the frustration of Senator Russ Feingold, who found himself overwhelmed by Senate support to push the Patriot Act forward, in his book, *Refuge Of A Scoundrel: The Patriot Act In Libraries*. Feingold, from the Senate floor, stated:

> If we lived in a country where the police were allowed to search your home at any time for any reason: if we lived in a country where the government was entitled to open your mail, eavesdrop on your phone conversations, or intercept your e-mail communications; if we lived in a country where people could be held in jail indefinitely based on what they write or think, or based on mere suspicion that they were up to no

good, the government would probably discover and arrest more terrorists... But that would not be a country in which we would want to live... Preserving our freedom is the reason we are now engaged in this new war on terrorism. We will lose that war without a shot being fired if we sacrifice the liberties of the American people in the belief that by doing so we will stop the terrorists. (pp. 50-51)

The enactment of the Patriot Act has brought confusion and, to some degree, frustration to many within the banking industry. This frustration is due to Section 326, which is an amendment of Section 5318 of Title 31 of the United States Code, and deals with the identification and verification of account holders. Under the Patriot Act, the standard is raised as to requirements and liability to banks in properly identifying account holders. The crux of the problem facing banks is due to the over 240 different types of valid drivers licenses now available, not to mention the "matricula," an identification card that Mexican consulates have been issuing Mexicans expatriates (Cocheo, 2003).

Derek D. Davis talks about the negative religious implication of the Patriot Act in his article, "The Dark Side To a Just War: The USA Patriot Act and Counterterrorism's Potential Threat to Religious Freedom," when talking about contrasting groups, such as the Ku Klux Klan and Neo-Nazis, and liability under the Patriot Act. Davis believes:

> Many more groups that approach the mainstream of American religious culture, including Jehovah's Witnesses and Christian Scientists, are at least passively resistant to certain public institutions, and occasionally even to what Americans would consider the basic requirements of citizenship. (2002, *Section I*)

In addition to the religious repercussions to ordinary organizations by the Patriot Act, the concern over the aggressive labeling by John Ashcroft that dissenters only "aid terrorists" and "erode our unity," could only be seen as a move that would ultimately lead to opposition (Davis, 2002). Davis also documented, as a great concern within the Patriot Act, Section 411 which elevates liability under law for giving material support to terrorists. This violation, which can be triggered through donations, among others activities, is criticized because individuals found in violation must prove that they did not know that the organization to which they donated assistance in some form was a terrorist organization (Davis, 2002).

As the various groups within the country have taken their shot at attacking the Patriot Act, Hollywood has not been an exception. Two months after the deadly attacks on the Twin Towers and the Pentagon, Barbra Steisand, while attending a birthday party for the Reverend Jesse Jackson, verbally attacked John Ashcroft for reducing civil rights through the Patriot Act (Streisand, 2001). Much more recently, Michael Moore was the recipient of the Cannes Film Festival best picture award for his film *Fahrenheit 9/11* which, among other Bush denigrating topics, included a harsh analysis of the Patriot Act.

One aspect of the Patriot Act's creation that should not be overlooked was the immense amount of pressure the government was under to take some action. Americans had died and there was a sense that retaliation was not only justified but necessary. Without a doubt, the Patriot Act took into account a personal factor. Barbara Olson, wife of Solicitor General Ted Olson, was one of many victims who died in the plane that crashed into the Pentagon. Olson, who was known by many members of the Justice Department, called her husband twice by cell phone before her plane went down into the Pentagon (Kettl, 2004). The Olson death, along with those which never received public attention, were critical factors that may have affected the speed and quality of review that the Patriot Act received.

While many of these groups have been at odds with the government on many issues prior to the adoption of the Patriot Act, some have not and are new to taking a stance opposite the government. Whether you agree with the different stances these groups take, the reader is educated by understanding the various arguments and how these different oppositions affect various portions of the Patriot Act.

References

American Civil Liberties Union [ACLU]. (n.d.). *About us*. Retrieved August 13, 2005, from http://www.aclu.org/about/aboutmain.cfm

American Civil Liberties Union [ACLU]. (n.d.). *Freedomwire: The USA Patriot Act: It could happen to you*. Retrieved August 13, 2005, from http://www.aclu.org/freedomwire/ patriotact/it_could_happen.pdf

American Civil Liberties Union [ACLU]. (n.d.). *List of communities that have passed resolutions.* Retrieved October 6, 2006, from http://www.aclu.org/safefree/resources/ 17102res20040610.html

American Civil Liberties Union [ACLU]. (n.d.). *The USA Patriot Act and government actions that threaten our civil liberties.* Retrieved August 13, 2005, from http://action.aclu.org/ site/DocServer/patriotactflyer.pdf?

American Civil Liberties Union [ACLU]. (2003, July 7). *Detention.* Retrieved August 13, 2005, from http://www.aclu.org/safefree/resources/16828res20030707.html

Amster, S. E. (2003). *Patriot Act redux: A second anti-terrorism proposal, further eroding Americans' civil liberties, comes under attack from both parties.* Retrieved August 12, 2005, from http://www.splcenter.org/intel/intelreport/article.jsp?pid=100

Beeson, A., & Jaffer, J. (2003, July 30). *Unpatriotic acts: The FBI's power to rifle through your records and personal belongings without telling you.* Retrieved August 12, 2005, from http://www.aclu.org/safefree/resources/16813pub20030730.html

Bohn, K. (2003, July 30). ACLU files lawsuit against Patriot Act. *CNN Washington Bureau.* Retrieved September 25, 2004, from http://www.cnn.com/2003/LAW/07/30/patriot.act

Caruba, A. (2005, June 13). *Can patriots survive the Patriot Act?* Retrieved September 23, 2006, from http://www.canadafreepress.com/2005/caruba061305.htm

Cocheo, S. (2003). License to fool? *ABA Banking Journal, 95*, 44-50. Retrieved January 27, 2005, from OCLC FirstSearch database.

Crotty, W. (2004). On the home front: Institutional mobilization to fight the threat of international terrorism. In W. Crotty (Ed.), *The politics of terror: The U.S. response to 9/11* (pp. 191-234). Boston: Northeastern University Press.

Davis, D. H. (2002). The dark side to a just war: The USA Patriot Act and counterterrorism's potential threat to religious freedom. *Journal of Church & State, 44*, 5-17. Retrieved January 27, 2005, from OCLC FirstSearch database.

Eggen, D., & Tate, J. (2005, June 12). U.S. campaign produces few convictions on terrorism charges. [Electronic Version]. *The Washington Post*, p. A01. Retrieved July 25, 2006, from http://www.washingtonpost.com

Essex, D. (2004). Opposing the USA Patriot Act: The best alternative for American librarians. *Public Libraries, 43*, 331-340. Retrieved January 27, 2005, from OCLC FirstSearch database.

Etzioni, A. (2003, May 2). Patriot Act is needed, but so are revisions. [Electronic Version]. *The Christian Science Monitor*, p. 11. Retrieved June 7, 2003, from http://www.gwu.edu/ ~ccps/etzioni/B419.html

Foerstel, H. N. (2004). *Refuge of a scoundrel: The Patriot Act in libraries*. Westport, CT: Libraries Unlimited. Rosenzweig, P., Kochems, A., & Carafano, J. J. (Eds.). (2004). *The Patriot Act: Understanding the law's role in the global war on terrorism*. Washington, DC: The Heritage Foundation.

Free Congress Foundation (2004, February 27). *Commentary: Gun owner takes aim at the USA-Patriot Act*. Retrieved August 13, 2005, from http://www.freecongress.org/centers/tp/ ccl/2004/040227.asp

Gun Owners of America. (2004, June 16). *Gun owners of America e-mail alert*. Retrieved August 13, 2005, from http://www.gunowners.org/statealerts/va061604.txt

Jaffer, J. (2003, August 26). *Patriot propaganda: Justice Department's Patriot Act Website creates new myths about controversial law*. Retrieved August 12, 2005, from http://www.aclu.org/safefree/resources/16761pub20030826.html

Keene, D. A. (2003, September 16). *Ashcroft shows shortcomings with 'victory'*. Retrieved September 23, 2006, from http://www.conservative.org/columnists/keene/ 030916dk.asp

Kettl, D. F. (2004). *System under stress: Homeland security and American politics.* Washington, DC: CQ Press.

Knight, P. (2005, April 8). *We must never let the terrorists win.* Retrieved September 23, 2006, from http://www.michnews.com/cgi-bin/artman/exec/view.cgi/141/7772

Levin, B. (2001). *Freedom and dissent: The nation struggles to balance civil liberties and police power in the aftermath of the September horror.* Retrieved August 12, 2005, from http://www.splcenter.org/intel/intelreport/article.jsp?aid=173

Lochhead, C. (2002, December 5). *Dick Armey leaves House with call for freedom.* Retrieved September 23, 2006, from http://www.mindfully.org/Reform/2002/Dick-Armey-Conservative-Liberty5dec02.htm

Lynch, T. (2003, September 10). *More surveillance equals less liberty: Patriot Act reduces privacy, undercuts judicial review.* Retrieved September 23, 2006, from http://www.cato.org/research/articles/lynch-030910.html

Madigan, M. (2002, October 16). ACLU campaign challenges Patriot Act. *P. C. World.* Retrieved September 20, 2004, from http://www.pcworld.com/article/id,106002-page,1/article.html

Minow, M. (2002, February 15). The USA Patriot Act and patron privacy on library Internet terminals. *Law Library Resource Xchange, LLC.* Retrieved August 13, 2005, from http://www.llrx.com/features/usapatriotact.htm

Preston, J. (2004, September 30). Judge strikes down section of Patriot Act allowing secret subpoenas of Internet data. [Electronic Version]. *The New York Times*, p. A26. Retrieved October 1, 2004, from http://www.nytimes.com

Rabinovitz, J. (2004). Taking the ACLU into the limelight: Can Anthony Romero '90 change the way Americans view civil liberties? *Stanford Lawyer, 68*, 14-18, 80. Retrieved September 23, 2006, from http://www.law.stanford.edu/publications/stanford_lawyer/issues/68/TakingTheACLU.pdf

Riba, E. (2002). *The USA Patriot Act: The response and responsibility of library management.* Retrieved August 13, 2005, from http://www.osmond-riba.org/lis/usapatriot.htm

Rice, R. (2002). The USA Patriot Act and American libraries. *Information for Social Change, 16.* Retrieved August 13, 2005, from http://libr.org/isc/articles/16-Rice.html

Streisand, B. (2001, December 11). *Rainbow/PUSH Coalition fourth annual awards dinner: Remarks by Barbra Streisand.* Retrieved August 13, 2005, from http://www.barbrastreisand.com/news_statementsArchives.html#rainbow

Vermont Library Association. (2002, October 21). *USA Patriot Act letter.* Retrieved August 13, 2005, from http://www.vermontlibraries.org/patriot.html

Weich, R. (2002, October 15). *Insatiable appetite: The government's demand for new and unnecessary powers after September 11.* Retrieved August 12, 2005, from http://www.aclu.org/safefree/resources/17042pub20021015.html

CHAPTER 8

Evaluating History

INSOFAR AS THIS CHAPTER'S TITLE is concerned, I have once again taken the liberty of utilizing a portion of a previously co-authored journal article published in Vol. 5, No. 6, of the *Illinois Law Enforcement Executive Forum, November* 2005, entitled "Countdown to Patriot Act II," to assist in presenting the history of the Patriot Act. I would like to take this opportunity to thank my co-author, Dr. Michael L. Birzer, for his contribution to the original article and for graciously allowing my adaptation of that article here. My deviations from the originally published article are simply to eliminate any material which might have already been presented in the book, and additions to make this chapter as concise as possible. While the changes to the published work are small, they may or may not represent my co-author's view. It was decided that certain speculations toward the end of the chapter, made at the time of this article's original publication about a then future Patriot Act renewal, are still relevant, if not educational, in giving readers a well-rounded historical accounting of the Patriot Act from this researcher's perspective. So, buckle up in our time machine and prepare to take a unique look at U.S. history from a point in time when the Patriot Act renewal was becoming a major media topic.

There are strong opposing views as far as support for the Patriot Act and potential future legislation, Patriot Act II. Currently, members of the Senate Intelligence Committee are preparing for the first rounds of closed-door sessions on what is to be known as the Patriot Reauthorization Act (Regan, 2005). These private meetings, in conjunction with numerous public sessions, mark what is sure to be one of the most hotly debated renewals of legislation in modern times.

The construction period of the Patriot Act took place in the direct aftermath of the most successful terrorist attacks on U.S. soil. Furthermore, the drafters of this legislation dealt with the issues of possible further attacks, an anthrax attack, and requested needs by government agencies to have adequate tools to protect a nation in crisis (Howell, 2004).

Many in opposition to the Patriot Act wonder how the nation could construct and ratify any one single document that contains so many potential civil liberty abuses. However, after a historical review, it may be seen that the U.S. government has often expanded its powers while temporarily suspending citizens' rights in times of war and national crisis. As often happens, these powers, which are considered by many as overreaching, are reined in after the crisis has abated. At the least, this is where the debate is situated. It is by placing the Patriot Act within the context of U.S. historical events that one can more fully understand not only present day governmental decisions, but also make more educated guesses on future actions (Lilly, 2003).

In 1798, shortly after the birth of the nation, while the United States was facing the crisis of war with France, the government passed the Alien and Sedition Acts. These acts gave the president the power to deport any alien he deemed dangerous. An individual was subject to arrest for offenses that included criticizing the government (Thomas, 2003). Within the writings of the Alien and Sedition Act was The Alien Enemy Act. This act allowed the government, in times of war, to seize all males 13 years and older within the U.S. who were citizens of warring countries (Engle, 2004). Furthermore, the Alien and Sedition Act stripped individuals of their ability to avoid deportation with a hearing and the presentation of evidence (Rosenzweig, Kochems, & Carafano, 2004).

In the 1860s, during the American Civil War, President Lincoln declared a state of national emergency. Furthermore, after suspending the writ of habeas corpus on eight different occasions (Rosenzweig et al., 2004), Lincoln used federal troops to imprison thousands of dissenters along key border states (Lilly, 2003). During this period of civil war, the executive branch sent out secret agents to track individuals opposing the war, and also participated in covert Confederate espionage and subversion (Kreimer, 2004).

In 1882, the government passed the Chinese Exclusion Act. This law dramatically curtailed the number of individuals of Chinese descent who were allowed to enter the country. It is believed that this action was taken to reduce a growing recession in the Western states (Sekhon, 2003). Other factors may have included a fear of a loss of American dominance in language and culture (Engle, 2004).

During World War I, the government, perceiving the nation at great risk, passed the Espionage Act of 1917. During this period, President Wilson authorized secret surveillance and wiretapping of German delegations in the United States (Lee, 2003).

On May 16, 1918, an amendment was made to Section 3 of the Espionage Act. This amendment was the creation of the Sedition Act of 1918, which made individuals liable for sanctions for interfering with operations of the military. Interference included publishing disloyal writings, utterances, and profane language about the government. Actions considered illegal included: urging, inciting, and advocating any curtailment of the war effort. This law was wide ranging in scope and carried heavy penalties, including $10,000 in fines and/or 20 years in prison. With this power, over 2,000 individuals were prosecuted for their opposition to the war. Although their convictions were later overturned, the arrests effectively squelched all public opposition to the war (Rosenzweig et al., 2004).

One of the most well known individuals to be charged under the Sedition Act of 1918 was labor union organizer, and member of the American Socialist Party, Eugene V. Debs. Eugene Debs, prior to 1918, formed the Social Democratic Party. Debs ran for president on the Socialist ticket in 1904, 1908, 1912, and 1920. In 1920 he received 6% of the popular vote (*Eugene V. Debs Internet Archive*, 2001). Debs was subsequently arrested, charged, and convicted of giving an anti-war speech in Ohio on June 16, 1918 (*Debs v. United States*, 1919).

Another important event that transpired during this era was the "Palmer Raids." The Palmer Raids took place in 1920 and were a government response to several bombings that had transpired within the U.S. in 1919. During these raids over 10,000 individuals were arrested for suspicions of being communists (Fisher, 2004). Suspects were herded into bullpens and questioned without representation (Cole, 2004). None of the arrestees were found to have been involved in the bombings. The arrests were orchestrated by a newly founded government organization called the General Intelligence Division (GID), managed by J. Edgar Hoover. This agency would later be called the Federal Bureau of Investigation (FBI) (Fisher, 2004).

As stated in Chapter 4, history will always reflect the Japanese internments of WWII and the damage that it caused to innocent lives. During World War II, by direct authority of President Roosevelt, approximately 110,000 people of Japanese descent were detained in internment camps (Lilly, 2003; Sekhon, 2003; Thomas, 2003). The detentions began on December 7, 1941, and lasted for more than a year. The justification for internment was based on a need to limit potential sabotage and pre-invasion collaboration between Japanese Americans and enemy forces (Lilly, 2003). Under Executive Order 9066, Japanese Americans were advised to sell their property before moving to the internment camps located in Arkansas, Arizona, California, Colorado, Idaho, Utah, and Wyoming (Sekhon, 2003). While the Supreme Court upheld Roosevelt's actions as legal, in 1988 President Ronald Reagan submitted an official apology and financial reimbursement to surviving Japanese-American internees (Rosenzweig et al., 2004).

Following World War II, the country entered into what was considered to be a new kind of warfare. The common term for this period of antagonisms between the U.S. and predominately the Soviet Union, was the "cold war" (Lilly, 2003). This period saw the House Un-American hearings, which were an attempt to use the rule of law to ferret out the disloyal within the country.

The red scare era of the cold war brought about several laws that were both cursed for breaching civil liberties, and embraced for being necessary tools for national security. One example was the 1947 Taft-Hartley Act, which had several highly controversial anti-communist provisions (Lilly, 2003). Another example was the McCarran Act of 1950. The McCarran Act sought to criminalize private membership in communist organizations (Lilly, 2003). This period also saw the passing of the Subversive Activities Control Act of 1950. This act made it illegal for members of communist organizations to get jobs in defense facilities (Thomas, 2003). Within this timeframe came the Emergency Detention Act, which gave the government the authority to detain an American citizen without charges being filed, and allowed the government to withhold information needed for the detainee's defense (Cole, 2004; Kubler, 2004). Other acts passed in a perceived climate of national crisis were the Internal Security Act, the Smith Act, and the McCarran-Walter Act of 1952. These acts embodied the philosophy of punishing American citizens who were perceived to have given their loyalty to another country (Engle, 2004).

During the 1960s-1970s, the U.S. saw a growing anti-war sentiment in response to the Vietnam conflict. Between 1967 and '68, the National Guard was used 83 times to restrain protests and riots. The Army was likewise mobilized four times for the purpose of stopping angry protesters (Kreimer, 2004). The year 1969 saw over 500 reported bombings in the U.S. These bombing statistics doubled in 1970, and then doubled again in 1971. This environment of war, combined with civil disobedience, cumulated into a massive government operation to monitor and control the populace. In his article, "Watching the Watchers: Surveillance, Transparency, and Political Freedom in the War on Terror," Seth F. Kreimer identifies this cooperative effort between the military and domestic law enforcement and its effect on the populace. Kreimer (2004), recounting a story he read at the Department of Defense Web site, states:

> The information collected on the persons targeted by Defense intelligence personnel was entered into a national data bank and made available to civilian law enforcement authorities. This produced a chilling effect on political expression by those who were legally working for political change in domestic and foreign policies. (p. 140)

Kreimer continues:

> On the civilian side, the NSA, the CIA, and the FBI deployed conventional investigative techniques against a variety of domestic critics and potential opponents, but engaged as well in break-ins, mail openings, warrantless wiretaps, and covert efforts to discredit groups viewed as potential sources of disruption. (p. 141)

It was in this environment, when portions of the general population were acting in direct defiance of the government, that President Nixon began to marshal a variety of federal law enforcement agencies, including the IRS, to deal with groups considered a threat (Kreimer, 2004). One such FBI-operated program to infiltrate, collect intelligence information, and sabotage domestic organizations was labeled COINTELPRO (Fisher, 2004; Hoffman, 2003). The CIA also had a similar program called CHAOS. Programs such as these, along with illegal FBI and CIA information sharing, led to actions such as the attempted destruction of anti-war groups, political campaigns, and civil rights leaders (Fisher, 2004).

By 1970, information was beginning to be made public on just how extensive government surveillance had been on political figures during the turbulent 1960s. Some have called the degree to which civil rights were protected or restrained by the government as the changing action of a swinging pendulum. This particular era of extensive government surveillance, with almost no review, appeared to be coming to an end. A visible effort was being made to separate law enforcement and intelligence agencies from working together. Specifically, the CIA was being removed from domestic activities (Becker, 2003).

From the creation of the CIA in 1947, its function as an intelligence gathering agency has both worked with and against the similar purpose of the FBI. The FBI's purpose is to ensure domestic security through reactive policing. The FBI's primary focus is on collecting information for prosecution (Banks, 2003). Conversely, the CIA acts to collect information that may be important in ongoing or future intelligence matters. Intelligence information gathering has historically not been prosecution oriented. While it has been long understood that both agencies may work together to some degree, the concern over the degree of overlap in investigations and the motivations for collaboration is a major concern to the present day (Banks, 2003).

In 1969, Congress enacted Title III of the Omnibus Crime Control and Safe Streets Act. This law gave uniform standards for warrant requirements for domestic surveillance (Lee, 2003). The overall goal of the law was to strengthen the privacy rights of individuals by requiring a probable cause standard for warrant application that a target was committing, had committed, or was about to commit a particular offense (Banks, 2003; Kollar, 2004; Lee, 2003).

The 1970s also saw several legal cases in which the courts attempted to define limitations and requirements to be placed on the government for searches and surveillance when national security was an issue. In *United States v. United States District Court* (1972) (the *Keith* case), the courts denied the validity of wiretaps conducted without a warrant based solely on a claim of inherent and extra-constitutional executive authority. This case set forth the precedent that a warrant was needed for domestic security intelligence gathering (Banks, 2003; Kollar, 2004; Kreimer, 2004).

By 1974, public attention over the congressional hearings on military surveillance, combined with the Watergate incident, compelled executive and legislative initiatives to curtail political surveillance. The same year, Congress passed the Federal Privacy Act (Kreimer, 2004). However, the courts still had to contend with difficult decisions when dealing with cases that had an overlap of intelligence and law enforcement activities. To demonstrate the complexities in the interpretations of the court, one can look at the case of *United States v. Truong Dinh Hung* (1980). In this case, the courts ruled that while intelligence agents could at times gather information without a warrant, once the surveillance became primarily a criminal matter a search warrant was required (Banks, 2003; Kollar, 2004). This ruling was based on what was termed the "primary purpose" doctrine. This doctrine reflected the court's belief that as the primary focus of an investigation changed from an intelligence gathering investigation to an investigation primarily focused for prosecution, the expectation to privacy by the target increased (Banks, 2003).

Beginning in 1978, the Foreign Intelligence Surveillance Act (FISA) set the procedures for conducting electronic surveillance. As the law was updated in 1994, it addressed physical searches as well as electronic searches within U.S. borders (Banks, 2003; Kollar, 2004). With the enactment of FISA, a secret court was constructed to look at wiretap and surveillance requests. FISA's primary goal was to clarify an area often in contention, that is, the president's foreign affairs power and the Constitution's safeguards on unreasonable search and seizure (Kollar, 2004). FISA states that electronic surveillance may take place when the target in question is a foreign power or the agent of a foreign power (Harrison, 2004; Kollar, 2004). The act also allowed for wiretapping of U.S. citizens, as well as non-citizens within the U.S., as long as the investigation was for foreign intelligence purposes and not for law enforcement. All actions had to be based on the probable cause standard (Harrison, 2004). The procedures under which FISA designates which circumstances will allow for surveillance and search warrants have been in place for 24 years (Banks, 2003).

Beginning in July 1995, Janet Reno, Attorney General for President Clinton, enacted procedures to further limit intelligence and law enforcement consultations (Banks, 2003; Kollar, 2004). The procedures were based on concerns over growing collusion between intelligence and law enforcement which had come to a head in the Aldrich Ames espionage investigation of 1993 (Banks, 2003). While the Aldrich Ames case was resolved in a plea bargain, the potential for corrupting future cases sparked the Clinton administration to take action. What the Clinton administration did was use the Justice Department's Office of Intelligence Policy and Review

(OIPR) as an intermediary for information being shared between intelligence and law enforcement. The OIPR screened information dissemination and served as a watchdog to stop situations where law enforcement would be leading any investigation involving intelligence agencies. OIPR was successful in separating intelligence and law enforcement coordination. Ironically, after the September 11, 2001, attacks, the Bush administration cited OIPR "walls" to detour information and coordination between intelligence and law enforcement as a critical component in the failure to stop the attacks (Banks, 2003). So, if it could be said that since the Nixon era the pendulum had swung more in the favor of civil liberties and government restraint, the terrorist attacks on September 11, 2001, put in motion events that would cause the pendulum to swing heavily toward expansion of government power and restrictions to civil liberty.

When reflecting on how the government, in times of crisis, has dealt with non-citizens, some interesting patterns are seen. It is initially observed that an environment of national crisis may be initiated by war, threat of war, or by economic strain. Historical examples that have been forwarded are the Alien and Sedition Acts, the Chinese Act, and the Alien Enemy Act. Currently, Sections 411 and 412, among others within the Patriot Act, have important implications to non-citizens. The Patriot Act does not in itself deny non-citizens entrance into the country, as did the Chinese Act. As well, the Alien Enemy Act does not appear to fit well as a match to the Patriot Act, in that the Patriot Act does not allow arbitrary seizure of in-country non-citizens during times of war. There does appear to be a closer match between components of Section 412 of the Patriot Act and the Alien and Sedition Act (Lithwick & Turner, 2004). The Alien and Sedition Act allowed the president to deem non-citizens dangerous and deport them. Likewise, the Patriot Act's Section 412, though there is an absence of actual use (Cole, 2004), addresses the authority of the attorney general to certify a non-citizen as a threat in which detention and deportation procedures begin (EPIC, 2001).

From the historical review provided, similarities may also be seen between Section 411 of the Patriot Act and the McCarran Act of 1950. For some it may be a small leap from the concept of communism to terrorism. Both laws deal out repercussions for affiliations with organizations deemed hostile to the government.

As well, many may see a parallel in law evolution between the Espionage Act and the Sedition Act of 1918, and more current laws such as the Foreign

Intelligence Surveillance Act and the Patriot Act. At the least, it could be argued that they are similar in that both sets of laws increased the power and authority of the government, and that both came during an environment of national crisis.

The historical concern over the information sharing between intelligence and law enforcement has been revived by the Patriot Act. The Patriot Act, by its construction, has been created in part to bring a closer working relationship between intelligence and law enforcement in the name of national security. Some say that the government's reluctance to disclose the uses of the Patriot Act sections that are reminiscent of the tools used to abuse civil liberties in the past is the fundamental reason for the increase of fear and suspicion over the law today (Lithwick & Turner, 2004).

Certainly not everyone fears this renewed collaboration between intelligence and law enforcement. Some view the Patriot Act's creation as a logical and long needed governmental upgrade to national security. Andrew McCarthy (2004) speaks to this in his article, "The Patriot Act Without Tears," when he says, "Contrary to widespread calumny, Patriot is not an assault on the Bill of Rights. It is, basically, an overhaul of the government's antiquated counter-terror arsenal, which had been haplessly fighting a 21st-century war with 20th-century weapons (p. 32). McCarthy articulates in support of breaking down the wall between intelligence and law enforcement when he asserts:

> The most essential improvement wrought by Patriot has been the dismantling of the intelligence wall. The bill expressly amended the government's national-security eavesdropping-and-search authority (under the Foreign Intelligence Surveillance Act or FISA) to clarify that intelligence agents, criminal investigators, and prosecutors not only may but should be pooling information and connecting dots. This is common sense: Along the way toward mass murder, terrorists inevitably commit numerous ordinary crimes... One could not surveil them as agents of a foreign power (as FISA permits) without necessarily uncovering such crimes, and this, far from being a problem, is a bonus since these lay the groundwork for prosecutions that can both stop terrorists before they strike and pressure them to turn state's evidence. (p. 33)

Time will tell if this controversial system will be seen as a successful bold step for fighting terrorism or a fallback to Nixon era abuses.

It may be premature at this point to designate the Patriot Act as doomed to repeat some of the more negative of government actions in the past. Paul

Rosenzweig (2004) talks on this subject in his article, "Civil Liberty and the Response to Terrorism," by saying,

> There are two over-arching themes that animate criticism of the Patriot Act... First, critics of the Patriot Act frequently decry the expansion of executive authority in its own right. They, generically, equate the potential for abuse of Executive Branch authority with the existence of actual abuse. They argue, either implicitly or explicitly, that the growth in executive power is a threat, whether or not the power has, in fact, been misused in the days since the anti-terrorism campaign began. In essence, these critics come from a long tradition of limited government that fears an expansion of executive authority, notwithstanding the potential for benign and beneficial results, because they judge the potential for the abuse of power to outweigh the benefits gained. (p. 664)

Rosenzweig justifies his second point by saying,

> The second theme of many criticisms of the Patriot Act and other government responses is one we might call a fear of technology. In service of our efforts to combat terrorism, the government has begun to explore ways of taking advantage of America's superior capacity to manage data through new information technologies. (p. 664)

It may be that certain aspects within the Patriot Act, such as technology advances for fighting terrorism, should be compared very cautiously to situations in the past. For some, this fear of technology stems from the examples of one of the more ominous additions recently seen in Europe. Currently, Britain has had a popularity boom for closed circuit surveillance cameras that are beginning to cover many aspects of their people's lives.

A more common theme may be seen in the perceived goals that these historical acts share with the Patriot Act. These eras represent a time when there was a mindset that could be considered a mentality of fighting a battle on two fronts. Past events may share with the present the feeling that the nation has an enemy in foreign locations while also perceiving enemies deep within the fabric of the country. This situation places extreme stress to shore up the home front defenses to avoid advances from an outside enemy. This situation appears to be seen throughout the historical perspectives forwarded. Many may see this same kind of environment today. There is little doubt that failure to adequately protect the country from terrorism will have adverse and long lasting ramifications.

It is unknown how the existing balance between national security and civil liberties will develop in the future. This issue is specific to the Patriot Act as many of the controversial sections are set to expire on December, 31 2005 (EPIC, 2001, *Section 224*).

It is possible that the Patriot Act situation will be resolved similarly to the situation in 1798 with the Alien and Sedition Act. The Alien and Sedition Act simply passed its expiration date and went away. This tension filled period for the U.S., which saw the potential danger to the country by the Napoleonic Wars, cycled away to different concerns. However, some of the immediate repercussions of the aftermath of the Alien and Sedition Act are pertinent when looking to the future of the Patriot Act. After the expiration of the Alien and Sedition Act that sparked President John Adams to label Thomas Jefferson guilty of "treason," several major changes were made. Thomas Jefferson, who replaced John Adams as president, pardoned everyone convicted of a violation of the act (Rosenzweig, 2004). That is, every effort was made to reverse the law and its effect. If, in fact, the Patriot Act does expire, all of the sections of the numerous laws that are currently amended by the Patriot Act will suddenly come back into effect. This landscape, and its unforeseen repercussions, has not been adequately identified and further study and evaluation are needed.

There is equal potential that the Patriot Act will not sunset. In fact, those who take an interest in the long term ramifications of the Patriot Act should acknowledge the potential that a sequel to the Patriot Act may lead to laws that become permanent parts of the culture. An example of this is relayed by Dana Keith's article, "In The Name of National Security or Insecurity? The Potential Indefinite Detention of Noncitizen Certified Terrorists in the United States and the United Kingdom in the Aftermath of September 11, 2001." Within the article Keith (2004) talks about some of England's temporary anti-terrorist measures that were expected to have a short life span, but became permanent due to the nature of terrorism warfare. Speaking specifically about the Prevention of Terrorism Act, England's response to terrorism in Northern Ireland, Keith said,

> The introduction of the PTA 1974 created a dual system of criminal justice in the United Kingdom...The British government originally intended these 'emergency powers' laws that were only applicable to suspected terrorist to last for the brief period it took to reestablish order in Northern Ireland. That brief period, however, never expired. (p. 428)

While Section 412 of the Patriot Act is currently being bypassed by the government for other existing immigration detainment laws, the Patriot Act is, without a doubt, a powerful tool for immigration control. Since September 11, 2001, over 5,000 non-citizens have been detained in the name of national security. Similar to the Palmer Raids and the World War II Japanese interment incident, the post 9-11 detentions are considered by some as the third historical example of mass suspicionless preventative detentions within the U.S. (Cole, 2004). Within the current sensitized environment in which we live, it is not beyond the realm of possibility that future terrorist attacks could initiate circumstances where a re-visiting of internment camps could come again. This is not said lightly or for the purpose of being provocative. In fact, the odds are against such a repetition of brutality. What is meant to be relayed is that a well rounded observer and researcher must not eliminate any of the possibilities and history is not without cases of repetition.

In the end, it would appear that there is as much diversity in opinion about the larger concepts of fighting terrorism, especially the rapid increase of intelligence and law enforcement cooperation (Solove, 2004), as there is with the Patriot Act. While there is ample literature in the field to show that the pendulum of justice is swinging in the direction of government access and control, it is unknown whether the pendulum will continue its swing forward to a point where government can encroach in more areas previously considered protected by civil liberties. Furthermore, it is unknown at this point if, or more likely when, the pendulum will swing back.

Ronald Weich, submitting a 2002 ACLU report entitled, "Insatiable Appetite: The Government's Demand for New and Unnecessary Powers after September 11," warned:

> Some national leaders downplay these concerns, saying that wartime limitations on civil liberties are temporary and normal conditions will return once hostilities end. But the war on terrorism, unlike conventional wars, is not likely to come to a public and decisive end. Both Homeland Security Director Tom Ridge and the newly appointed drug czar, John Walters, recently equated the war on terrorism with the nation's continuing wars on drugs and crime. So restrictions on civil liberties may be with us for a very long time. So long, in fact, that they may change the character of our democratic system in ways that very few Americans desire. (p. 16)

It is with the knowledge of the past that we consider the proper actions for future implementations in the struggle with terrorism. Recent proposals to deal with national crisis, such as the "emergency constitution" (Ackerman, 2004), are examples of current constructs that may be present in a future Patriot Act sequel. There is no doubt that the collective input of both further research and debate will strengthen not only the quantity of information to review but the quality of the final decisions that will be made to affect the future of our country.

As for the Patriot Act, we find ourselves at a historical crossroads. The renewal or sunset of many of the controversial sections of the act will have long lasting implications to the country. Even now, the battle over the future of the Patriot Act is brewing. However, in actuality, the arguing and fighting may be much shorter than the act's implications to the future. It is at this moment, this relatively quiet moment, when deep reflection should be made as to the history of government's action in times of crisis as well as the products of that action.

In concluding this chapter, we can reflect that history shows a tendency for the government to limit civil liberties in times of crises as a defense mechanism for the protection of the nation. As with the historical events chronicled in this chapter, after the crisis has abated civil liberties were restored and, in some cases, additional safeguards were put in place. To some readers, after digesting this most interesting historical review of U.S. history, the Patriot Act, when compared to the legislative acts of the past, may no longer seem as such a damaging piece of legislation to civil liberties as previously believed. However, as has been a running theme in this book, the final call of where the Patriot Act should be placed in history as a potential threat to civil liberties or tool for national defense will be up to the individual. The difference now is that the readers of this book can make valid comparisons of the Patriot Act with laws enacted throughout history when America was under the stress and strain of perceived crisis.

References

Ackerman, B. (2004). The emergency constitution. *Yale Law Journal, 113*, 1029-1091.

Banks, W. C. (2003). And the wall came tumbling down: Secret surveillance after the terror. *University of Miami Law Review, 57*, 1147-1194.

Becker, S. W. (2003). "Mirror, mirror on the wall...": Assessing the aftermath of September 11th. *Valparaiso Law Review, 37*, 563-626.

Cole, D. (2004). The priority of morality: The emergency constitution's blind spot. *Yale Law Journal, 113*, 1753-1800.

Debs v. United States, 249 U.S. 211 (1919).

Electronic Privacy Information Center [EPIC]. (2001). *HR 3162 RDS: 107th Congress.* Retrieved September 25, 2004, from http://www.epic.org/privacy/terrorism/hr3162.html

Engle, K. (2004). Constructing good aliens and good citizens: Legitimizing the war on terror(ism). *University of Colorado Law Review, 75*, 59-114.

Eugene V. Debs Internet Archive. (2001). Retrieved February 10, 2005, from http://www. marxists.org/archive/debs

Fisher, L. E. (2004). Guilt by expressive association: Political profiling, surveillance and the privacy of groups. *Arizona Law Review, 46*, 621-675.

Harrison, D. L. (2004). The USA Patriot Act: A new way of thinking, an old way of reacting, higher education responds. *North Carolina Journal of Law & Technology, 5*, 177-211.

Hoffman, G. A. (2003). Litigating terrorism: The new FISA regime, the wall, and the Fourth Amendment. *American Criminal Law Review, 40*, 1655-1682.

Howell, B. A. (2004). The future of Internet surveillance law: A symposium to discuss Internet surveillance, privacy & the USA Patriot Act: Surveillance law: Reshaping the framework: Seven weeks:

The making of the USA Patriot Act. *George Washington Law Review, 72,* 1145-1207.

Keith, D. (2004). In the name of national security or insecurity? The potential indefinite detention of noncitizen certified terrorists in the United States and the United Kingdom in the aftermath of September 11, 2001. *Florida Journal of International Law, 16,* 405-428.

Kollar, J. F. (2004). USA Patriot Act, the Fourth Amendment, and paranoia: Can they read this while I'm typing? *Journal of High Technology Law, 3,* 67-93.

Kreimer, S. F. (2004). Watching the watchers: Surveillance, transparency, and political freedom in the war on terror. *University of Pennsylvania Journal of Constitutional Law, 7,* 133-181.

Kubler, J. (2004). U.S. citizens as enemy combatants; indication of a rollback of civil liberties or a sign of our jurisprudential evolution? *St. John's Journal of Legal Commentary, 18,* 631-674.

Lee, L. T. (2003). The USA Patriot Act and telecommunications: Privacy under attack. *Rutgers Computer and Technology Law Journal, 29,* 371-403.

Lilly, J. R. (2003). National security at what price?: A look into civil liberty concerns in the information age under the USA Patriot Act of 2001 and a proposed constitutional test for future legislation. *Cornell Journal of Law and Public Policy, 12,* 447-471.

Lithwick, D., & Turner, J. (2004). From a guide to the Patriot Act. In N. Smith & L. M. Messina (Eds.), *Homeland security* (pp. 94-103). Bronx, NY: H.W. Wilson Co.

McCarthy, A. C. (2004, June 14). The Patriot Act without tears. *National Review, 56,* 32-35.

Regan, T. (2005, June 6). 'Secret' Senate meeting on Patriot Act. [Electronic Version]. *The Christian Science Monitor.* Retrieved June 6, 2005, from http://www.csmonitor.com/ 2005/0606/dailyUpdate.html

Rosenzweig, P. (2004). Civil liberty and the response to terrorism. *Duquesne University Law Review, 42,* 663-723.-

Rosenzweig, P., Kochems, A., & Carafano, J. J. (Eds.). (2004). *The Patriot Act: Understanding the law's role in the global war on terrorism.* Washington, DC: The Heritage Foundation.

Sekhon, V. (2003). The civil rights of "others": Antiterrorism, the Patriot Act, and Arab and South Asian American rights in post-9/11 American society. *Texas Forum on Civil Liberties & Civil Rights, 8,* 117-148.

Solove, D. J. (2004). The future of Internet surveillance law: A symposium to discuss Internet surveillance, privacy & the USA Patriot Act: Surveillance law: Reshaping the framework: Electronic surveillance law. *George Washington Law Review, 72,* 1264-1305. -

Thomas, P. A. (2003). Emergency and anti-terrorist power: 9/11: USA and UK. *Fordham International Law Journal, 26,* 1193-1229.

United States v. Truong Dinh Hung, 629 F.2d 908 (4th Cir. 1980).

United States v. United States District Court, 407 U.S. 297 (1972).

Weich, R. (2002, October 15). *Insatiable appetite: The government's demand for new and unnecessary powers after September 11.* Retrieved August 12, 2005, from http://www.aclu.org/safefree/resources/17042pub20021015.html

CHAPTER 9

What Writers Write: A Content Analysis

IT IS WITH GREAT HAPPINESS that this chapter is presented to readers interested in looking at the Patriot Act from unique and interesting perspectives. While there will be ample explanation of the study forthcoming, there should be a moment spent to clarify a few things about this chapter. First, when making assumptions or determinations about another's work, a certain amount of humility should be exercised. With that in mind, let it be said that each of the articles examined in this study was of a very high quality and, without a doubt, worthy of the peer-review acceptance that brought about its publication. Second, it should also be stated that while this pre-Patriot Act renewal content analysis was undertaken with the zest and vigor that always embodies the search for new knowledge, it is also understood that it reflects a learning experience. Like early day pioneers breaking new ground through the untraveled wilderness, there were many unforeseen pitfalls and perils experienced along the course of this research project. However, the adventure was illuminating in many respects and the fruits of that journey are now passed on to you.

In previous chapters, the positions and opinions of individuals and groups on opposing sides of the Patriot Act have been examined. Looking at different opinions on aspects of the Patriot Act has been important as it helps to give readers a more rounded view of the issues. In this chapter, this same philosophy is carried to a new level. Once again, if you see some core statistics about the law repeated, it is because they have been deemed important to make sure that some of the basic facts concerning the Patriot

Act do not get lost in the creative and "out of the box" approach to studying the Patriot Act that is being presented in this book.

The origins of the Patriot Act remain a mystery to the public to date. Even more perplexing is the lack of knowledge of how this diverse and complex document impacts the country now, and its potential implications for the future. This lack of public education has exacerbated misunderstandings about the law and served to deepen already existing divides between groups in America. As with many things following 9-11, fear has moved faster than knowledge (DeBecker, 2002).

By now, we have established the daunting physical size of the Patriot Act. Most readers also understand the complexities involved in understanding each of the laws and their various changes from original versions. What about the Patriot Act's function? The Patriot Act has been, and continues to be, plagued by a perceived duality of function. On the one hand, the Patriot Act was constructed as a response to 9-11 and serves to not only bring the nation together, but also to protect the nation by allowing the government the ability to combat terrorism in a modern world. This representation of the Patriot Act's function is abundantly portrayed in the expanded version of its title, "The Uniting and Strengthening America by Providing Appropriate Tools Required to Intercept and Obstruct Terrorism Act" (EPIC, 2001). Apart from this function, the Patriot Act is also perceived as a bold, if not reckless, expansion of government power into the privacy of its people. These dual roles of the Patriot Act are perceived in different ways by different people. While some believe that the Patriot Act serves only one of the two functions mentioned, others see the law serving both functions in differing situations. It is the combination of the complex nature of the Patriot Act, in conjunction with its broad expanse of government powers, which requires further evaluation and analysis.

It has been commonly expounded that only through research and evaluation can a civilized culture draw from the knowledge of the past to make viable decisions for the future. The issue of the Patriot Act research gives a unique opportunity for such an exercise. Not only does the Patriot Act deal with such timely issues as terrorism, national security, and civil rights, but also, through built-in preventative measures in Section 224 (EPIC, 2001), the Patriot Act offers an opportunity to research the viability and relevance of a unique and dynamic law for the future.

Purpose of Study

The Patriot Act, by its construction, is not a single coherent law (Kerr, 2003). The Patriot Act, by the nature of its learner "unfriendly" construction, has the ability to turn off the inquisitive seeker from further in-depth research and, even worse, send people out into the field with inaccurate information on the law. If this were not the case, everyone would be fully versed on the Patriot Act and this book would not be necessary. However, there is a small motivated group of individuals who spend their time in search of every document pertaining to the Patriot Act. This small group sifts through the simplest and most ambiguous documents in what is often a never ending search for a more refined knowledge of the Patriot Act. These individuals are known as researchers. For researchers reporting on Patriot Act issues, the goal is often to recognize that the Patriot Act is a literal minefield of ambiguity and, to be able to traverse the law carefully and comprehensively, one step at a time, and hopefully mark the way for others as they go.

Just as the public is diverse in backgrounds, opinions, and concerns over the Patriot Act, the same can be said for researchers. Researchers, like the public, tend to focus on certain areas within the vast realm of the Patriot Act. Sometimes this concentrated research becomes overly repetitious with an overabundance of information in one area, while other areas of equal importance appear like a desert. This is yet another reason why a comprehensive book like this was created. In the end, whether the topic researched was "feast or near famine," it was created by an individual who felt there was something worth saying to someone else. The goal of this study is to look at the communications made by those researchers as they report over different topics within this law.

The specific purpose of this study is to perform a content analysis of scholarly articles written about the Patriot Act. The goal of the content analysis is to answer two research questions:

1. Are the majority of the Patriot Act articles within our journal sample negative toward Patriot Act usage?
2. If the majority of the Patriot Act articles are negative toward its usage, on what section(s) of the Patriot Act do they focus that negative argument on?

Methodology

"Content Analysis," as a term, has been in existence for approximately 50 years. While content analysis has been in practice for a long time, Webster's Dictionary for the English language had content analysis recorded and defined starting in 1961 (Krippendorff, 1980). Content analysis is a research technique for the comprehension of data as a collection of symbolic phenomena (Krippendorff, 1980). Content analysis has the ability to incorporate research studies on written forms of communications in various formats including, but not limited to, the following: newspapers, magazine articles, movies, political speeches, cartoons, and the list goes on an on. In our study, we will be studying scholarly articles. Specifically, articles pertaining to the Patriot Act.

Our sample was collected from 7 scholarly journals : *Oklahoma Law Review, Texas Journal on Civil Liberties & Civil Rights, Cornell International Law Journal, Harvard Journal of Law & Public Policy, Wisconsin Law Review, Brigham Young University Law Review* and *Brigham Young University Education and Law Journal*. Of these selected journals, all Patriot Act related articles were collected from October 27, 2001, to November 20, 2005. This collection equaled a total of 17 Patriot Act related articles. The sample was collected using the LexisNexis database, a well recognized source for collecting journal articles (Krippendorff, 2004).

Careful consideration was given to the sampling technique. While the usage of the database might fit into the basis for a labeling of our sample as a convenience sample (Krippendorff, 2004), the actuality is that the collection of our sample was based on relevance for our research questions, and would more adequately be called a purposeful sample. Because the sample was not randomly collected, the findings of this research project will only be stated as an observance within this specific sample. In fact, this lack of data inferences, along with strategic sampling, is a known hallmark of qualitative analysis (Roberts, 1997).

With this sample a Qualitative Content Analysis was conducted. It is important to explain some of the differences between "quantitative" and "qualitative" content analysis. It would be reasonable to say that both techniques are for "…capturing the essence…what is the perfume, the flavor, the *nature* of the phenomenon" (Neill, 2006). One solid difference is that qualitative analysis utilizes quasi-quantitative methods. That is, in our report, while we will be coding words that will be identified and counted (frequency counting) during the analysis of the journal text, we will be focusing our results on the thematic schemes found within the text. Quantitative analysis is often done on large samples with rigid data collection guidelines, while our sample, representative of qualitative analysis, will be conducted on a smaller sample and incorporate less strict guidelines to enhance the versatility of research techniques (Berelson, 1971). Qualitative analysis often relies more on the intent of the communicator and goes beyond the simple word counting found in quantitative analysis (Berelson, 1971).

The process of completing the qualitative content analysis will be executed by observing content units. Simply put, the journals serve as a collection of content units. While there are many types of content units (Berelson, 1971; Holsti, 1969; Krippendorff, 2004; Neuendorf, 2002), we will primarily focus on two. The first is the smallest unit known as the "word." The second unit, known as the "theme," is found within complete sentences and word groupings (Berelson, 1971). We will also be cognizant of the "tone," often called the "direction" or the "orientation," of the communication. These terms describe the pro or con treatment of the subject matter (Berelson, 1971).

As the text of each of the journals is analyzed, words will be coded by negative indicators such as: corruption, ineptness, deceit, greed, and so forth. Any overlapping indicator categories will be collapsed for simplicity. Word groupings will be evaluated for themes and those collected will also be evaluated for existing trends that will be reported. This information will allow us to answer the first research question: Are the majority of the Patriot Act articles within our journal sample negative toward Patriot Act usage? From the words and/or sentences that are collected, both will be analyzed to see which section of the Patriot Act corresponds with the data unit. Each data unit will either fall into one or more of the 10 titles in the Patriot Act or, if the negative communication of the Patriot Act is not being centered on a specific section of the law, an alternative explanation will be forwarded to answer the second research question: If the majority of the Patriot Act articles are negative toward its implementation, what themes are these arguments based on?

Although quantitative, and some qualitative, analysis utilize computer programs to assist with analyzing massive amounts of data, this research project will not incorporate this software. However, dictionaries will be utilized to assist with avoiding misinterpretations among confusing words.

This is a common practice within content analysis (Krippendorff, 2004; Neuendorf, 2002).

Findings

During the course of this research project, 17 law journals were reviewed. As mentioned previously, the journals were part of a purposeful selection process and the findings in this case are not being generalized to a larger population. This fact alone does not void the research project's viability. Several interesting findings were gleaned from the content analysis process that are pertinent to this and future studies. It is important to note that the presentation of the Patriot Act as a subject was not conveyed in a single fashion throughout our sample. Of the 17 journals, the Patriot Act was presented as a subject in the following ways: as a simple footnote supporting a non-terrorism subject in 2 articles; as a component of an argument within the text in at least 1 paragraph, but no more than 3 paragraphs, in 11 articles; and presented as the main focus of the text in 4 articles.

The complexity of the Patriot Act places this law in the proximity of many subject topics. Within the sample, the Patriot Act was placed in the context of the following subjects: religious freedom, foreign exchange students and collegiate issues, school safety issues, world trade, civil and human rights, indefinite detention, Haitian asylum issues, military tribunals, grand juries, function of the Central Intelligence Agency, and interagency intelligence sharing. This variety in the presentation format and the subject matter served as an interesting mix and gave a rounded display of the different ways the Patriot Act is being presented today.

Title Analysis

The first stage of the content analysis was a review of the titles of the journal articles. Journals with negative, positive, and neutral titles toward the Patriot Act were logged. It is important to note that the term "negative title" is a subjective term. For this study, the term "negative" was defined making negative judgments about the implementation or use of the Patriot Act. An articulated positive judgment in the title was also categorized. In addition to these two categories, neutral titles were also logged. Neutral title categories included titles that made no judgments, either positive or negative, to the Patriot Act or the related topics of which the Patriot Act was a part. While the neutrality of some statements and titles may be debatable, it was felt that an accurate observation could be made.

During the research it was found that the tone, that is, the mood, purposely or not, set by the author, was a fundamental factor in the later component of the theme. While the tone of the articles stayed fairly consistent throughout the texts of the journals, the tone within the titles of the journal articles was not a reliable factor for what the tone of the text would be. An analysis of the titles of the 17 journal articles found the following tone classifications: negative-9, positive-1, neutral-7. There were disparities with these findings and the findings for the tone of the text of the journals which were tabulated as: negative-13, positive-2, neutral-2.

Analyzing Units within the Text

During the process of analyzing the tone and identifying the underling themes within the text, 4 sets of units of texts were identified and categorized. These units included the following: single words, word strings of 2-4 words, word strings of more than 4 words but less than a sentence, and complete sentences. These words were tone driven. That is, based on the overriding tone of the article, these words were placed in one of three confidence levels. The three confidence levels were: high, medium, and low. The confidence level was based on the research question. All unit entries in the "high" category reflected units evidencing a negative tone against the implementation of the Patriot Act. Medium confidence levels most often reflected a neutral tone, and low confidence level units were units found in positive articles. There was a small amount of overlap due to tone shifts within the articles, but the shifts were minimal and most often found in the text. Another specific factor concerning tone shifts in this sample was the fact that the tone shifts were consistent, from positive to negative, regarding the Patriot Act. Within the sample, the tone shifts were preceded by the following words: yet-2, however-3, nonetheless-2, although-1, and but-1. Because the underlying themes were not always readily recognized, a comprehensive approach to unit collection was necessary.

Single Word Units

The following unit(s) and frequency of occurrence were categorized at the "high" confidence level:

danger - 2	reprisals - 1	race - 1	intimidate - 1	failed - 1
insufficient - 1	vigilantism - 1	negligent - 1	demand - 1	expands - 4
expanded - 4	destructive - 1	vague - 1	vagueness - 4	inappropriate - 1
self-delusion - 1	alienate - 1	overreact - 1	excessive - 1	failure - 1
unprecedented - 1	arrogance - 1	error - 1	quasi-war - 1	implications - 1
trigger - 3	punishing - 1	torture - 1	repression - 2	rushed - 1
problems - 1	expansion - 1			

The following unit(s) were categorized at the "medium" confidence level:
defective - 1

The following unit(s) were categorized at the "low" confidence level:
There were no units collected for this category.

The following 2-4 word groupings were categorized at the "high" confidence level:

preemptive determination - 1	discouraging impact - 1
Chinese exclusion case - 3	despite assurances offered - 1
Chinese exclusion & Japanese internment - 1	discouragement of perjury - 1
fear and suspicion - 1	scare tactics - 1
has generated much confusion - 1	moral dilemmas - 1
Big Brother - 1	hastened to initiate legislation - 1
rubber stamp - 1	expands this power - 1
disproportionate harm - 1	disproportionate manner - 1
broad and vague - 1	immense potential risk - 1
unrestrained use - 1	fragility of democracy - 1
challenge to democracy - 1	democracy must safeguard itself - 1
push the envelope - 1	overboard generalizations - 1
blanket prohibitions - 1	unjustified imposition on innocents - 1
perhaps more troubling - 1	vague statute - 1
vaguely defined - 1	relaxes the secrecy rule - 1
immune from judicial review - 1	legal fictions - 1
unconstitutionally void for vagueness - 1	serious constitutional concerns - 1
serious consequences - 1	unchecked surveillance power - 1
sweeping constitutional language - 1	perceived terrorist threat - 1

sounding the death knell - 1	consequential refocusing of power - 1
unregulated power - 1	unlimited access - 1
general hostility - 1	fear retribution - 1
danger of leaks increase - 1	suffer reputational harm - 1
backdoor expansion - 2	unauthorized expansion - 1
potential for misuse - 1	significant danger - 1
de facto authorization - 1	expanded government power - 1
ideological test - 1	due process shortcomings - 1
bigotry and ignorance - 1	erosion of constitutional rights - 1
unconstitutional imposition - 1	unconstitutionally vague - 1
stifles liberty - 1	collateral damages - 1
theory of bad tendencies - 1	surge of discretionary powers - 1
offensive behavior - 1	collateral consequences - 2
draconian measures - 1	draconian rules - 1
emotion reigns over reason - 1	secretly apply - 1
secretly arrested - 1	secret police powers - 1
dangers to democracy - 1	zealots from the right - 1
deceiving the American people - 1	repression measure - 1
grotesque unfairness - 1	repressive legal action - 1
headstrong Supreme Court - 1	

The following 2-4 word groupings were categorized at the "medium" confidence level:

adversarial relationship - 1	less trust - 1
more distance relationship - 1	burden on importers & shippers - 1
proper balance - 1	slippery slope - 1
hurried enactment - 1	Caligulan in its inaccessibility - 1
widespread surveillance - 1	

The following 2-4 word groupings were categorized at the "low" confidence level:

constant clamor - 1	American Gestapo - 1

The following word groupings are over 4 words but less than a full sentence. These word grouping were categorized at the "high" confidence level. In addition, because of the length of word groups, citations were placed with each individual word groups.

"...it fails to cite the First Amendment as a source of protection" (Mousin, 2003, p. 542).

"...we may turn a blind eye towards the violence of the state in our midst" (Mousin, 2003, p. 557).

"Students in some of the groups subject to this registration burden..." (Mantle, 2003, p. 820).

'...serves as a check on corrupt practices by exposing the judicial process to public scrutiny' (*Simone*, 14 F.3d at 839, as cited in Mantle, 2003, p. 827).

"...international students are at a distinct disadvantage" (Mantle, 2003, p. 832).

"...the only protection deportees have against government action" (Mantle, 2003 p. 832).

"...there was no rational factual basis for sacrificing rights in favor of security needs and that the lifting of the constitutional restrictions was no more than the emotional product of panic, paranoia, and fear" (Gross, 2004, p. 30).

"...the unequivocal tilting of the constitutional balance in favor of national security needs at the expense of individual rights" (Gross, 2004, p. 73).

"The judicial supervision of the exercise of the power is a pretense..." (Gross, 2004, p. 74).

"...far ranging surveillance powers available..." (Gross, 2004, p. 75).

"...application is vague, there is a danger that it will be constructed broadly..." (Gross, 2004, pp. 75-76).

"...despite the significant expansion of its powers..." (Gross, 2004, p. 76).

"...were these measures the outcome of panic and paranoia lacking any factual basis" (Gross, 2004, p. 89)?

"The most extreme and far-reaching renunciation of the system of checks and balances..." (Gross, 2004, p. 90).

"...democracy fights with one hand tied behind its back" (Gross, 2004, p. 91).

"The more the measure violates the core aspects of privacy..." (Gross, 2004, p. 91).

"...unnecessary restrictions imposed in times of emergency..." (Gross, 2004, p. 92).

'the ongoing struggle between control and discretion...' (Cole & Dempsey, 2002, as cited in Harris, 2003, p. 138).

"...latitude for investigation of political activity..." (Harris, 2003, p. 139).

"...political spying remain largely unrestricted..." (Harris, 2003, p. 139).

"...threat to Americans' privacy and First Amendment freedoms" (Harris, 2003, p. 140).

"...increased invasions of privacy and incursions on civil liberties..." (Harris, 2003, p. 140).

"…expansion of government surveillance is unnecessary and even counter-productive to the effort to prevent terrorism." (Harris, 2003, p. 141).

"When one treats a whole group of people as presumptively suspicious…" (Harris, 2003, p. 141).

"…less is actually more when it comes to preventing terrorism…" (Harris, 2003, p. 141).

"…recent legislative trend insulting administrative immigration decisions from judicial review…" (Gardner, 2003, p. 179).

"The government started this questionable practice …" (Gardner, 2003, p. 192).

"While Arab and Muslim communities have reason to protest…" (Amorosa, 2005, p. 264).

"Attorney General's complete casting aside of the contrary determinations, of both fact and law… (Amorosa, 2005, p. 265).

"…unreasonable exercise of unchecked power…" (Amorosa, 2005, p. 266).

"…exceeds even the constitutional maxim…" (Amorosa, 2005, p. 275).

"…D-J- is a dangerous aberration from the legitimate use of administrative power" (Amorosa, 2005, p. 275).

"…justification as a pretext for punishing…" (Amorosa, 2005, p. 282).

"…unreasonable and unjustifiable blanket detention" (Amorosa, 2005, p. 284).

"…unreasonable abuse of discretion that should be checked by the judiciary…" (Amorosa, 2005, p. 292).

"In D-J-, the Attorney General abused his power…" (Amorosa, 2005, p. 292).

"…most significant risks to political and personal freedoms…" (Heymann, 2002, p. 443).

"…monitor effectively every individual or group who may possibly be planning such an attack" (Heymann, 2002, p. 443).

'Unjustified investigations of political expression…' (Senate Select Comm. On Intelligence, The FBI and Cispes, S. Rep. No. 101-46, at 102, as cited in Heymann, 2002, p. 444).

"New problems of civil liberties and equal protection quickly emerge…" (Heymann, 2002, p. 445).

"…by detaining aliens illegally in the United States or removable for cause (or on the basis of the new detention power claimed in President Bush's 'military order')…" (Heymann, 2002, p. 448).

"…the effect of alienating a much larger group than were originally sympathetic to the terrorists." (Heymann, 2002, p. 449).

"…with large numbers of those concerned with civil liberties withdrawing support from government measures against terrorists" (Heymann, 2002, p. 449).

"…the gravest danger to civil liberties and human rights…" (Heymann, 2002, p. 456).

"The mantra of the Bush team…" (Fletcher, 2002, p. 635).

"…the White House has found it easy to invoke the rhetoric of armed aggression and collective self-defense" (Fletcher, 2002, p. 635).

"...we are in a state of collective confusion..." (Fletcher, 2002, p. 637).

"...we run the risk of committing great moral and legal error" (Fletcher, 2002, p. 638).

"...a deprivation of basic constitutional rights..." (Fletcher, 2002, p. 638).

"...tribunals lack credibility and severely curtail the rights of criminal defendants..." (Fletcher, 2002, p. 652).

"...some damage to the interests traditionally served by grand jury secrecy, especially reputational interests, may occur" (Beale & Felman, 2002, p. 710).

"The USA Patriot Act defines these terms broadly..." (Beale & Felman, 2002, p. 715).

"The blurring of the line between crime and war..." (Beale & Felman, 2002, p. 718).

"...they raise red flags concerning fundamental constitutional rights" (Aziz, 2003, p. 47).

"...the means currently utilized by the federal government in pursuing these legitimate ends are highly questionable..." (Aziz, 2003, p. 47).

"...may violate organizations' and individuals' constitutional Due Process and First Amendment rights" (Aziz, 2003, p. 47).

"...a form of political protest against the United States'..." (Aziz, 2003, p. 48).

"...past and ongoing targeting of Arab and Muslim individuals and organizations..." (Aziz, 2003, p. 49).

"...trigger an array of other punitive laws..." (Aziz, 2003, p. 55).

"...the stakes are high and the consequences can be severe..." (Aziz, 2003, p. 56).

"...have potentially adverse foreign policy consequences..." (Aziz, 2003, p. 57).

"Therefore, terrorism-related charges serve as powerful tools to avoid an individual's First, Fourth, and Fifth Amendment rights..." (Aziz, 2003, p. 59).

"The bona fide risk of deprivation of liberty..." (Aziz, 2003, p. 60).

"Another illuminating example of the U.S. government's double standards..." (Aziz, 2003, p. 71).

"...the Bill of Rights exists precisely to protect vulnerable minority groups from the majority's prejudices..." (Aziz, 2003, p. 92).

"...frivolous, baseless, time-consuming, or unnecessary actions is just one collateral consequence of strictly disciplining student expression" (Nappen, 2003, p. 115).

"...students feel that they have no voice and that their opinions are not valid" (Nappen, 2003, p. 116).

'zero tolerance takes away discretion...' (Texas Association of School Boards, Inc., Can Our Discipline Policies Help? as cited in Nappen, 2003, p. 120).

"Protest the government's unjustified invasion of our liberties..." (Traynor, 2005, p. 28).

"...leaders in Congress who are expressing their disquiet concerning the Patriot Act and seeking to rein it in" (Traynor, 2005, p. 33).

"...attack on our civil liberties..." (Lewis, 2003, p. 260).

"To the already arbitrary aspects of immigration law, the Bush administration added new burdens..." (Lewis, 2003, p. 262).

"The conservative majority on the U.S. Supreme Court may instinctively incline toward giving the President the war-making authority..." (Lewis, 2003, p. 271).

"...the Bush administration's attempt to brush constitutional rights aside in the war on terrorism" (Lewis, 2003, p. 271).

"...the breadth and rigidity of its position" (Lewis, 2003, p. 271).

The following word groupings are over 4 words but less than a full sentence. These word groupings were categorized at the "medium" confidence level. In addition, because of the length of word groups, citations were placed with each individual word groups.

"...tension between liberty and security..." (Heymann, 2002, p. 441).

"The costs in terms of privacy..." (Heymann, 2002, p. 441).

"The risks to American civil liberties—and to the human rights of others..." (Heymann, 2002, p. 442).

"...the USA Patriot Act has generated confusion and controversy" (Seamon & Gardner, 2005, p. 321).

"...the Patriot Act was meant to expand executive power..." (Seamon & Gardner, 2005, p. 326).

"...even the compromise version was unconstitutional"(Seamon & Gardner, 2005, p. 378).

The following word groups are over 4 words but less than a full sentence. These word groups were categorized at the "low" confidence level. In addition, because of the length of word groups, citations were placed with each individual word groups.

"…narrower, more xenophobic and insular views promoted by other government agencies" (Glick, 2002, p. 638).

"…a cry to unleash the CIA…" (Hitz, 2002, p. 765).

"…authority of the Executive Branch…" (Iraola, 2003, p. 573).

Identifying Tone

The analyses of the content units within the text were of major importance to understanding tone. During the study, three features of tone were identified in the sample articles:

1. Tone would fluctuate to some degree through all the articles.
2. Tone was identified through the usage of content units.
3. The consistency and the totality of tone elements assisted in theme identification.

After totaling the tone categories for the 17 articles in the study sample, 13 articles had a totality of negative tone, 2 articles had a totality of positive tone, and 2 articles had a totality of neutral tone. When reviewing the articles, elements of tone became apparent immediately; however, to identify the overall tone of the article required repeated analysis. Articles within the sample would have fluctuations as the writers pushed home important points in the text, in this case aspects of the Patriot Act, with passion. This passion would involve strong elements of tone, either positive or negative. Places that would precede major points in the text would be mixed in how tone was implemented. At times, the text would be negatively or positively tone driven, possibly preparing the reader for a major point. At other times, tone before major points in the text would be preceded by neutral tone text. It was seldom seen that combinations of positive followed by negative tone elements were seen in preparation of major point presentations within the text. Conversely, following major points in the text, a change in tone would occur. To place tone in an analogy that identifies its potential deceptiveness, following and analyzing tone within the articles was like riding a river. Quite often the wave action would be distinct and turbulent; while at other times the river appeared calm. The challenge to traversing this dynamic environment was to immerse oneself within the text.

Working within the parameters of this study, negative judgments on the implementation of the Patriot Act constituted negative tone. Positive judgments which supported the implementation of the Patriot Act constituted positive tone. While it is acknowledged that it is open to debate, a lack of an overt negative or positive judgment as to the implementation of the Patriot Act constituted neutral tone. While respecting the challenges involved with tone categorization, the process of identifying tone served as an important path to one of the main objectives of the study--the identification of themes.

Theme Summation

Within the study, theme served as the main idea(s) or point(s) being expressed in the articles. Some of the articles had multiple themes and, when this was the case, a totality of the themes was tabulated to make the decision of how the article would be categorized. The breakdown of positive, negative, and neutral themes ran the same as the tone totals. That is, by the parameters of the study: 13 articles had negative themes, 2 articles had positive themes, and 2 articles had themes that were non-judgmental as to the implementation of the Patriot Act and were deemed neutral. Specifically, the repeated reoccurring negative themes included the following:

1. The Patriot Act was rushed into legislation.
2. The Patriot Act gives the government uncontrolled surveillance power.
3. The Patriot Act violates civil rights.
4. The civil rights violations created by the Patriot Act may be irreversible.
5. The Bush administration is creating a police state.
6. History will reflect negatively on the Patriot Act.
7. A collective effort is needed to stop the Patriot Act.

Positive themes found in the text included the following:

1. The Patriot Act allows the government the tools to fight terrorism.
2. Opposition to the Patriot Act is a baseless overreaction.
3. Detention authorities within the Patriot Act are vital to national security.

Neutral themes were benign in nature and involved non-judgmental information themes. These themes included the following:

1. International trade strategies.
2. Historical review of intelligence and law enforcement cases.

The limited number of negative themes is a testament to the amount of overlap and repetition of themes found in the articles. In addition, some variations of similar themes were collapsed in order to create s simpler and more encompassing theme set. An example of two similar themes that were collapsed would be "the Patriot Act was a rush to legislate" and the "Patriot Act is full of legal deficiencies." Since there is a close and logical progression between the two themes, they were collapsed into one theme.

The greatest majority of the articles had two themes, while none of the articles had more than three themes. Themes most often supported one another; however, theme development was varied. Some of the articles ran two themes concurrently and built up the themes throughout the text by the use of content units and tone. The majority of the articles separated themes into sections or halves of the text. Themes were always stressed at the end of the articles in the form of a passive or non-passive call to action.

Implications

While it was expected that there would be a sizable number of negative articles on the Patriot Act, the existence of neutral articles involving this highly contentious subject matter was unexpected since the majority of articles take a strong "for" or "against" attitude.

The nature of content analysis has exciting implications to further study. Foremost, the Patriot Act, by the nature of its complexity, will remain in the forefront of analysis from several fields of study. Continued content analysis has the potential not only to document the pulse of the symbols of communication of this subject, but also contribute to a higher level of honesty in the dissemination of this information. This study was but a snapshot, a literal dipping of a toe into a massive river of information. While the findings in this study were interesting for the sample collected, the limits of the purposeful sample do not allow for generalization to a larger population. As well, while this study strove to incorporate elements of quantitative content analysis, the main focus was to look at the hidden, and sometimes abstract, meanings within the text in a qualitative manner. Future studies would be enhanced by the collection of a random sample in combination with analysis in other mediums of communication. Multiple studies in this fashion would also be able to analyze if there is a pattern of writing, with regard to tone and themes, which are geographically based. A challenging, and possibly the most rewarding combination of efforts, would be a mixed method approach. Incorporating this method would flesh out both the quantitative and qualitative aspects of content analysis on the Patriot Act.

Conclusion

The future impact of the Patriot Act is unknown. It is from this uneasy vantage point that scholars and practitioners alike analyze, speculate, and prognosticate on what living under this law will mean tomorrow, and for many years to come. The Patriot Act, and the subsequent impact of responses thereto, is only one example of an event in U.S. history that begs the questions, "What is being written?" and "What is really being said?" For content analysis, many things can be learned as events unfold involving the Patriot Act and communications begin to flow with their unique symbols and meanings. In this respect, the journey may be as rewarding as the destination.

References

Amorosa, J. (2005). Dissecting in re D-J-: The attorney general, unchecked power, and the new national security threat posed by Haitian asylum seekers. *Cornell International Law Journal, 38*, 263-292.

Aziz, S. (2003). The laws on providing material support to terrorist organizations: The erosion of constitutional rights or a legitimate tool for preventing terrorism? *Texas Journal on Civil Liberties & Civil Rights, 9*, 45-92.

Beale, S. S., & Felman, J. E. (2002). Responses to September 11 attacks: The consequences of enlisting federal grand juries in the war on terrorism: Assessing the USA Patriot Act's changes to grand jury secrecy. *Harvard Journal of Law & Public Policy, 25*, 699-718.

Berelson, B. (1971). *Content analysis in communication research.* New York: Hafner Publishing Co.

DeBecker, G. (2002). *Fear less: Real truth about risk, safety, and security in a time of terrorism.* New York: Little, Brown and Company.

Electronic Privacy Information Center [EPIC]. (2001). *HR 3162 RDS: 107th Congress.* Retrieved September 25, 2004, from http://www.epic.org/privacy/terrorism/hr3162.html

Fletcher, G. P. (2002). The military tribunal order: On justice and war: Contradictions in the proposed military tribunals. *Harvard Journal of Law & Public Policy, 25,* 635-652.

Gardner, J. W. (2003). Halfway there: Zadvydas v. Davis reins in indefinite detentions, but leaves much unanswered. *Cornell International Law Journal, 36,* 177-206.

Glick, L. A. (2002). World trade after September 11, 2001: The U.S. response. *Cornell International Law Journal, 35,* 627-638.

Gross, E. (2004). The struggle of a democracy against terrorism—protection of human rights: The right to privacy versus the national interest—the proper balance. *Cornell International Law Journal, 37,* 27-93.

Harris, G. C. (2003). Terrorism and the Constitution: Sacrificing civil liberties in the name of national security. *Cornell International Law Journal, 36,* 135-150.

Heymann, P. B. (2002). Civil liberties and human rights in the aftermath of September 11. *Harvard Journal of Law & Public Policy, 25,* 441-456.

Hitz, F. P. (2002). Responses to the September 11 attacks: Unleashing the rogue elephant: September 11 and letting the CIA be the CIA. *Harvard Journal of Law & Public Policy, 25,* 765-780.

Holsti, O. R. (1969). *Content analysis for the social sciences and humanities.* Reading, MA: Addison-Wesley Publishing Co.

Iraola, R. (2003). Enemy combatants, the courts, and the Constitution. *Oklahoma Law Review, 56,* 565-619.

Kerr, O. S. (2003). Internet surveillance law after the USA Patriot Act: The big brother that isn't. *Northwestern University Law Review, 97,* 707-673.

Krippendorff, K. (1980). *Content analysis: An introduction to its methodology.* Beverly Hills, CA: Sage Publications.

Krippendorff, K. (2004). *Content analysis: An introduction to its methodology* (2nd ed.). Thousand Oaks, CA: Sage Publications.

Lewis, A. (2003). Civil liberties in a time of terror. *Wisconsin Law Review, 2003,* 257-272.

Mantle, D. R. (2003). What foreign students fear: Homeland security measures and closed deportation hearings. *Brigham Young University Education and Law Journal, 2003,* 815-834.

Mousin, C. B. (2003). Standing with the persecuted: Adjudicating religious asylum claims after the enactment of the International Freedom Act of 1998. *Brigham Young University Law Review, 2003,* 541-591.

Nappen, L. P. (2003). School safety v. free speech: The seesawing tolerance standards for students' sexual and violent expressions. *Texas Journal on Civil Liberties & Civil Rights, 9,* 93-127.

Neill, J. (2006, July 5). *Analysis of Professional Literature.* Retrieved January 1, 2006, from http://www.wilderdom.com/OEcourses/PROFLIT/Class8Qualitative3.htm# Content

Neuendorf, K.A. (2002). *The content analysis guidebook.* Thousand Oaks, CA: Sage Publications.

Roberts, C. W. (1997). Text analysis for the social sciences: Methods for drawing statistical inferences from texts and transcripts. In C. W. Roberts (Ed.), *Introduction* (pp. 1-8). Mahwah, NJ: Lawrence Erlbaum Associates.

Seamon, R. H., & Gardner, W. D. (2005). The Patriot Act and the wall between foreign intelligence and law enforcement. *Harvard Journal of Law & Public Policy, 28*, 319-386.

Traynor, M. (2005). Citizenship in a time of repression. *Wisconsin Law Review, 2005,* 1-34.

CHAPTER 10

A Sociological Perspective of the Patriot Act

BY NOW READERS ARE AWARE that the Patriot Act is one of the most controversial pieces of legislation to be implemented in the War on Terrorism since the terrorist attacks of September 11, 2001. It cannot be overstated that part of the controversy behind the Patriot Act issue is based on its ambiguity and complexity. As well, it may be that another reason there is so much debate about the law has to do with the differences in how individuals, as well as groups, think about the differing aspects of life that the Patriot Act affects. Simply put, we as individuals have our own views about life that we take into every situation that confronts us.

The goal of this chapter is to analyze the Patriot Act from a sociological perspective. To do this, a brief synopsis of three well known theories will be given. As well, the Patriot Act will be compared and contrasted with these sociological theories, which include: Structural Functionalism, Conflict Theory, and Marxism. This is not meant to imply that other sociological theories should not, or could not, be examined in the context of the Patriot Act. Furthermore, the analysis of these three theories from the perspective of the Patriot Act is not meant to be completely definitive. It is a working project of the author and embodies his perception of both the theories forwarded and the law in question at this time.

So why use theory to analyze the Patriot Act? It is believed that analyzing the Patriot Act from this unique perspective may serve to illuminate some previously hidden aspects of the law, as well the possible mindset of people deliberating these issues. It is important to note that apart from the educational references, some of the citations in this chapter reflect the ideas and beliefs of individuals who may or may not fall in line, to some degree, with the theory being observed. The source material in a specific area may simply back up an idea or concept and has no direct relation to a specific theory. This is simply an interpretation of the author and is not meant to imply more than that. In the end, it is hoped that this creative approach will spark future debate and contemplation, which will lead to a fuller knowledge of this complex law.

While considered by many as a theory of the 30s, 40s, and 50s, structural functionalism is still the dominant paradigm of organizations today. In fact, unconsciously, structural functionalism is often used by people to explain how the world works. Specifically, structural functionalism views society as an organism. Within this organism are several sub-components that work together for the greater good (Farganis, 2004). In short, people are dependent on one another. Differentiation within the system is seen only as a tool to increase the efficiency and productivity of the collective. Everyone has a specific function, but that function works together with others in a cooperative division of labor. Change is not a common event within this system, as structural functionalism strives to maintain the status quo. Individuals who threaten the society, or organism, are considered dysfunctional because of a lack of socialization, and are a threat to the whole (Parsons, 1954). The solution to this problem is re-socialization, combined with eventual reintegration, or incarceration (Farganis, 2004).

Conflict theory centers on the ongoing conflict between groups for scarce resources (Ritzer & Goodman, 2004). Groups that have access to these resources, whether money, food, prestige, etc., have greater power and are able to dominate the groups lacking these resources. For the dominant groups, a continual struggle ensues to maintain the top position of power. Dominance is maintained in part by restricting the less fortunate groups' access to resources (Farganis, 2004). Specifically, access is established by organizations that work to gain access to those in authority of resources. The more powerful and effective interest groups are reflected in the power of the dominant groups. Within this dynamic and fluctuating system, change is inevitable. As well, in this system people do things that they would not do by their own nature. That is, people conform to unnatural tendencies because someone with dominant power makes them conform.

Marxian theory looks at human nature, on both the individual and societal levels, as being based on material existence. That is, survival is determined by the ability to produce and control production. Under this theory, classes are formed and maintained in an exploitation process in which non-producers force producers to strive for maximum production of goods, to create a surplus (Farganis, 2004). The collection of surplus is the ultimate goal of non-producers. Surplus begins when the level of production exceeds the amount needed to reproduce the producer (Ritzer & Goodman, 2004). Non-producers strive to limit the surplus that non-producers receive. While both groups, producers and non-producers, are in constant conflict, they are also reliant on each other. In Marxism, change comes from within the battle between the two classes. It is important to note that within Marxism, class is not so much a position, but the extraction of surplus.

When looking at these three sociological theories within the topic of the Patriot Act, we find several areas wherein each can be argued to have a niche of viability. Within structural functionalism, there is always a drive to maintain the status quo. That is, change is not expected nor accepted as a regular occurrence. In fact each individual is seen as a sub-unit working in a group effort. A threat to one group would be seen as a threat to the entire organism, and action would be taken to eliminate that problem and restore maximum efficiency. There is little doubt that the 9-11 terrorist attacks, commonly known as a precursor for the development of the Patriot Act, shook America's belief in the notion of safety within the homeland (DeBecker, 2002).

Beyond the emotional insecurity was the financial insecurity that followed the attacks. The stock market responded to the attacks with radical fluctuations and even wilder speculations of the future. Airlines, one of the most pivotal travel industries in the country, were going bankrupt because people were gripped with fear of flying, as well as other aspects of everyday life (DeBecker, 2002). The Patriot Act, in its many facets of surveillance, detection, and detention capabilities, served as a practical measure, as well as symbolic feature, to calm the nation for a strategic purpose. The purpose was to tell the people, through legislation, that the government was on the problem and that people should continue to fulfill their function in the workplace.

Few are aware how the definitional sections within the Patriot Act were used to head off mass insurance claim refusals. Prior to 9-11, most insurance carriers had no liability to cover the majority of insurance claims under current definitions of terrorism. The restructuring of definitions of terrorism, in combination with emergency government action, avoided a mass defaulting by insurance companies that would have crippled the country (Ibbetson, 2005). These actions by the government are salient examples of structural functionalism. If one component of society (insurance companies) fails, it is understood that it will take other components with it. Thereby, structural functionalism demands that insurance carriers, as well as the airlines, be saved to protect the viability of the society (organism) as a whole.

The stock market, airlines, and insurance companies are examples of large corporate entities; however, structural functionalism is seen on the individual level, too, in regard to the Patriot Act. It is important to understand that under structural functionalism, the individual is considered a sub-unit, with a specific function, who operates in a system of integration for the survival of the whole (Ritzer & Goodman, 2004). So how does a terrorist fit into structural functionalism? The fact is, under structural functionalism, a terrorist might very well be seen as a dysfunctional element. Under this theory, a terrorist in the United States would be a terrorist because he or she had not been properly socialized. This description would be applicable to both the U.S. citizen as well as non-U.S. citizens. These individuals would be seen as people seeking their own self interest, in total opposition to the betterment of the society. The solution would be reintegration or elimination. Thus enters the Patriot Act to fulfill this requirement.

Under the Patriot Act, the government has extended authority to detain, sometimes indefinitely, individuals who are considered involved in terrorist activities (EPIC, 2001). Furthermore, Title VIII of the Patriot Act allows for lifetime supervision of released terrorists after incarceration (EPIC, 2001; Ibbetson, 2005). In this way, the government has a powerful tool, both to incarcerate and also to monitor individuals after release, to see if they are reintegrating into society properly to fulfill the sub-unit role.

It would be remiss to fail to speak of the financial allocations found in the Patriot Act. The Patriot Act, from Title I through Title X, is heavily laden with allocations of funds, from a terrorist fund for victims of terrorism, to funds for additional border security personnel. While other sociological theories, by the nature of their construction, might take issue with aspects of the many funds dispersed through this law, structural functionalism is not hampered by that problem.

Under structural functionalism, if a large amount of money is spent to pay border guards to monitor the border, the question of whether it is an exorbitant amount is not guaranteed to be challenged. On the contrary, under structural functionalism at the sub-unit level, it is more than likely to be perceived that the border security personnel are highly trained individuals who face a higher danger of death than the average person, thus deserving higher pay. At another level, the border security personnel, in general, would be seen as fulfilling a necessary function among other functions for the protection of the society (organism). This would be an example of organic solidarity (Giddens, 1977), which is a core element of structural functionalism.

Conflict theory illuminates different aspects of the Patriot Act which are a direct result of the fundamental difference between the two theories. While structural functionalism looks at everyone being interdependent and aims to hold the group together, conflict theory observes groups all in competition for the same scarce resources. Groups with access to resources can, and do, exploit those with less access. Terms like "power" and "authority" have extreme significance under this theory (Farganis, 2004).

Compared to structural functionalism, conflict theory embodies many of the dissenting arguments found in the Patriot Act literature. If we juxtapose the arguments against the Patriot Act found in the literature today with conflict theory, we see an interesting story develop. Under conflict theory, those in power would be the government and their mission would be to keep the poor from having access to resources.

Conflict theory would definitely allow for the present day expansion of power by the attorney general. Under the Patriot Act, the attorney general, the chief law enforcement officer, not the president, wields the added authority of this legislation. However, while it takes the Congress to pass laws, it is the president who the public often acknowledges as having the authority to bring about the legislation that the attorney general is then charged with carrying out.

President Bush, as commander in chief of the military and the highest ranking government official to throw support behind the Patriot Act, is often considered a charismatic authority by the public. Some of the stirring precursors to Patriot Act legislation are well documented; for example, the president standing at Ground Zero promising the dejected citizens of New York a response to the terrorist attacks. It can be argued that such charismatic moments by the president in the early periods following the terrorist attacks lead to the additional authority acquired by the president, and the congressional support for Joint Resolution 107-40, authorizing the use of military force (Block, 2005). Conversely, as the president's poll numbers begin to wane, it is speculated that the events that propelled him as a charismatic leader are losing their luster, and he will also lose some of the tools his authority allowed him to use (i.e., the Patriot Act).

Because conflict theory is centered on power and authority, the ability of one group to subordinate another group against its wishes is observed. Some would say that the Patriot Act falls under the model of traditional authority in that it is sometimes viewed as arbitrary and favoring those with citizenship or money. Others might say that the Patriot Act is an exercise in rational-legal authority in which the laws are a set of procedures and guidelines that treat all the same and give rationality to how things are done. However, as previously stated, and throughout the Patriot Act literature, it is documented that the Patriot Act was the product of an emotionally-charged event. Many believe President Bush harnessed the dynamic environment of 9-11 to consolidate his authority to benefit himself and the special interest groups that previously supported him.

While this theory fits conflict theory, and is prolific in the literature, an alternative is now presented. It starts with the query of whether a charismatic leader need be a politician, Republican, or even a human being at all? It is submitted that 9-11, as an event, is the actual charismatic leader, and that the president, government, and political parties are the special interest groups that serve to keep the event forefront in the public mind. Functioning similarly to the event of the "Alamo," the term alone speaks to individuals in strong tones that drive emotions to a crescendo to which some action is inevitable. The special interest groups then steer the course of that action, in line with their desires, to maintain themselves as the superordinate group within conflict theory (Ritzer & Goodman, 2004).

This event as charismatic leader has been more recently paralleled with such happenings as Pearl Harbor. As with the terrorist attacks of 9-11, Pearl Harbor was seen as an unprovoked attack that required a strong response (Crockatt, 2003). All that needed to be said was "remember Pearl Harbor." The images of Pearl Harbor, and the events of 9-11, are as motivational to the subordination process as any presidential speech. Their existence dictates a subconscious solution in the form of retribution or "setting a wrong right." The difference between the two proposals within conflict theory is that the president, as charismatic leader, is heard because of the event in which he finds himself. The event, as charismatic leader, is heard because of its own unique existence. Both examples suffer from the need to maintain a high charismatic level.

There is little doubt that the Patriot Act extends the power and authority of law enforcement, as well as future missions of the military. This is accomplished by the joining of efforts of the intelligence community with that of domestic security. In particular, groups like domestic security (FBI) can now work more freely with intelligence agencies, such as the CIA. Because politicians legislate laws that affect the civil liberty guarantees of the public, such as the Patriot Act, politicians also reinforce their power over those with limited resources. A prime example of this power building is seen in the Nixon-era collaborations between intelligence and domestic security in the investigation and harassment of activist groups in the U.S. (Kreimer, 2004). Many detractors of the Patriot Act have adopted, at least subconsciously, conflict theory as part of their warning that the Patriot Act may bring about the same kind of Nixon-era abuses (Kreimer, 2004).

Under conflict theory, the allocation of funds within the Patriot Act is seen as another example of those with the strongest interest groups, hypothesized as the security industries and Bush family members, being supplied with resources, while those without access to resources, namely the lower class and non-citizens, being denied the benefits of such funding (Pike, 2003).

The most salient example between the Patriot Act and the battle for access to resources and domination is seen in the Patriot Act renewal process that has recently taken place. Officially, only 16 of the most controversial sections of the Patriot Act were slated for debate; however, the renewal process in some ways placed the entire law under review. If there has been a transfer of dominance between the dissenters and supporters of the Patriot Act, it would be reflected in the renewal process. This would ultimately be a decision that readers would make individually.

When the Patriot Act in relation to Marxian theory is analyzed, other arguments and points of view are seen within the literature. These arguments again differ from conflict theory in that Marxian theory deals primarily with the inequalities of capitalism and the effect of capitalism on the relationships between the producers (proletariat) and the non-producers (bourgeoisie) (Farganis, 2004). Two components are forwarded in Marxist theory on the Patriot Act. The first is that the Patriot Act and the war in Iraq are seen as working in conjunction with one another as tools for the expansion of capitalism. The war in Iraq is seen as a strategic plan by non-producers, (i.e., government officials, oil companies, and large-scale developers) to secure oil production resources to create a surplus and secure their survival within the capitalistic system. Within this scenario, both the soldiers, as well as the populace at home, serve as the workers (proletariat). These workers, who are securing and ultimately producing the surplus, have supervisors and foremen, in the form of sergeants and field commanders within the U.S. military. However, neither the soldiers nor the citizens benefit from their actions. The capitalists are the only groups that benefit in the system (Gorz, 1976). The soldiers and the public, under capitalism, sell their labor as the working class. The capitalist pays for the labor of the working class and then uses that labor to create capital which is used to create more capital. This capital is referred to in western society most often by its transformed state, "money."

Under the capitalist system, which is based on the unrelenting drive of the capitalist to acquire excess surplus, many creative maneuvers must be made by non-producers to stay viable within the system. War can be a very financially productive endeavor under the capitalist system. Some believe that the economic sanctions placed on Iraq by the United States and Great Britain were the first stages of an ultimate goal of securing oil production. In fact, the need under capitalism for a constant expanding market makes expansion into places like Iraq inevitable. Within this scenario, the Patriot Act might be seen as the legal hammer to knock down the opposition. Exploitation can be seen in the fact that the workers (soldiers) have to die to secure the oil fields (Mitchell, 2005), and then have no control over, or benefit from, the oil production. This separation from true ownership of labor and identity plants the seeds of alienation (Lewis, 1972) that threaten to demoralize the troops. The great demands placed on the military to secure infrastructure, from a Marxian perspective, might be seen as an act to create surplus labor time and increase profits (Little, 1986), even at the cost of American lives.

The second part of this Marxian-related scenario not only embodies the multifaceted purposes behind the Patriot Act, but also identifies capitalism on a macro level. This would be the idea of the Patriot Act and the war in Iraq as a tool of freedom. The Patriot Act is touted as a tool to protect the nation against terrorism, which is seen as a direct threat to our freedom. However, the Patriot Act is not only seen as a domestic tool of freedom, but a tool for use abroad. The Patriot Act is therefore utilized abroad under the philosophy that it serves to protect the homeland as well as to stop terrorists who threaten the expansion of democracy. Under Marxian theory, the spread of democracy that President Bush says is craved by middle-eastern countries, such as Iraq (Bush, 2003), in reality would be the expansion of capitalism on a macro level. In fact, the U.S.-directed war in Iraq, under the idea of a true capitalist operation, could very well see a mass *proletarianization* not observed since the U.S. industrial revolution.

Both parts of this scenario involve an exploitation of the working class which is inevitable under the capitalist system. As Marxian theory points out, the capitalist system is plagued with contradictions. These contradictions come about because of the differences in the class system; specifically, the exploitation of the working class. Capitalism cannot progress without the exploitation of the working class. These contradictions are believed to be what will cause the working class to rise up and overthrow the system and replace it with a new system. However, a capitalist system, in times of war, uses some very interesting tactics to delay a change in the system through revolution. We will examine these diversionary tactics while looking at the contradictions in the Patriot Act and the war in Iraq.

The first contradiction is seen in that the workers (soldiers) have secured the massive oil fields of Iraq, yet U.S. residents now pay some of the highest fuel prices in western history. Within the U.S., the exorbitant fuel prices have the greatest impact on the low wage earning proletariat (Nyhan, 2005). Though rapidly increasing fuel prices are unsettling to the populace, revolt is unlikely in a wartime environment. An accepted element of war is sacrifice for the greater good (i.e., national survival). Another contradiction is that the Patriot Act and the war in Iraq are both products to secure democracy and freedom. The government expresses not only the idea that people abroad want our form of democracy, but also that the U.S. will be more secure by preemptive military action on foreign soils. This insinuates peaceful relations both at home and abroad because each has what each wants. This would also insinuate that the tools of that war (i.e., the Patriot Act) are also legitimized. From the Marxian perspective, among others, this could not be further from reality. The Patriot Act, as well as the war in Iraq, has received scathing reviews, both domestically (Prager, 2004) and abroad. Currently the U.S. government is scrambling to find officials to assist with quelling the rise in anti-Americanism (Baker, 2005). In the U.S., this feeling of isolation from the international community, especially in a created time-of-war atmosphere, creates an "us vs. them" mentality which serves to bond the producers and non-producers together. Even if this bonding is based on false assumptions and is viable only for a limited time, it allows the capitalist to exploit the worker with limited fear of revolution. In fact, related to the concerns over the reduction of civil rights seen in the Patriot Act, the United States has a long history of reducing civil liberties in times of crisis. Through Marxian theory, we can reflect historically on crisis events in the U.S. as either opportunities to secure capitalism or, worse, to simply expand the capitalist system under the guise of national security.

To anyone interested in the expanding perceptions of both the Patriot Act and sociology, the following exercise in analyzing these well-recognized sociological theories must be considered intellectually nutritious. It is important that readers understand what this chapter is trying to accomplish. This exercise was not intended to sway readers to endorse a specific theory in relation to the Patriot Act. In reality, the author believes that all the theories forwarded are brilliantly flawed. That is, not one of them is perfect, but all serve a positive function to sociological theory.

Structural functionalism may be the most versatile in its application to everyday life. However, structural functionalism does not deal well with social change. The problem with structural functionalism and change comes from the fact that the theory is so firmly rooted in the idea of all the elements in society working together for a common benefit. If elements start changing, structural functionalism can't always explain adequately why it happens. Within the Patriot Act scenario, structural functionalism has trouble answering why so many people from so many walks of life are offended by the law. Structural functionalism seems to be portrayed as a mirror reflection of society; when, in fact, it may be more of a conservative ideological system.

Conflict theory is criticized for failing to be a clear reflection of Marxian theory. In fact, conflict theory is more closely related to structural functionalism. More importantly, conflict theory is under-developed and places the bulk of its theoretical foundation on a somewhat radical ideology.

When looking at the Marxian theory, one has to look critically at its real-life applicability. If one says that the countries that have applied Marxian theory in practice have done so in true conformance with his ideas, then many would say that it has been an utter failure as a theory in practice. While Marx's insights into the various processes regarding capitalism are unique and insightful, Marx has a tendency to place the working class in the position of social change leading to communism. This idea has been found to be lacking, as the working class has had a tendency to oppose communism. This has left the responsibility of social change to liberal intellectuals, and the effect has not been as fruitful as assumed by Marx. Also, the vision seen by Marx of the capitalistic system progressing by stages to socialism, and eventually to communism, turned out to be wrong. Lastly, Marxian theory does not have ample safeguards to avoid recreating a new bourgeoisie in the form of the state.

When examining the theories for a best fit to the Patriot Act and its relationship to the war on terror, difficulties abound. The paramount problem is that they all fit to some extent. Conversely, they all exclude themselves from total conformity by the nature that no theory has reached the level of perfection. However, when stepping forward with the theory that best fits the topic, structural functionalism may be the most applicable. In the Patriot Act scenario, it would seem there was consensus in the need to defend the nation from a threat to the whole country. The events of 9-11 showed that terrorists included every American as targeted for death. The 9-11 attacks served as confirmation of the written request for American deaths found in the 1996 fatwa constructed by al-Qaeda leader Osama bin Laden (bin Laden, 1996). The response to 9-11 in its various forms, including the Patriot Act, appear most logically as the tools to allow each member of the society to participate in their specific function in the protection of the society (organism) from actual annihilation. A lack of socialization would appear to explain the anti-American voices within the country, at least to the extent to make this theory the best fit of the three presented.

There is little doubt that further analysis of the sociological perspective of the Patriot Act is needed. As well, this assertion of a theoretical best fit only survives until a better argument is forwarded. This is but a first tentative step in the quest for further enlightenment on the unique and dynamic law known as the Patriot Act.

References

Baker, P. (2005, March 12). Karen Hughes to work on the world's view of U.S. [Electronic Version]. *The Washington Post,* p. A03. Retrieved April 15, 2005, from http://www.washingtonpost.com

bin Laden, O. (1996). *Declaration of war against the Americans occupying the land of the two holy places.* Retrieved October 22, 2005, from http://www.pbs.org/newshour/ terrorism/international/fatwa_1996.html

Block, F. (2005). Civil liberties during national emergencies: The interactions between the three branches of government in coping with past and current threats to the nation's security. *New York University School of Law Review of Law and Social Change, 29,* 459-524.

Bush, G. (2003, November 6). *President Bush discusses freedom in Iraq and Middle East.* Retrieved October 22, 2005, from http://www.whitehouse.gov/news/releases/2003/11/ 20031106-2.html

Crockatt, R. (2003). *America embattled: September 11, anti-Americanism, and the global order.* New York: Routledge.

DeBecker, G. (2002). *Fear less: Real truth about risk, safety, and security in a time of terrorism.* New York: Little, Brown and Company.

Electronic Privacy Information Center [EPIC]. (2001). *HR 3162 RDS: 107th Congress.* Retrieved September 25, 2004, from http://www.epic.org/privacy/terrorism/hr3162.html

Farganis, J. (Ed.). (2004). *Readings in social theory: The classical tradition to post-modernism* (4th ed.). New York: McGraw-Hill.

Giddens, A. (1977). *Studies in social and political theory.* New York: Basic Books Inc.

Gorz, A. (1976). The tyranny of the factory: Today and tomorrow. In A. Gorz (Ed.), *The division of labour: The labour process and class-struggle in modern capitalism* (pp. 55-62). Atlantic Highlands, NJ: Harvester Press.

Ibbetson, P. (2005). The Patriot Act: Title VII: Analyzing the quiet giants. *Illinois Law Enforcement Executive Forum, 5,* 83-96.

Kreimer, S. F. (2004). Watching the watchers: Surveillance, transparency, and political freedom in the war on terror. *University of Pennsylvania Journal of Constitutional Law, 7,* 133-181

Lewis, J. (1972). *The Marxism of Marx.* London, England: Lawrence & Wishart.

Little, D. (1986). *The scientific Marx*. Minneapolis, MN: University of Minnesota Press.

Mitchell, L. (2005, August 15). *Blood for oil: The only justification that makes sense*. Retrieved October 22, 2005, from http://harpers.org/BloodForOil.html

Nyhan, P. (2005, April 27). *High gas prices really sting low-wage workers*. Retrieved October 21, 2005, from http://seattlepi.nwsource.com/local/221825_gasprices27.html

Parsons, T. (1954). *Essays in sociological theory* (Rev. ed.). New York: Free Press.

Pike, J. (2003, October 22). *How the Bush family profits from the Patriot Act*. Retrieved October 18, 2005, from http://www.evote.com/?q=node/1630

Prager, D. (2004, July 6). *Michael Moore and American self-hatred*. Retrieved October 20, 2005, from http://www.wnd.com/news/printerfriendly.asp?ARTICLE_ID=39300

Ritzer, R., & Goodman, D. J. (2004). *Sociological theory* (6th ed.). New York: McGraw-Hill.

CHAPTER 11

Polling the Patriot Act

IN CHAPTER 6, READERS WERE presented with polling information on the Patriot Act. This polling was a joint *USA Today*/CNN/Gallup Poll taken on August 29, 2003. The poll numbers in Chapter 6 are a favorite of the government. The results tend to support the government's claim that people support the law and the law was perceived as doing its job on the date of the poll. While presentation of that particular polling data is very legitimate for a chapter supporting the Patriot Act, further polling data is needed to give a fuller and more rounded view of the Patriot Act landscape. However, it would be remiss to submit substantial polling data without clarifying a few things.

First, it is believed that understanding polling data as it pertains to the Patriot Act can be educational in becoming a more learned observer. Why? Well, there are several reasons. For one, people are a naturally curious species and, while we personally gather and evaluate information on just about every subject, we also tend to watch and see how those around us are responding as well. People also like seeing questions answered through statistics. The most common method is the use of percentages. This makes sense as percentages are easy to understand and simple to compare with one another. In fact, many human events that take place in the United States, if not the world, are implicitly tied to statistics. One example is political elections. Imagine how people would respond if only the winners of an election were reported. It would probably not be a pretty picture.

Today, percentages are used to report not only the percentage difference between losing and winning candidates in political contests, but percentages are often reported in stages during the election tally to give viewers a breakdown of the differences in political opinion in different geographical areas. People just like to know what other people think about issues.

Do politicians look at polls? Yes, quite often they do. If you watch media reports on the Patriot Act, you have probably seen reports about groups challenging the law on various grounds. Does that basically mean people just don't like the law? Maybe only the fringe groups support or oppose the Patriot Act? What are the feelings about the Patriot Act from the average person? Polling can be viewed as an attempt to answer these questions.

If you have not recently attended a statistics class, here are a few additional words on polling. Not all polls are created equal (Sprinthall, 2003). In fact, anyone can attempt to conduct polling. Just step outside your house and ask, let's say, the next 10 people who walk by "Hey, do you like the Patriot Act?" Write down the answers and, walla! you're polling. However, your results would not be usable to infer anything except that you probably have some neighbors who walk by your house and are willing to talk to you.

Polls are complex systems utilizing internal safeguards that check for quality and reliability of the findings. Polls have been around for some time. In 1824 the first political poll took place. The contest was for the presidency and the candidates were John Quincy Adams and Andrew Jackson. A newspaper in Pennsylvania attempted to predict the winner of the presidential race using on the street interviews. In short, their results that Jackson would win were completely wrong (Sprinthall, 2003).

By 1936, George Gallup of the American Institute of Public Opinion in Princeton, New Jersey, stepped into the forefront of the polling spotlight. Due to innovative sampling techniques, Gallup became one of the premier polling institutions which remains true to this day (Sprinthall, 2003). A lot of refining has taken place in the technology of polling since the 1930s. Still, even today, professional pollsters, as well as all researchers, have to be wary that their samples are not biased. That is, that they have a truly representative sample of individuals being observed or surveyed (Frankfort-Nachmias & Leon-Guerrero, 2006). That is one reason why our residence sidewalk survey scenario does not work. Our results would only reflect what the people near our home thought, and a poor reflection at that. Scientific polling, which is the only polling we want to pay attention to when studying the Patriot Act, will have several quality protocols in play that we will identify.

When polling is done on subjects such as the Patriot Act, they are often labeled as "opinion polls" because that is just what they are, peoples' opinions on the issues related to the Patriot Act. Do opinions change over time? You bet. Polls are similar to a snapshot, a picture of a moment in time.

One point of this chapter is to show that one poll cannot give a researcher a reasonable perspective on the attitudes of people toward a law that has been in effect for many years. For this purpose, you are given polling perspectives from differing polling organizations on the Patriot Act. These polls will incorporate unique questions that come at the Patriot Act from different angles. Some of the polling questions you will read will include questions you have probably asked yourself, and some may be totally new to you. As importantly, years of polling data are covered which include the most current polls in conjunction with enlightening analysis. Most of the polls forwarded show the reader the methodology used to collect the sample. This includes things such as how many people were surveyed, the kind of sample (i.e. adults, voters, etc.), the way in which the sample was collected, and when the sample was collected. All polling data can be further examined at any time by following the citations. Readers are invited to do so. The goal of looking at polling data is to utilize yet another aspect of the literature available to widen the scope of understanding this controversial issue. So, what do opinion polls say about how people think about the Patriot Act? Keep reading.

A lot of polling data on the Patriot Act begins to accumulate starting in 2003. That is not to say that some older data is not around. However, one must remember that the Patriot Act became a law on November 26, 2001, so by 2003 the law had been in action a little over a year. Public opinion was then at a point of development where polling could start to get a sense of how people felt about this new and dynamic piece of legislation.

A final word before we jump into the numbers. As we look at different aspects of public opinion of the Patriot Act, often we will move back and forth in time. Don't let this confuse you. In fact, this is done purposely to separate the issues as best as possible as the Patriot Act debate is much more complex than is often reported. Breaking the issues down will allow the reader to understand the various issues pollsters, as well as the public, have come to focus on with this law. Here we go.

A rather abundant period of polling was conducted by various major polling groups in early 2003. One such poll was conducted by the long recognized Gallup Organization. This poll was conducted during Attorney

General John Ashcroft's promotional tour of the country promoting the Patriot Act. Conducted on August 25-26, 2003, the poll utilized telephone interviews with individuals 18 years of age or older. The sample had a 95% confidence level and the maximum margin of error was plus or minus 3 percentage points (Moore, 2003, September 9).

Within the poll, 67% of respondents said that the government should not take action to prevent terrorism if those actions would violate basic civil liberties. However, 55% of the people polled thought that the Bush administration had gone "about right" in restricting civil liberties in order to fight terrorism, as opposed to 21% who stated that the government has gone "too far." While this is a wide margin of difference, three Gallup Polls taken from June 21-22, 2002, to August 25-26, 2003, saw a 5% decrease in those responding "about right" and a 10% increase in those responding that the Bush administration was going "too far" in restricting civil liberties in order to fight terrorism (Moore, 2003, September 9). Specific to the Patriot Act, 48% of respondents felt the law restricted civil liberties "about right" in order to fight terrorism (Moore, 2003, September 9). Interestingly enough, almost as many respondents, 21%, felt the law did not go "far enough" to restrict civil liberties in order to fight terrorism. Some of these changes can be put into more perspective when looking at polls that were taken on November 26-27, 2001, approximately two months after 9-11, when 60% of respondents thought the Bush administration had gone "about right" in restricting civil liberties in order to fight terrorism, compared to a paltry 10% that felt the administration had "gone too far" (Saad, 2001, December 10).

A continual focus of many polling organizations was an attempt to ascertain the level of knowledge average citizens really had about the Patriot Act. According to Moore (2003, September 9), on August 25-26, 2003, an even split was seen between those claiming to be "very familiar" and "somewhat familiar" with those claiming to be either "not too familiar" or "not at all familiar" with the law. By November 10-12, 2003, the poll numbers were 53% to 47% (Carlson, 2004) and by February 16-17, 2004, the percentage of respondents claiming familiarity with the Patriot Act increased again to 59% to 41% (Saad, 2004).

Several interesting findings were taken from this poll regarding the question of just how much knowledge people really had about the Patriot Act. Over half of respondents thought incorrectly that the Patriot Act gave the president the power to detain terrorism suspects indefinitely without charges or a lawyer. In reality, the president uses his war powers authority for that purpose and not the Patriot Act (Saad, 2004). Over half of respondents wrongly believed that the Patriot Act gave authority for the use of military tribunals for non-U.S. citizens suspected of terrorism. Actually, this is a current policy of the Bush administration (Saad, 2004), which is currently being evaluated by the Supreme Court. Saad's (2004) Gallup report, *"Americans Generally Comfortable with Patriot Act,"* began to dig for citizens' specific knowledge on the Patriot Act. The findings support the assertion that there is a fundamental difference between general knowledge and really knowing the facts. The creation of this book is a testament to that belief.

An August 25-26, 2003, Gallup included 5 polls dealing with the question of whether the government should take all steps necessary to fight terrorism, even if certain steps would violate basic civil liberties. Using poll data collected on January 25-27, 2002, to August 26-26, 2003, poll numbers steadily dropped from 47% to 29% for respondents saying that the government should take steps, even if those steps included violating basic civil liberties. Conversely, the same polling data saw an increase from 49% to 67% for respondents wanting steps taken by the government that were void of civil liberty violations (Moore, 2003, September 9).

To put some of the polling data from 2003 in perspective, one has to take into account the general turbulence surrounding the Patriot Act in 2003. The Patriot Act 16-city promotional tour conducted by Attorney General John Ashcroft in 2003, which included lectures as well as "Patriot Rocks" concerts (Kettl, 2004), most certainly was brought about by a feeling of necessity on the part of governmental officials to build support for a law that was increasingly coming under attack by civil liberties groups (Lynch, 2003). As well, in the same month of August, 2003, the Patriot Act was being actively opposed by 120 American cities that defiantly designated themselves as "civil liberties safe zones" (Lynch, 2003). In conjunction with the promotional tour, the Department of Justice would also launch an informational Web site, www.lifeandliberty.gov, for the purpose of educating citizens about the positive aspects of this highly contentious piece of legislation.

At this point, it is important to note some poll data on Attorney General John Ashcroft. Due to the nature of the office, it is common for the Patriot Act to be equated solely with President George W. Bush; however, this tendency does not do justice to the impact of the Patriot Act as implemented by the chief law enforcement officer, Attorney General John Ashcroft. The *USA Today*/CNN/Gallup organizations conducted at least three years of polling which asked 1,006 national adults questions that pertained to the highly controversial attorney general. From January 15-16, 2001, pre-Patriot Act, to February 16-17, 2004, when asked about the favorability of John Ashcroft, the attorney general always maintained a majority favorable rating. In fact, over the three-year period of polling in which respondents came to know and increase their opinions on the attorney general, his favorable rating went through peaks and valleys but ended higher in 2004 at 42% than it was in 2001 at 34% (Saad, 2004). Of course, the attorney general's unfavorable rating, while never surpassing his favorable rating, increased as well from 28% in 2001 to 36% in 2004 (Saad, 2004).

While Ashcroft was often under attack by various liberal groups for things ranging from his steadfast defense of the Patriot Act to his personal religious beliefs (Lynch, 2003), the attorney general may have had no greater nemesis than the ACLU. The constant battling between the civil liberties group and the attorney general made for interesting polls as well. While there is little doubt that the assertion is highly contentious, Attorney General John Ashcroft appears to have triumphed over the ACLU in the category of trust. Noting the attorney general's resignation from office in November of 2004, a *USA Today*/CNN/Gallup Poll from February 16-17, 2004, illuminates a strong level of trust by respondents for the embattled attorney general. Specifically, according to the *USA Today*/CNN/Gallup Poll, Ashcroft received a higher confidence rating over that of the ACLU by respondents with a fairly large margin of 57% to 43% (Saad, 2004).

Moving back to the public at large, according to Saad (2004), women were less likely than men to think that the Patriot Act went too far in sacrificing civil liberties by a difference of 32% to 17% for men. In addition, while there was not a majority of any political or demographic group that opposed the Patriot Act, certain groups had stronger support, as well as opposition percentages, to the law. Of the groups who believed that the Patriot Act went "too far" in sacrificing civil liberties, 33% or more were: self-described liberals, Americans with postgraduate degrees, Democrats, and military veterans (Saad, 2004). Conversely, groups least likely to think the Patriot Act went "too far" included: Republicans, conservatives, people from rural areas, and those without a college education (Saad, 2004).

By 2005 several things had transpired that opened the door to interesting polling questions. For one thing, even more years had now passed since the terrorist attacks of 9-11. A reasonable question for pollsters would be if the memory of the horrific events of September 11, 2001, would continue or disappear over time. As well, the Gallup Organization would look at how terrorist events abroad would affect the U.S. populace.

The bitter fighting among members of Congress over the Patriot Act, among other issues in 2005, appeared to be weighing on the patience of the American people. A Fox Poll of 900 registered voters released on June 16, 2005, found that over 50% of voters thought that Congress had grown out of touch with the country (Blanton, 2005). According to Blanton, 50% of voters thought that the Patriot Act had been instrumental in preventing terrorist attacks in the U.S. as opposed to 35% who felt it had not been a factor. In this environment of dissatisfaction with political stalemates over passing legislation, including the Patriot Act, it was not surprising that 63% of respondents thought congressional members were "petty politicians fighting for personal gain" (Blanton, 2005).

Most certainly the public was aware of the political debate over the Patriot Act's renewal which, by June 2005, was approximately 6 months out. The question was if the anger the public felt at their politicians' inability to come to a consensus on a renewal package for the Patriot Act was based on a frustration over political squabbling, a fear for national security, or both.

The 2005 terrorist subway bombings in London kept the reality of terrorism in the forefront for U.S. Americans. To gauge Americans' opinions on the Patriot Act after a major international incident, as well as growth of public knowledge on the law, the Gallup Poll conducted another Patriot Act opinion poll. As of June 24-25, 2005, 64% of respondents said that they were "very" or "somewhat familiar" with the Patriot Act (Carlson, 2005, July 19). According to Carlson, partisan opinions remained as strong as ever about the law with 37% of Democratic respondents saying the law went to "too far" in restricting civil liberties. Independent voters polled even higher dissent at 40%, with only 12% of Republicans thinking the law went "too far" (Carlson, 2005, July 19). Not surprisingly, the 2005 poll found that the more education an individual had, the more likely they were to be familiar with the law (Carlson, 2005, July 19). What was more interesting was that the 2005 poll brought forth some evidence that familiarity might cause more discontent with the law as 45% of respondents who marked "very familiar" with the law, thought it went too far in restricting civil liberties, as opposed to 33% of those who responded "somewhat familiar" with the law (Carlson, 2005, July 19). The results of the poll were based on telephone interviews with a randomly selected sample of 1,009 adults 18 or over (Carlson, 2005, July 19).

The year 2005 also marked the 10th anniversary of the Oklahoma City bombing. The Oklahoma City bombing of the Murrah Federal Building, while not reaching the scope of destruction as the events of 9-11, was an interesting event to compare fear of terrorism over time. According to Carroll (2005), directly after the Oklahoma bombing 90% of respondents polled felt "very" or "somewhat" worried that future bombings would take place in the U.S. Years later, 35% of respondents still retained the same concern for similar style attacks. This 55% reduction would indicate that as time passes people start to become less concerned about terrorism.

Following the September 11, 2001, terrorist attacks, respondents saying they felt "very" or "somewhat worried" about future terrorist attacks was again raised by the event itself and then appeared to level off. Using yearly averages, Carroll (2005) reported the following percentages for respondents being "worried or somewhat worried" as the following: 48% in 2001, 39% in 2002, 38% in 2003, 39% in 2004, and 38% in 2005. Though a leveling off in percentages for this general category is noted, future upward swings in fear of terrorism when new terrorist acts occur would be noted in other polls.

On June 16, 2005, Fox News released its newest Opinion Dynamics Poll to date which, among other questions, gauged public opinion over the Patriot Act. The poll involved 900 registered voters who were interviewed by telephone on the evenings of June 14-15, 2005. Results had a margin of error of plus or minus 3 percentage points. When asked if respondents felt the Patriot Act was good or bad for America, 57% responded "good" while 30% responded that the law was a "bad" thing for America. When looking at whether the Patriot Act had assisted in preventing additional terrorist attacks in the U.S., 50% responded that they believed it had while 35% felt it had not (FOX News, 2005). According to the same poll, support for renewing the law had increased 3 percentage points from 53% on April 21-22, 2004, to 56% in June 14-15, 2005. Conversely, those respondents not supporting the renewal showed a small drop from 32% to 31% during the same time period.

Once again, it should be stated that polls are just a single tool used to try and gauge public opinion. We have seen several polls that have asked for individuals' opinions on several different aspects of the Patriot Act. Many similar questions have been addressed by different polls during different time periods. This has been done to give a fuller picture of the Patriot Act debate. However, in displaying some of the long-term polling sequences as we have done, have we illuminated the complete landscape? That is, has public opinion surrounding the events which have shaped the alleged need for a Patriot Act been completely disclosed? The answer is no, and probably no one book can do that; however, the goal of this book is to take readers to a new level of understanding.

To give a more comprehensive context to the way people think, or have thought, about issues directly related to the Patriot Act, we have to delve further. To do this, polling data that encompasses issues linked in various ways to the Patriot Act debate are provided. In the end, from a polling perspective, not only will you have an idea of how people feel about the Patriot Act, but also about the environment that surrounds the Patriot Act, the war on terror.

One of the factors being revealed from our polling research is that people appear to fluctuate in opinions over time. To look at this in the context of the war on terror, of which the Patriot Act is considered a primary tool, it is helpful to look at U.S. opinion during other historical conflicts. When an event happens that places the nation in a state of fear, at least in America, people appear to rally to the call of defense. However, as time passes, views tend to fluctuate up and down depending on a number of seen and unforeseen variables. Historically, there was virtually no polling data collected during World War I. However, polls taken by Gallup following the Japanese attacks at Pearl Harbor found that 97% of those who responded thought going to war with Japan was proper. A similar poll, taken two weeks later, found 84% thought that President Roosevelt had done everything to avoid war (Moore, 2001).

In June 1950, 78% of Americans approved when President Truman inevitably took the country into the Korean War when he sent U.S. troops as a peace force. However, by 1951, 49% of Americans thought it had been a mistake for the U.S. to become militarily involved, compared to 38% who still supported the operation (Moore, 2001).

A similar swell and decline was seen with Vietnam when 61% of Americans originally supported sending troops to fight in 1964, dropping dramatically by 1971 to a two-to-one margin against military involvement (Moore, 2001).

Considering that the Persian Gulf War had a long buildup before forces were deployed, initially Americans were skeptical. In 1990, only 31% favored using planes to bomb Iraq. However, when Americans were given the information that Iraq had been given a formal resolution and had failed to take the opportunity to avoid conflict, support for the war rocketed to 62% (Moore, 2001). When President George H.W. Bush sent grounds troops into Iraq, American support was polled at 84%. Even post-event polling indicates a highly positive response compared to the dismal post conflict numbers for the police actions of Vietnam and Korea. One caveat should be noted. The Persian Gulf War lasted a matter of weeks, while Korea and Vietnam lasted years (Moore, 2001).

In the war on terror, George W. Bush's initiative to take military action following the terrorist attacks of September 11, 2001, has received an 89% approval rating, rivaling the support given for war following the Japanese attacks on Pearl Harbor (Moore, 2001). A short time after the terrorist attacks, Americans were still riding a wave of concern over the potential of repeat attacks in the United States. To deal with the myriad of potential weaknesses in security seen in the events of 9-11, authorities enacted a number of security protocols with the full blessing of the general public. The following are a list of Gallup Poll issues collected from a survey conducted on October 19-21, 2001. The polling was an attempt to gauge how citizens felt about increased security measures brought forth by the government following 9-11. One should note that the Patriot Act would be signed into law approximately one month later. When polled, 68% of respondents said that increased security, such as the National Guard at airports and visible inspections by the Coast Guard at major ports, made them feel more secure. Respondents seemed, at this early stage following the 9-11 attacks, to be willing to suffer certain discomforts, if not infringements, in return for a stronger feeling of security. For example, 75% of respondents favored requiring airline passengers to go through heightened security procedures that could take as long as two to three hours before taking a flight (Saad, 2001, October 31). In addition, 80% of respondents favored limiting passengers to only one small carry-on piece of luggage (Saad, 2001, October 31). Respondents were more divided, 49% in favor and 49% against supporting "profiling" measures, such as requiring U.S. as well as non-U.S. Arabs to carry a special type I.D. (Saad, 2001, October 31).

In 2001 when polled, respondents showed little readiness to allow the government additional powers to tap phones and read e-mail without a person's knowledge (Saad, 2001, October 31). This reluctance to allow eavesdropping measures was an example of opposition that was few and far between in an environment that was moreover strongly supportive of enhanced security measures. During the same time period, there was large-scale support at 96% for strengthening airline cockpit doors and 90% support for placing armed sky marshals on commercial airliners (Saad, 2001, October 31). As well, 85% of people polled agreed that it was more important to place the pilot in a position to have additional control over the plane, even if it meant a loss of passenger comfort (Saad, 2001, October 31). Barring the use of the Army or National Guard, 77% of individuals polled were in favor of the federal government taking over airport security (Saad, 2001, October 31).

While Americans were originally very concerned over terrorism issues, a few weeks after 9-11, concerns started to wane. However, a new terrorist related threat on October 4, 2001, in the form of an anthrax scare, quickly re-ignited public fears (Saad, 2001, December 10). As of December 10, 2001, only 8% of respondents thought they were "very worried" about terrorism, a large reduction from 23% as reported on September 11, 2001.

As well as fears, confidence in the war on terror was beginning to wane. From September 21-22, 2001, to November 26-27, 2001, respondents who reported being very confident that the U.S. would be able to prevent future terrorist attacks in the U.S. fell from 32% to 29%. Those "not very" or "not at all confident" that every global terrorist organization would eventually meet with defeat went up from 40% to 46% (Saad, 2001, December 10).

As previously mentioned, significant differences in the polling responses concerning fear of terrorism are seen in three specific societal areas among respondents: gender, income, and education. Women were more likely than men to have a fear of becoming a victim of terrorism. In households earning less that $20,000, 48% responded being "somewhat or very worried," compared to only 28% of those earning $50,000. There was also a noticeable gap between respondents with college educations and those without college educations, with those less educated having more fear of terrorism (Saad, 2001, December 10). While 18% of respondents polled on October 11-14, 2001, felt "very worried" that they, or someone in their family, would be a victim of terrorism, within approximately two months the number would drop to 8% (Saad, 2001, December 10). At the other extreme, those respondents "not worried at all" would increase as well from 14% to 30% (Saad, 2001, December 10).

By June 7, 2002, a CNN/USA/Gallup Poll would reflect that respondents no longer felt as strongly that the United States was winning the war on terror. This growing pessimism grew after some time had passed since the victories in Afghanistan and the defeat of the Taliban (Saad, 2002). While most respondents polled believed that neither the United States nor the terrorists were winning, during this period people were less reluctant to fly on planes, go into skyscrapers, and travel overseas (Saad, 2002).

Following the terrorist bombings in 2003 in Saudi Arabia and Morocco, some Democrats began to blame the president for inadequacies in the war on terror. However, in polling results from this period, U.S. citizens were slow to blame the president for these attacks (Kiefer, 2003). While the majority of Americans, Democrats (54%) and Republicans (89%), did not place very much blame on the president for the attacks in Saudi Arabia and Morocco, a larger percentage of Democrats blamed the president a "great deal" more than Republicans (Kiefer, 2003). Although the president enjoyed large amounts of support initially from both political parties directly after 9-11, by May 2003, political divisions were more evident. However, these divisions between Democrats and Republicans over presidential decision making were more evident on matters not related to terrorism (Kiefer, 2003).

In a CNN/*USA Today*/Gallup Poll released on September 8, 2003, the poll found media coverage of repeated car bombings in Iraq had sparked a renewed sentiment of fear in the American populace (Moore, 2003, September 8). This poll illuminated several somber reactions among Americans. Of those polled, 80% believe that there are terrorists inside the U.S. and also 80% of respondents believe that the U.S. will have to use military force in another country in the war on terror within the next few years. As disheartening, 70% believe that suicide bombings will take place within the U.S. sometime in the next five years (Moore, 2003, September 8). As many as 50% of respondents felt the U.S. would be the victim of a chemical or biological attack by terrorists in the next five years, while only 20% expected the U.S. to be the victim of a nuclear attack by terrorists in the next five years (Moore, 2003, September 8).

We have seen the fluctuating opinions on the support for the war on terror as well as the opinions of how much people fear being a victim of terrorism. Just how far is the U.S. public willing to allow its government to go to secure the nation? This question echoes around the Patriot Act in nearly all debates. The following surveys would give a glimpse at the answer to this question.

In a CNN/*USA Today*/Gallup Poll released on March 1, 2005, respondents were asked their willingness to have the U.S. government conduct certain measures if the government thought it would help to combat terrorism. The results were interesting. When asked in 2001 if respondents were willing to allow the government to assassinate known terrorists, 77% said they were however, by 2005, the number had dropped to a still strong 65% (Carlson, 2005, March 1). From October 5-6, 2001, to January 7-9, 2005, public opinion would change from 52% of respondents willing to allow the government to assassinate leaders of countries that harbor terrorists to 37%. A steady "non-willingness" to allow the government to take action if they thought it was necessary to combat terrorism was polled on actions such as prisoner torture and use of nuclear weapons (Carlson, 2005, March 1). Specific to torture and interrogation, the March 8, 2005, release of a CNN/*USA Today*/Gallup Poll asked respondents if they thought certain specific interrogation techniques were "right" or "wrong." The following techniques rated the following percentage responses: 79% of respondents felt that making prisoners remain naked and chained in uncomfortable positions in cold rooms for several hours was "wrong" (Carlson, 2005, March 8). Forcing Muslim males to have physical contact with female interrogators in violation of their religious codes was seem as "wrong" by 85% of respondents (Carlson, 2005, March 8). While respondents were deadlocked on interrogation techniques such as sleep deprivation, more aggressive techniques such as threatening prisoners with dogs were seen as "wrong" (Carlson, 2005, March 8).

An ABC News/*Washington Post* Poll released June 9, 2005, which looked at a national sample of 1,002 adults, found that respondents were largely in favor, 59% to 39%, of renewing the Patriot Act (Langer, 2005). However, respondents were showing a growing concern that the government was not doing everything it could to protect their civil liberties in regard to tactics in the war on terror (Langer, 2005). On issues such as requiring the postal service to allow agencies, such as the FBI, to make copies of the outsides of envelopes, 54% were opposed to such action while 44% approved (Langer, 2005). Stronger opposition, 68% to 31%, was seen on the issue of records collection made by the FBI without the consent of a judge (Langer, 2005). The ABC News/*Washington Post* Poll confirmed the continuing partisan division among the political parties on the Patriot Act renewal with 80% of Republicans supporting the renewal versus 43% of Democrats (Langer, 2005).

Starting on August 4, 2005, and ending on August 22, 2005, the Center for Survey Research and Analysis (CSRA), located at the University of Connecticut, conducted a comprehensive national telephone survey centered on Patriot Act issues. The survey was based on a sample of 800 Americans. As stated previously, attempting to gauge the knowledge of citizens on the Patriot Act has been a goal of many polling organizations. The CSRA would use three techniques to attempt to glean citizen knowledge of the law. The techniques included the following: self-report data, ability to identify the law's basic intent, and a quiz on the basic safeguards of the law (Best & McDermott, 2005). From the sample, 57% of respondents said they were familiar with the law while a lower percentage, 42%, were able to identify the law's primary intent (Best & McDermott, 2005). When given a quiz on the basic safeguards, a quiz that determined respondent's ability to identify specific information on the law, only 31% of respondents passed the quiz (Best & McDermott, 2005). When gauging support for the law, 64% of Americans were found to support the law (Best & McDermott, 2005; Lester, 2005). When looking at support for the law based on political affiliation, Republicans showed more support for the Patriot Act at 85%, than Democrats at 50% (Best & McDermott, 2005). An interesting piece of data not collected by other surveys was that Republicans appeared to be more knowledgeable about the law at 44%, than Democrats at 36% (Best & McDermott, 2005). However, in general, being more informed about the law reduced support for the Patriot Act (Best & McDermott, 2005; Lester, 2005).

One of the focuses of the study was to determine if respondents separated the Patriot Act from the war on terror. The determination made by the CSRA was that in general people equate the two together (Best & McDermott, 2005; Lester, 2005).

Respondents of the CSRA survey were also asked to list what groups were considered most likely to be investigated by the government using the Patriot Act. While there was little shock that "suspected terrorists" were prioritized first at 85%, and "ordinary Americans" were designated as the least likely to be investigated at 13% by way of the Patriot Act (Best & McDermott, 2005), some of the other categories and percentages were of more interest. From the survey, the second highest likelihood of being investigated, 78%, was for "Americans who send money to a charitable organization that has ties to a terrorist group" (Best & McDermott, 2005). Both "Americans who visit terrorist websites" and "Americans who check out bombing making books from the library" tied for third most likely to be investigated under the Patriot Act at 69% (Best & McDermott, 2005). Finishing out the list were "Muslim Americans" at 50%, "Arab Americans" at 49% and "Americans who protest the Iraq war" at 40% (Best & McDermott, 2005). Only 13% of respondents felt that individuals considered "ordinary Americans" would be investigated using the Patriot Act (Best & McDermott, 2005). It might appear from the wording of the survey that ordinary Americans are not considered to be those who would protest the war in Iraq but, of course, that would most assuredly be contentious in many circles.

In summary, a few comments are forwarded about the polling data. First, it appears that the differences in opinion over the Patriot Act can be seen among groups that differ in education, gender, political affiliation, and income to name a few. It appears that there is a disparity between those who support the Patriot Act and those who really have detailed knowledge of the law. However, regardless of those who can and cannot be designated as truly knowledgeable about the Patriot Act, the overall majority of respondents have, and continue to, support the law.

There does appear to be a correlation between fear of terrorism and concerns over civil liberties abuses. Specifically, when people are the most concerned about being victims of terrorism there is a tendency to be less stringent about civil liberty concerns. Conversely, as threats of terrorism begin to wane, an increase in civil liberties concerns, most notably reducing the government's ability to encroach on civil liberties, start to increase.

On the subject of public fear of terrorism, it appears that U.S. citizens are affected by both domestic and international incidents. It also appears that the public has a limited tolerance for political deadlocks when it comes to renewing pieces of legislation for national security. The future renewal process of the Patriot Act would test politicians and the public alike in ways that many would not have foreseen. We will soon move into the next stage of the Patriot Act story, namely the highly contentious renewal of the law. But before we can learn the details about the epic struggle to renew the Patriot Act, we must take a moment to address what is often considered a side note in the Patriot Act story. This side note, which is often overlooked or forgotten entirely, is affectionately called, "The little law that wasn't."

References

Best, S., & McDermott, M. (2005, August 26). *University of Connecticut releases new national poll on the USA Patriot Act.* Retrieved June 26, 2006, from http://www.csra.uconn.edu/ pdf/PATRIOTACT-PRESSRELEASE.pdf

Blanton, D. (2005, June 16). *Fox poll: Congress 'out of touch'; Majority supports renewing Patriot Act.* Retrieved June 28, 2006, from http://www.foxnews.com/story/ 0,2933,159790,00.html

Carlson, D. K. (2004, January 20). *Far enough? Public wary of restricted liberties.* Retrieved August 15, 2005, from http://www.gallup.com

Carlson, D. K. (2005, March 1). *Would Americans fight terrorism by any means necessary? Two-thirds willing to let government assassinate terrorists.* Retrieved August 16, 2005, from http://www.gallup.com

Carlson, D. K. (2005, March 8). *Americans frown on interrogation techniques: Sleep deprivation most acceptable to Americans.* Retrieved August 16, 2005, from http://www.gallup.com

Carlson, D. K. (2005, July 19). *Liberty vs. security: Public mixed on Patriot Act: Majority familiar with the law.* Retrieved August 15, 2005, from http://www.gallup.com

Carroll, J. (2005, April 19). *American public opinion about terrorism.* Retrieved August 16, 2005, from http://www.gallup.com

FOX News. (2005, June 16). *FOX news/opinion dynamics poll, 16 June 05.* [Data File] Retrieved June 6, 2005, from www.foxnews.com/projects/pdf/poll_061605.pdf

Frankfort-Nachmias, C., & Leon-Guerrero, A. (2006). *Social statistics for a diverse society* (4th ed.). Thousand Oaks, CA: Pine Forge Press.

Kettl, D. F. (2004). *System under stress: Homeland security and American politics.* Washington, DC: CQ Press.

Kiefer, H. M. (2003, June 3). *Public's partisanship evident on terror issue.* Retrieved August 16, 2005, from http://www.gallup.com

Langer, G. (2005, June 9). *Poll: Support seen for Patriot Act.* Retrieved June 28, 2006, from http://abcnews.go.com/US/print?id=833703

Lester, W. (2005, August 29). *Poll: Info shrinks Patriot Act support.* Retrieved June 28, 2006, from http://www.sfgate.com/cgi-bin/article.cgi?file=/news/archive/2005/08/29/ national/w151949D27.DTL

Lynch, T. (2003, August 21). *Patriotic questions.* Retrieved June 29, 2006, from http://cato.org/ research/articles/lynch-030821.html

Moore, D. W. (2001, October 3). *Support for war on terrorism rivals support for WWII: Vietnam War received least support.* Retrieved August 16, 2005, from http://www.gallup.com

Moore, D. W. (2003, September 8). *Worry about terrorism increases: Fifty-four percent of Americans expect new acts of terrorism in the United States in the next several weeks.* Retrieved August 16, 2005, from http://www.gallup.com

Moore, D. W. (2003, September 9). *Public little concerned about Patriot Act: Wants civil liberties respected, but feels Bush administration has not gone "too far" in restricting liberties.* Retrieved August 15, 2005, from http://www.gallup.com

Saad, L. (2001, October 31). *Americans want tighter airport security at any cost: Majority supports every major proposal.* Retrieved August 16, 2005, from http://www.gallup.com

Saad, L. (2001, December 10). *Fear of terrorism subsides despite persistent concerns about nation's security: Only 29% are highly confident future attacks can be prevented.* Retrieved August 16, 2005, from http://www.gallup.com

Saad, L. (2002, June 7). *Fewer Americans perceive anti-terror war as successful: But Americans' fear of being a victim holds stead.* Retrieved August 16, 2005, from http://www.gallup.com

Saad, L. (2004, March 2). *Americans generally comfortable with patriot act: Few believe it goes too far in restricting civil liberties.* Retrieved August 15, 2005, from http://www.gallup.com

Sprinthall, R. C. (2003). *Basic statistical analysis* (7th ed.). Boston, MA: Pearson Education Group, Inc.

Part II

The Road to Patriot Act II

CHAPTER 12

The Little Law That Wasn't

MOST PEOPLE HAVE HEARD THE children's story about the little engine that could. Basically, it is the story about a little train with a big heart that beat the odds and achieved its goal of climbing a huge mountain. Well "the little law that wasn't" pertains to the first publicized attempt for a Patriot Act sequel. This law, the Domestic Security Enhancement Act of 2003 (DSEA 2003), which surfaced early in that year, was coined by several different names including Patriot Act II, and Son of Patriot (Electronic Frontier Foundation, n.d.). The draft, created by John Ashcroft's Department of Justice, marked "confidential," was leaked and first made public by The Center for Public Integrity.

Upon the draft's unintentional debut, the Justice Department originally denied its existence until it was proved that House Speaker Dennis Hastert and Vice President Dick Cheney had received a copy (Domestic Security Enhancement Act [DSEA], 2004; Neas, 2003). Wild debate followed as to the Justice Department's true plan for DSEA 2003. Many believed Attorney General John Ashcroft's true plan was for actual legislation of the 2003 version. Some speculated that Ashcroft never really thought this new upgraded version of the Patriot Act would pass scrutiny as it was muscled up with more governmental powers than its predecessor. It was not beyond the realm of possibility for some to think that Ashcroft was plotting to unleash what civil liberty advocates saw as his little 120-page monster after a future terrorist attack (DSEA, 2004). It was even pondered whether a renewal action had been planned to take place after the Iraq conflict had begun.

Let it be stated that the Domestic Security Enhancement Act of 2003 did not become a law. There also is no compelling proof in the literature that this leaked draft was ever intended to be promoted as a finished product for legislative support. In fact, what little evidence can be gleaned from investigations of the DSEA 2003 tend to support the assumption that it was more than likely a rough draft. With that knowledge it may be wondered why we should even look at this issue at all. The answer is the leak and discovery of the DSEA 2003 is part of the Patriot Act history. A piece of history that few people have analyzed in the full totality of the complete Patriot Act story. Even when removing the majority of unnecessary hype that was produced by the media, DSEA 2003 remains a bit mysterious.

As a person learns more about the "little law that wasn't," certain reflections might be prudent. If this law had gone into effect, how would things be today? What were the concerns that the Domestic Security Enhancement Act of 2003 sparked in civil liberties groups? Were they legitimate complaints considering the country was, and is, in a state of war? Finally, special notice should be paid to see that while this "little law" failed the first time around, would any of these modifications be seen in the true sequel?

The Domestic Security Enhancement Act of 2003 was a 120-page document which had 87 pages of actual bill material, including 33 pages of section-by-section analysis (Jones, 2003). The legislation itself was believed to have been leaked from someone within the Justice Department; however, the source of the leak has not been identified. The bill contains the following sections that were considered contentious.

Section 101 - Individual Terrorists as Foreign Powers. This section placed individuals who were categorized as terrorists into the status of foreign powers and took away standard U.S. citizen rights under the definition of "enemy combatants" (DSEA, 2003; Jones, 2003).

Section 102 - Clandestine Intelligence Activities by Agent of a Foreign Power placed a lower standard on information gathering that could be considered a violation of this section. This could include clandestine intelligence activities for a foreign power. This also included information gathering, regardless of whether or not those activities were legal or illegal (DSEA, 2003; Edgar, 2003; Jones, 2003).

Section 103 - Strengthening Wartime Authorities under FISA. This section gives authority to the federal government to implement martial law powers inside the United States and abroad without an official Congressional declaration of war (Cole, 2003; DSEA, 2003; Jones, 2003).

Section 104 - Strengthening FISA's Presidential Authorization Exemption. In certain situations, this section allows the attorney general to authorize electronic surveillance for up to one year without FISA court prior approval (DSEA, 2003).

Section 106 - **Defense of Reliance on Authorization** created a defense for agents who commit unauthorized searches or surveillance, or who disclose unauthorized information if they are relying on an order issued by the FISA court (DSEA, 2003). Some forward that this section ultimately says that government agents must be given immunity for carrying out search warrants with no prior court approval (Jones, 2003). Others saw this section as a shelter for federal agents' activity engaged in illegal surveillance (Edgar, 2003).

Section 107 - **Pen registers in FISA Investigations** makes pen registers available in cases of non-U.S. persons for the express purpose "to obtain foreign intelligence information." The standard for receiving pen registers for U.S. citizens had a higher requirement. Pen registers were not allowed unless "to protect against international terrorism or clandestine intelligence activities" (DSEA, 2003). This eliminated many protections in the current FISA for U.S. citizens. One concern was that this section would, in effect, allow pen registers on U.S. citizens for any foreign intelligence investigation without designating the difference between criminal and terrorist cases (Cole, 2003).

Section 109 - Enforcement of Foreign Intelligence Surveillance Court Orders.
This section gave the Foreign Intelligence Surveillance Court the same authority as the United States district court to enforce their court orders. These powers included the ability to enforce contempt charges in cases of disobedience (DSEA, 2003). This section was considered a strong-arm tactic to force individuals to incriminate themselves and others, and an attack on the Fifth Amendment (Jones, 2003).

Section 110 - Technical Correction Related to the USA Patriot Act. This section makes adjustments to sections within the Patriot Act, including removing the sunset clause from certain sections (DSEA, 2003). Some saw this as an action to make the Patriot Act permanent (Jones, 2003).

Section 111 - International Terrorist Organizations as Foreign Powers. This section expanded the definition of foreign combatants (Jones, 2003).

Section 121 - Definition of Terrorist Activities. This section adds a definition of "terrorist activities" to the definitional section of Chapter 119, the chapter of criminal code for electronic surveillance. The definition encompasses criminal acts of domestic and international terrorism as defined in 18 U.S.C. § 2331, together with related preparatory, material support, and criminal activities (DSEA, 2003). The major concern with this section was that it eliminated the distinction between domestic and international terrorism. The concern was that traditional restrictions related to criminal investigations would be bypassed (Cole, 2003).

Section 123 - Extension of Authorized Period Relating to Surveillance and Searches in Investigations of Terrorist Activities. This section extended the period for "domestic terrorism" searches and surveillance. Compared to the previous limit of 30 days, electronic surveillance under this section could last for up to 90 days. This section also limited the frequency in which a judge could request a progress report from government officials (Electronic Frontier Foundation, n.d.).

Section 129 - Strengthening Access to and Use of Information in National Security Investigations. This section deals with correcting problems and weaknesses with the authorization of use of "national security letters." These are a form of subpoena that allow officials to receive information and evidence for use in national security investigations. This section sets rules of punishment for non-disclosure of sensitive information during national security investigations (DSEA, 2003). Detractors felt that this was an attempt to be able to silence possible whistle blowers in the future by federal agents (Jones, 2003).

Section 201 - Prohibition of Disclosure of Terrorism Investigation Detainee Information. Due to the possible negative impact of the disclosure of certain detainee information to national security, the government need not release detainees of terrorist related investigations until natural disclosure comes from criminal charges (DSEA, 2003). Many saw this as nothing short of secret arrests (Cole, 2003). Others scoffed at the idea that one of the government's justifications for non-disclosure was for the protection of the detainee (Electronic Frontier Foundation, n.d.). Still others were concerned with the non-disclosure in combination with detention without definite criminal charging (Edgar, 2003).

Section 302 - Collection and Use of Identification Information from Suspected Terrorists and Other Sources. This section allows for the collection and storage of the DNA of suspected terrorists, including individuals currently detained in Guantanamo Bay (DSEA, 2003). Some believed that the expansion of the national DNA database would inevitably increase the chances of errors that might mislabel individuals as terrorists (Electronic Frontier Foundation, n.d.). Many were concerned that the DNA collection of individuals only suspected, or possibly mere innocent associates of terrorists, was a civil rights violation (Cole, 2003; DSEA, 2004; Edgar, 2003).

Section 321 - Authority to Seek Search Warrants and Orders to Assist Foreign States. Because 28 U.S.C. § 1782 only allows the United States to respond to requests by foreign governments with the service of subpoenas within the U.S., this section was enacted. This section would modify federal law so that the United States may seek pen/trap orders, warrants, and ECPA orders in response to a request by a foreign government (DSEA, 2003). Some felt that this gave free license for foreign governments to be able to spy on American citizens (Edgar, 2003; Jones, 2003). Amply as discouraging was the fact that now even governments with which the U.S. did not have treatises could take advantage of the power of this section (Edgar, 2003).

Section 402 - Providing Material Support to Terrorism. Under 18 U.S.C. § 2339A, the current definition of providing material support to terrorism was considered to be too narrow, and not a viable definition, as it did not cover crimes of international terrorism. The definition was expanded to cover a larger range of categories (DSEA, 2003). The deluge of opposition to this section was that the element of "intent" to give material support had been removed from the definition (Edgar, 2003; Electronic Frontier Foundation, n.d.; Jones, 2003). This would be considered an expansion of Section 411 of the original Patriot Act.

Section 408 - Post Release Supervision of Terrorists. This section expanded on the first Patriot Act's Section 812 to include more crimes that could result in sentences to post release supervision of 10 years to life. Some saw this statute as putting people into perpetual slavery to the government (Jones, 2003).

Section 411 - Penalties for Terrorist Murders replaces existing law which was not deemed to have adequate penalties, so the death penalty was put in place. Sentences of up to life in prison or the death penalty were to be used for cases such as those that caused the major loss of life through the sabotage of a nuclear facility, national defense installation, or an energy facility (DSEA, 2003). Many saw this section as just another government action to increase the death penalty (Cole, 2003). This was seen as an extension of Section 802 of the original Patriot Act (Jones, 2003).

Section 501 - Expatriation of Terrorists dealt with lowering the threshold for an American citizen to be expatriated, from the previous verbal request by the citizen, to the government's observance (through authority of the attorney general) that a citizen's unlawful activities were in conjunction with a "terrorist organization." These activities would serve as an "inferred intent to be expatriated" (Lewis & Mayle, 2003).

Section 504 - Expedited Removal of Criminal Aliens. This section allows for the quick removal of aliens convicted of crimes which make them ineligible for "discretionary relief." This section would expand the removal capabilities of the government beyond only non-permanent citizens to include all aliens. Second, it would expand the removal triggering crimes to include the following: possession of controlled substances, firearms offenses, sabotage, espionage, treason, threats against the president, violation of the Trading with the Enemy Act, and certain alien smuggling crimes (DSEA, 2003). This section was attacked by some as having nothing to do with the war on terror and just another unjust addition to existing immigration law (Cole, 2003).

When confronted with questions about the legislation, Barbara Comstock, the Department of Justice's Director of Public Affairs said,

> The President expects all his cabinet departments that are involved in homeland security, including the Department of Justice, to make sure we are doing everything we can to protect the American people. It should not be surprising that the Department of Justice takes that responsibility seriously and discusses additional tools to protect the American people. We are continually considering anti-terrorism measures and would be derelict if we were not doing so. The Department's deliberations are always undertaken with the strongest commitment to our Constitution and civil liberties. (Comstock, 2003)

She continued by saying,

> We are continually asking our field prosecutors, investigators and experts what tools they need to prevent future acts of terrorism. During our internal deliberations, many ideas are considered, some are discarded and new ideas emerge in the process along with numerous discussion drafts. Department staff have not presented any final proposals to either

the Attorney General or the White House. It would be premature to speculate on any future decisions, particularly ideas or proposals that are still being discussed at staff levels. (Comstock, 2003)

While in the official governmental response the Department of Justice did not take direct ownership of the DSEA 2003 document, the Justice Department alluded to the fact that potential rough drafts on Patriot Act related legislation would be a part of the administration's game plan to continue to protect the country.

The potential Patriot Act sequel was met with strong opposition by civil rights activists and the government dropped any direct pursuits with the bill. Within a short time, DSEA 2003 fell off the public radar. However, many of the new powers found in the DSEA 2003 were incorporated into an attempted alternate bill, entitled the Vital Interdiction of Criminal Terrorist Organizations Act of 2003, or the Victory Act (Neas, 2003).

Two additional issues were present in the DSEA 2003 draft that would come back again in the actual Patriot Act in 2005. The DSEA 2003 was written to sidestep the sunset provision. That is, the Patriot Act upgrade in the DSEA 2003 would have made all the laws permanent. This was a bone of contention in 2003, and would again be pivotal in 2005, when the sun would be setting on the Title II provisions.

Another topic more quickly forgotten by historians would be the issue of intelligence leaks to the media. The DSEA 2003 leak sparked the short lived story of a potential "back door" upgrade to the Patriot Act being orchestrated by the Bush administration. In 2005, a similar event would take place, but this time with potentially devastating effects to the Patriot Act, and the nation, in a time of war.

References

Cole, D. (2003, February 10). *What Patriot II proposes to do*. Retrieved February 15, 2005, from http://www.cdt.org/security/usapatriot/030210cole.pdf

Comstock, B. (2003, February 7). *Statement of Barbara Comstock, Director of Public Affairs*. Retrieved January 2, 2006, from the Department of Justice Web site: http://www.usdoj.gov/opa/pr/2003/February/03_opa-082.htm

Domestic Security Enhancement Act of 2003 [DSEA]. (2003, January 9). Retrieved February 15, 2005, from The Center For Public Integrity Web site: http://www.publicintegrity.org/ docs/PatriotAct/story_ 01_020703_doc_1.pdf

Domestic Security Enhancement Act of 2003 [DSEA]. (2004, December 5). In *Wikipedia, The Free Encyclopedia.* Retrieved February 15, 2005, from http://en.wikipedia.org/w/index. php?title=Domestic_ Security_Enhancement_Act_of_2003&oldid=13993637

Edgar, T. H. (2003, February 14). *Interested persons memo: Section-by-section analysis of Justice Department draft "Domestic Security Enhancement Act of 2003," also known as "Patriot Act II".* Retrieved February 15, 2005, from the ACLU Web site: http://www.aclu.org/safefree/general/17203leg20030214.html

Electronic Frontier Foundation. (n.d.). *EFF analysis of "Patriot II," provisions of the Domestic Security Enhancement Act of 2003 that impact the Internet and surveillance.* Retrieved August 19, 2005, from http://www.eff.org/Censorship/Terrorism_militias/patriot-act-II-analysis.php

Jones, A. (2003, February 10). *A brief analysis of the Domestic Security Enhancement Act 2003.* Retrieved January 30, 2004, from http: www.rickieleejones.com/political/patriotact.htm

Lewis, C., & Mayle, A. (2003, February 7). *Justice Dept. drafts sweeping expansion of anti-terrorism act.* Retrieved February 15, 2005, from The Center for Public Integrity Web site: http://www.publicintegrity.org/report.aspx?aid=94

Neas, R. G. (2003, September 9). *Two years after 9/11: Ashcroft's assault on the Constitution.* Retrieved July 1, 2005, from http://www.pfaw.org/pfaw/dfiles/file_232.pdf

CHAPTER 13

Viewing the Political Landscape

THE FUTURES OF ALL LAWS are dependent upon the prevailing winds of politics. The Patriot Act is different. There have been, and will continue to be, political events that will affect the Patriot Act at its core. For the original Patriot Act, obviously the terrorist attacks were instrumental in projecting the Patriot Act. However, after the Patriot Act exited the starting gate, politics became the second most important factor in its development. The Justice Department, under Attorney General John Ashcroft, brought the original draft out. This draft was tempered to some extent by Representative Sensenbrenner of the House of Representatives. On the Senate side, the Patriot Act moved forward primarily by the political maneuverings of Senator Leahy (D) and Senator Hatch (R). The entire Patriot Act process was observed and endorsed by President Bush.

With that in mind, Patriot Act II must be, at least for a moment, examined for the implications of the presidential elections of 2004. Would a different outcome of the presidential race between president-elect George Bush and presidential candidate John Kerry have affected the Patriot Act? The answer is, decidedly, yes.

To validate this answer one must follow the political courses of action pertaining to John Kerry and the Patriot Act. John Kerry was an early supporter of the Patriot Act. This support went well beyond him simply voting for the Patriot Act (H.R. 3162). John Kerry was one of the official architects of the Patriot Act. His contribution to Patriot Act legislation pertained to the anti-money laundering provisions (Kerry, n.d.). Nevertheless, John

Kerry's support began to waiver for the Patriot Act and, especially, its chief enforcer, Attorney General John Ashcroft.

On December 2, 2003, while speaking at Iowa State University, Kerry stated that he would end the "John Ashcroft era" (Neznanski, 2003). Continuing in that speech, Kerry gave somewhat mixed messages attacking the uses of the Patriot Act while supporting his vote for the contentious law (Neznanski, 2003). In fact, the inconsistency of John Kerry on campaign issues was also relevant to the Patriot Act. Michael Grunwald addresses the issue in his article, "John Kerry's Waffles: If you Don't Like the Democratic Nominee's View, Just Wait a Week," when he says, "Kerry's supporters cite his reversals as evidence of the senator's capacity for nuance and complexity, growth and change. His critics say they represent a fundamental lack of principles" (2004).

This duality of thinking was used against Kerry in presidential ads, one of which documented the potential first 100 days of Kerry's presidency. In this ad, approved by the president, among a series of bad things that would befall the country was a weakening of the Patriot Act (Lessmann, 2004). No matter how much true mileage the Bush campaign received from Patriot Act issues, the end result was a resounding victory for President George W. Bush. When the final polls came in on the 2004 presidential election, it became clear that the Patriot Act would live to see another day, and a sequel. The question that then remained was what kind of sequel would it be? To understand that, we must look at the full range of players as they line up for the Patriot Act renewal.

For a law to pass, it must pass the House of Representatives, the Senate, and then be signed by the president. Due to the fact that the Patriot Act had to renew by December 31, 2005, or sunset, the issue would be dealt with by the 109th Congress. As with the 108th Congress, individual members of both the House and Senate certainly stood out as pivotal players. Major pieces of legislation that the 109th Congress had already passed included, but were not limited to the following: Class Action Fairness Act of 2005, Bankruptcy Reform Act of 2005, CAFTA Implementation Act, and the Energy Policy Act of 2005 (109th Congress, 2005).

As of August, 2005, the House leadership was as follows:

Speaker of the House	Dennis Hastert (R)		
Minority Leader	Nancy Pelosi (D)	Majority Leader	Tom DeLay (R)
Minority Whip	Steny Hoyer (D)	Majority Whip	Roy Blunt (R)

and the Senate leadership was as follows:

President	Richard Cheney (R)	President *pro-tempore*	Theodore Stevens (R)
Majority Leader	William Frist (R)	Minority Leader	Harry Reid (D)
Majority Whip	A. McConnell Jr. (R)	Minority Whip	Richard Durbin (D)

The Senate consisted of 55 Republicans, 44 Democrats, and 1 Independent (109th Congress, 2005). The Senate consisted of the following members:

Daniel Akaka	Hawaii (D)	Lamar Alexander	Tennessee (R)
A. Wayne Allard	Colorado (R)	George Allen	Virginia (R)
Max Baucus	Montana (D)	B. Evans "Evan" Bayh III	Indiana (D)
Robert Bennett	Utah (R)	Joseph Biden Jr.	Delaware (D)
Jeff Bingaman Jr.	New Mexico (D)	Christopher "Kit" Bond	Missouri (R)
Barbara Boxer	California (D)	Sam Brownback	Kansas (R)
James Bunning	Kentucky (R)	Conrad Burns	Montana (R)
Richard Burr	North Carolina (R)	Robert Byrd	West Virginia (D)
Maria Cantwell	Washington (D)	Thomas Carper	Delaware (D)
Lincoln Chafee	Rhode Island (R)	C. Chambliss	Georgia (R)
Hillary Clinton	New York (D)	Tom Coburn	Oklahoma (R)
W. Cochran	Mississippi (R)	Norman Coleman	Minnesota (R)
Susan Collins	Maine (R)	Kent Conrad	North Dakota (D)
John Cornyn	Texas (R)	Jon Corzine	New Jersey (D)
Larry Craig	Idaho (R)	Michael Crapo	Idaho (R)
Mark Dayton	Minnesota (D)	Jim DeMint	South Carolina (R)
Michael DeWine	Ohio (R)	Christopher Dodd	Connecticut (D)
Elizabeth Dole	North Carolina (R)	Peter Domenici	New Mexico (R)
Byron Dorgan	North Dakota (D)	Richard Durbin	Illinois (D)
John Ensign	Nevada (R)	Michael Enzi	Wyoming (R)
Russ Feingold	Wisconsin (D)	Dianne Feinstein	California (D)
William Frist	Tennessee (R)	Charles Grassley	Iowa (R)
Lindsey Graham	South Carolina (R)	Judd Gregg	New Hampshire (R)
Charles Hagel	Nebraska (R)	Thomas Harkin	Iowa (D)

Orrin Hatch	Utah (R)	Kay Hutchison	Texas (R)
James Inhofe	Oklahoma (R)	Daniel Inouye	Hawaii (D)
Johnny Isakson	Georgia (R)	James Jeffords	Vermont (I)
Tim Johnson	South Dakota (D)	Ted Kennedy	Massachusetts (D)
John Kerry	Massachusetts (D)	Herbert Kohl	Wisconsin (D)
Jon Kyl	Arizona (R)	Mary Landrieu	Louisiana (D)
Frank Lautenberg	New Jersey (D)	Patrick Leahy	Vermont (D)
Carl Levin	Michigan (D)	Joseph Lieberman	Connecticut (D)
Blanche Lincoln	Arkansas (D)	Trent Lott	Mississippi (R)
Richard Lugar	Indiana (R)	M. Martinez	Florida (R)
John McCain III	Arizona (R)	A. McConnell Jr.	Kentucky (R)
Barbara Mikulski	Maryland (D)	Lisa Murkowski	Alaska (R)
Patricia Murray	Washington (D)	Benjamin Nelson	Nebraska (D)
C. William Nelson	Florida (D)	Barack Obama	Illinois (D)
Mark Pryor	Arkansas (D)	John F. Reed	Rhode Island (D)
Harry Reid	Nevada (D)	C. Patrick Roberts	Kansas (R)
John Rockefeller IV	West Virginia (D)	Ken Salazar	Colorado (D)
Richard Santorum	Pennsylvania (R)	Paul Sarbanes	Maryland (D)
Charles Schumer	New York (D)	Jefferson Sessions III	Alabama (R)
Richard Shelby	Alabama (R)	Gordon Smith	Oregon (R)
Olympia Snowe	Maine (R)	Arlen Specter	Pennsylvania (R)
Debbie Stabenow	Michigan (D)	Theodore Stevens	Alaska (R)
John Sununu	New Hampshire (R)	James Talent	Missouri (R)
Craig Thomas	Wyoming (R)	John Thune	South Dakota (R)
David Vitter	Louisiana (R)	George Voinovich	Ohio (R)
John Warner	Virginia (R)	Ronald Wyden	Oregon (D)

(109th Congress, 2005).

The House of Representatives had 231 Republicans, 202 Democrats, and 1 Independent with 1 vacancy to be filled (109th Congress, 2005). These members included the following:

Jo Bonner	Alabama (R)		Terry Everett	Alabama (R)
Mike Rogers	Alabama (R)		Robert Aderholt	Alabama (R)
Robert Cramer	Alabama (D)		Spencer Bachus	Alabama (R)

Arthur Davis	Alabama (D)	Don Young	Alaska (R)
Rick Renzi	Arizona (R)	Trent Franks	Arizona (R)
John Shadegg	Arizona (R)	Ed Pastor	Arizona (D)
J. D. Hayworth	Arizona (R)	Jeff Flake	Arizona (R)
Paul Grijalva	Arizona (D)	Jim Kolbe	Arizona (R)
Marion Berry	Arkansas (D)	Vic Snyder	Arkansas (D)
John Boozman	Arkansas (R)	Mike Ross	Arkansas (D)
Mike Thompson	California (D)	Wally Herger	California (R)
Dan Lungren	California (R)	John Doolittle	California (R)
Doris Matsui	California (D)	Lynn Woolsey	California (D)
George Miller	California (D)	Nancy Pelosi	California (D)
Barbara Lee	California (D)	Ellen Tauscher	California (D)
Richard Pombo	California (R)	Tom Lantos	California (D)
Pete Start	California (D)	Anna Eshoo	California (D)
Mike Honda	California (D)	Zoe Lofgren	California (D)
Sam Farr	California (D)	Dennis Cardoza	California (D)
George Radanovich	California (R)	Jim Costa	California (D)
Devin Nunes	California (R)	Bill Thomas	California (R)
Lois Capps	California (D)	Elton Gallegly	California (R)
Howard McKeon	California (R)	David Dreier	California (R)
Brad Sherman	California (D)	Howard Berman	California (D)
Adam Schiff	California (D)	Henry Waxman	California (D)
Xavier Becerra	California (D)	Hilda Solis	California (D)
Diane Watson	California (D)	Lucille Roybal-Allard	California (D)
Maxine Waters	California (D)	Jane Harman	California (D)
Juanita McDonald	California (D)	Grace Napolitano	California (D)
Linda Sanchez	California (D)	Edward R. Royce	California (R)
Jerry Lewis	California (R)	Gary Miller	California (R)
Jo Baca	California (D)	Ken Calvert	California (R)
Mary Bono	California (R)	Dana Rohrabacher	California (R)
Loretta Sanchez	California (D)	Darrell Issa	California (R)
Randy Cunningham	California (R)	Bob Filner	California (D)
Duncan Hunter	California (R)	Susan Davis	California (D)
Diana DeGette	Colorado (D)	Mark Udall	Colorado (D)

John Salazar	Colorado (D)	Marilyn Musgrave	Colorado (R)
Joel Hefley	Colorado (R)	Thomas C. Trancredo	Colorado (R)
Bob Beauprez	Colorado (R)	John Larsons	Connecticut (D)
Rob Simmons	Connecticut (R)	Rosa DeLaura	Connecticut (D)
Christopher Shays	Connecticut (R)	Nancy Johnson	Connecticut (R)
Michael Castle	Delaware (R)	Jeff Miller	Florida (R)
Allen Boyd	Florida (D)	Corrine Brown	Florida (D)
Ander Crenshaw	Florida (R)	Ginny Brown-Waite	Florida (R)
Cliff Stearns	Florida (R)	John Mica	Florida (R)
Rick Keller	Florida (R)	Michael Bilirakis	Florida (R)
Bill Young	Florida (R)	Jim Davis	Florida (D)
Adam Putnam	Florida (R)	Katherine Harris	Florida (R)
Connie Mack IV	Florida (R)	Dave Weldon	Florida (R)
Mark Foley	Florida (R)	Kendrick Meek	Florida (D)
Ileana Ros-Lehtinen	Florida (R)	Robert Wexler	Florida (D)
Debbie Schultz	Florida (D)	Lincoln Diaz-Balart	Florida (R)
Clay Shaw	Florida (R)	Alcee Hastings	Florida (D)
Tom Feeney	Florida (R)	Mario Diaz-Balart	Florida (R)
Jack Kingston	Georgia (R)	Sanford Bishop	Georgia (D)
Jim Marshall	Georgia (D)	Cynthia McKinney	Georgia (D)
John Lewis	Georgia (D)	Tom Price	Georgia (R)
John Linder	Georgia (R)	Lynn Westmoreland	Georgia (R)
Charlie Norwood	Georgia (R)	Nathan Deal	Georgia (R)
Phil Gingrey	Georgia (R)	John Barrow	Georgia (D)
David Scott	Georgia (D)	Neil Abercrombie	Hawaii (D)
Edward Case	Hawaii (D)	C. L. Otter	Idaho (R)
Michael Simpson	Idaho (R)	Bobby Rush	Illinois (D)
Jesse Jackson Jr.	Illinois (D)	Daniel Lipinski	Illinois (D)
Luis Gutierrez	Illinois (D)	Rahm Emanuel	Illinois (D)
Henry Hyde	Illinois (R)	Danny Davis	Illinois (D)
Melissa Bean	Illinois (D)	Janice Schakowsky	Illinois (D)
Mark Kirk	Illinois (R)	Jerry Weller	Illinois (R)
Jerry Costello	Illinois (D)	Judy Biggert	Illinois (R)
Dennis Hastert	Illinois (R)	Timothy Johnson	Illinois (R)

Living Under The Patriot Act: Educating A Society | 193

Donald Manzullo	Illinois (R)	Lane Evans	Illinois (D)
Ray LaHood	Illinois (R)	John Shimkus	Illinois (R)
Peter Visclosky	Indiana (D)	Chris Chocola	Indiana (R)
Mark Souder	Indiana (R)	Steve Buyer	Indiana (R)
Dan Burton	Indiana (R)	Mike Pence	Indiana (R)
Julia Carson	Indiana (D)	John Hostettler	Indiana (R)
Mike Sodrel	Indiana (R)	Jim Nussle	Iowa (R)
Jim Leach	Iowa (R)	Leonard Boswell	Iowa (D)
Tom Latham	Iowa (R)	Steve King	Iowa (R)
Jerry Moran	Kansas (R)	Jim Ryan	Kansas (R)
Dennis Moore	Kansas (D)	Todd Tiahrt	Kansas (R)
Ed Whitfield	Kentucky (R)	Ron Lewis	Kentucky (R)
Anne Northup	Kentucky (R)	Geoff Davis	Kentucky (R)
Harold Rogers	Kentucky (R)	Ben Chandler	Kentucky (D)
Bobby Jindal	Louisiana (R)	William Jefferson	Louisiana (D)
Charlie Melancon	Louisiana (D)	Jim McCrery	Louisiana (R)
Rodney Alexander	Louisiana (R)	Richard Barker	Louisiana (R)
Charles Boustany	Louisiana (R)	Tom Allen	Maine (D)
Mike Michaud	Maine (D)	Wayne Gilchrest	Maryland (R)
Dutch Ruppersberger	Maryland (D)	Ben Cardin	Maryland (D)
Albert Wynn	Maryland (D)	Steny Hoyer	Maryland (D)
Roscoe Bartlett	Maryland (R)	Elijah Cummings	Maryland (D)
Chris Van Hollen	Maryland (D)	John Olver	Massachusetts (D)
Richard Neal	Massachusetts (D)	Jim McGovern	Massachusetts (D)
Barney Frank	Massachusetts (D)	Marty Meehan	Massachusetts (D)
John Tierney	Massachusetts (D)	Ed Markey	Massachusetts (D)
Mike Capuano	Massachusetts (D)	Stephen Lynch	Massachusetts (D)
Bill Delahunt	Massachusetts (D)	Bart Stupak	Michigan (D)
Peter Hoekstra	Michigan (R)	Vern Ehlers	Michigan (R)
David Camp	Michigan (R)	Dale Kildee	Michigan (D)
Fred Upton	Michigan (R)	Joe Schwarz	Michigan (R)
Mike Rogers	Michigan (R)	Joe Knollenberg	Michigan (R)
Candice Miller	Michigan (R)	Thaddeus McCotter	Michigan (R)
Sander Levin	Michigan (D)	Carolyn Kilpatrick	Michigan (D)

John Conyers	Michigan (D)	John Dingell	Michigan (D)
Gil Gutknecht	Minnesota (R)	John Kline	Minnesota (R)
Jim Ramstad	Minnesota (R)	Betty McCollum	Minnesota (D)
Martin Olav Sabo	Minnesota (D)	Mark Kennedy	Minnesota (R)
Collin Peterson	Minnesota (D)	James Oberstar	Minnesota (D)
Roger Wicker	Mississippi (R)	Bennie Thompson	Mississippi (D)
Chip Pickering	Mississippi (R)	Gene Taylor	Mississippi (D)
William Clay Jr.	Missouri (D)	Todd Akin	Missouri (R)
Russ Carnahan	Missouri (D)	Ike Skelton	Missouri (D)
Emanuel Cleaver	Missouri (D)	Sam Graves	Missouri (R)
Roy Blunt	Missouri (R)	Jo Ann Emerson	Missouri (R)
Kenny Hulshof	Missouri (R)	Denny Rehberg	Montana (R)
Jeff Fortenberry	Nebraska (R)	Lee Terry	Nebraska (R)
Tom Osborne	Nebraska (R)	Shelley Berkley	Nevada (D)
Jim Gibbons	Nevada (R)	Jon Porter	Nevada (R)
Jeb Bradley	New Hampshire (R)	Charlie Bass	New Hampshire (R)
Rob Andrews	New Jersey (D)	Frank LoBiondo	New Jersey (R)
Jim Saxton	New Jersey (R)	Chris Smith	New Jersey (R)
Scott Garrett	New Jersey (R)	Frank Pallone	New Jersey (D)
Mike Ferguson	New Jersey (R)	Bill Pascrell Jr.	New Jersey (D)
Steve Rothman	New Jersey (D)	Don Payne	New Jersey (D)
Rodney Frelinghuysen	New Jersey (R)	Rush Holt Jr	New Jersey (D)
Robert Menendez	New Jersey (D)	Heather Wilson	New Mexico (R)
Steve Pearce	New Mexico (R)	Tom Udall	New Mexico (D)
Tim Bishop	New York (D)	Steve Israel	New York (D)
Peter King	New York (R)	Carolyn McCarthy	New York (D)
Gary Ackerman	New York (D)	Gregory Meeks	New York (D)
Joseph Crowley	New York (D)	Jerrold Nadler	New York (D)
Anthony Weiner	New York (D)	Edolphus Towns	New York (D)
Major Owens	New York (D)	Nydia Velazquez	New York (D)
Vito Fossella	New York (R)	Carolyn Maloney	New York (D)
Charles Rangel	New York (D)	Jose Serrano	New York (D)
Eliot L. Engel	New York (D)	Nita Lowey	New York (D)
Sue Kelly	New York (R)	John Sweeney	New York (R)

Michael McNulty	New York (D)	Maurice Hinchey	New York (D)
John McHugh	New York (R)	Sherwood Boehlert	New York (R)
James Walsh	New York (R)	Thomas Reynolds	New York (R)
Brian Higgins	New York (D)	Louise Slaughter	New York (D)
Randy Kuhl	New York (R)	G. K. Butterfield	N. Carolina (D)
Bob Etheridge	N. Carolina (D)	Walter Jones	N. Carolina (R)
David Price	N. Carolina (D)	Virginia Foxx	N. Carolina (R)
Howard Coble	N. Carolina (R)	Mike McIntyre	N. Carolina (D)
Robin Hayes	N. Carolina (R)	Sue Myrick	N. Carolina (R)
Patrick McHenry	N. Carolina (R)	Charles Taylor	N. Carolina (R)
Mel Watt	N. Carolina (D)	Brad Miller	N. Carolina (D)
Earl Pomeroy	North Dakota (D)	Steve Chabot	Ohio (R)
Jean Schmidt	Ohio (R)	Michael Turner	Ohio (R)
Michael Oxley	Ohio (R)	Paul Gillmor	Ohio (R)
Ted Strickland	Ohio (D)	David Hobson	Ohio (R)
John Boehner	Ohio (R)	Marcia Kaptur	Ohio (D)
Dennis Kucinich	Ohio (D)	Stephanie Jones	Ohio (D)
Patrick Tiberi	Ohio (R)	Sherrod Brown	Ohio (D)
Steven LaTourette	Ohio (R)	Deborah Pryce	Ohio (R)
Ralph Regula	Ohio (R)	Timothy Ryan	Ohio (D)
Robert Ney	Ohio (R)	John Sullivan	Oklahoma (R)
Dan Boren	Oklahoma (D)	Frank Lucas	Oklahoma (R)
Tom Cole	Oklahoma (R)	Ernest Istook	Oklahoma (R)
David Wu	Oregon (D)	Greg Walden	Oregon (R)
Earl Blumenauer	Oregon (D)	Peter DeFazio	Oregon (D)
Darlene Hooley	Oregon (D)	Bob Brady	Pennsylvania (D)
Chaka Fattah	Pennsylvania (D)	Phil English	Pennsylvania (R)
Melissa Hart	Pennsylvania (R)	John Peterson	Pennsylvania (R)
Jim Gerlach	Pennsylvania (R)	Curt Weldon	Pennsylvania (R)
Mike Fitzpatrick	Pennsylvania (R)	Bill Shuster	Pennsylvania (R)
Don Sherwood	Pennsylvania (R)	Paul Kanjorski	Pennsylvania (D)
John Murtha	Pennsylvania (D)	Allyson Schwartz	Pennsylvania (D)
Michael Doyle	Pennsylvania (D)	Charles Dent	Pennsylvania (R)
Joseph Pitts	Pennsylvania (R)	Tim Holden	Pennsylvania (D)

Tim Murphy	Pennsylvania (R)	Todd Platts	Pennsylvania (R)
Patrick Kennedy	Rhode Island (D)	James Langevin	Rhode Island (D)
Henry Brown Jr.	S. Carolina (R)	Joe Wilson	S. Carolina (R)
Gresham Barrett	S. Carolina (R)	Bob Inglis	S. Carolina (R)
John Spratt	S. Carolina (D)	Jim Clyburn	S. Carolina (D)
Stephanie Herseth	South Dakota (D)	Bill Jenkins	Tennessee (R)
John Duncan	Tennessee (R)	Zach Wamp	Tennessee (R)
Lincoln Davis	Tennessee (D)	Jim Cooper	Tennessee (D)
Bart Gordon	Tennessee (D)	Marsha Blackburn	Tennessee (R)
John Tanner	Tennessee (D)	Harold Ford Jr.	Tennessee (D)
Louie Gohmert	Texas (R)	Ted Poe	Texas (R)
Sam Johnson	Texas (R)	Ralph Hall	Texas (R)
Jeb Hensarling	Texas (R)	Joe Barton	Texas (R)
John Culberson	Texas (R)	Kevin Brady	Texas (R)
Al Green	Texas (D)	Michael McCaul	Texas (R)
Mike Conaway	Texas (R)	Kay Granger	Texas (R)
Mac Thornberry	Texas (R)	Ron Paul	Texas (R)
Ruben Hinojosa	Texas (D)	Silvestre Reyes	Texas (D)
Chet Edwards	Texas (D)	Sheila Jackson-Lee	Texas (D)
Randy Neugebauer	Texas (R)	Charlie Gonzalez	Texas (D)
Lamar Smith	Texas (R)	Tom DeLay	Texas (R)
Henry Bonilla	Texas (R)	Kenny Marchant	Texas (R)
Lloyd Doggett	Texas (D)	Michael Burgess	Texas (R)
Solomon Ortiz	Texas (D)	Henry Cuellar	Texas (D)
Gene Green	Texas (D)	Eddie Johnson	Texas (D)
John Carter	Texas (R)	Pete Sessions	Texas (R)
Rob Bishop	Utah (R)	Jim Matheson	Utah (D)
Chris Cannon	Utah (R)	Bernie Sanders	Vermont (I)
Jo Ann Davis	Virginia (R)	Thelma Drake	Virginia (R)
Robert Scott	Virginia (D)	Randy Forbes	Virginia (R)
Virgil Goode	Virginia (R)	Bob Goodlatte	Virginia (R)
Eric Cantor	Virginia (R)	Jim Moran	Virginia (D)
Rick Boucher	Virginia (D)	Frank Wolf	Virginia (R)
Thomas Davis	Virginia (R)	Jay Inslee	Washington (D)

Rick Larsen	Washington (D)	Brian Baird	Washington (D)
Doc Hastings	Washington (R)	Cathy McMorris	Washington (R)
Norman Dicks	Washington (D)	Jim McDermott	Washington (D)
Dave Reichert	Washington (R)	Adam Smith	Washington (D)
Alan Mollohan	West Virginia (D)	Shelley Capito	West Virginia R
Nick Rahall	West Virginia (D)	Paul Ryan	Wisconsin (R)
Tammy Baldwin	Wisconsin (D)	Ron Kind	Wisconsin (D)
Gwen Moore	Wisconsin (D)	Jim Sensenbrenner	Wisconsin (R)
Tom Petri	Wisconsin (R)	Dave Obey	Wisconsin (D)
Mark Green	Wisconsin (R)	Barbara Cubin	Wyoming (R)

This concludes the number of voting members in the Senate and House of Representatives. The House of Representatives has additional members who do not have voting power. The seats are filled areas including: American Samoa, District of Columbia, Guam, Puerto Rico, and the Virgin Islands (109th Congress, 2005).

While it is understood that perusing the names of the various members of Congress may have been both interesting and arduous at the same time, let it be stated that there is a specific reason for the chapter. This reason is best explained by highlighting two points. First, each of these members of Congress would have the chance to cast a vote of some form regarding the Patriot Act. For that reason alone they should be documented as part of Patriot Act history. Secondly, and probably more importantly, the Patriot Act is, and will be, a product of these members who, by personal conviction, party affiliation, and constituent obligation, choose to step forward and play an intricate part in the process. Some played the part of support and construction while others opposed and sought to eliminate the Patriot Act in a grand play of political maneuverings and showmanship. This was absolutely true of the original Patriot Act, and it would be no different for the renewal.

Feel free to use this chapter as a reference to gain additional insights on the political party, state of origin, and position within Congress of the main players in both the Patriot Act and Patriot Act II.

References

109th United States Congress. (2005, August 3). In *Wikipedia, The Free Encyclopedia*. Retrieved August 8, 2005, from http://en.wikipedia.org/w/index.php?title=109th_United_ States_ Congress&oldid=20213103

Grunwald, M. (2004, March 3). *John Kerry's waffles: If you don't like the democratic nominee's views, just wait a week*. Retrieved August 8, 2005, from http://www.slate.com/id/ 2096540

Kerry, J. (n.d.). *John Kerry's Senate record*. Retrieved January 1, 2005, from http://www. johnkerry.com/about/john_kerry/senate.html#safer

Lessmann, K. (2004). *Bush negative ad against Kerry's "first 100 days."* Retrieved August 8, 2005, from http://www.gradfree.com/kevin/bushnegativeadagainstkerry.htm

Neznanski, M. (2003, December 2). *Kerry speaks against Patriot Act legislation*. Retrieved August 8, 2005, from http://www.archives2004.ghazali.net/html/kerry_on_patriot_ act.html

CHAPTER 14

The House of Representatives

IF THE SCRIPT OF THE first Patriot Act was to be repeated, observers were likely to see a House bill followed by a Senate bill pertaining to the Patriot Act. These two bills would be molded into a single bill that would be presented to the president to be signed into law. The question was whether things would unfold the same way a second time around. Things were brewing for a highly contentious battle, and the fate of the Patriot Act was unknown (Curry, 2004). As we travel down the road of actions taken by the 109th Congressional House of Representatives and others, let's take a quick moment to review where the battles over Patriot Act II would fall.

In the battle over whether or not to renew the Patriot Act, the landscape was wide and complex. For civil liberties groups there were several issues to address. They included delineating between the sunsetting sections they hated, and the non-sunsetting sections with which they also had issues. In general, the spotlight had stayed focused on what, for a better term, will be called the "big sixteen." These are the 16 sunsetting provisions originally stated within the Patriot Act. They included the following:

- Section 201 - various terrorist crimes as wiretap predicate
- Section 202 - computer fraud as a wiretap predicates
- Section 203(b,) - intelligence agency cooperation
- Section 203(d,)-information sharing between law enforcement agencies
- Section 204 - clarifications on lack of conflict between Title III and FISA
- Section 206 - the FISA court and the use of roving wiretaps

- Section 207 - FISA tap extensions
- Section 209 - the use of warrants for the purpose of capturing voice mail
- Section 212 - the use of emergency e-mail disclosure not requiring a court order
- Section 214 - pen registers, trap and trace standards reduced
- Section 215 - library records collection under FISA
- Section 217 - warrantless interception of computer trespasser information
- Section 218 - the "significant purpose" provision
- Section 220 - extend limits for service of search warrants for electronic evidence
- Section 223 - civil liabilities for violations of disclosure procedures
- Section 225 - FISA wiretap immunity for complying with FISA warrant (CDT, n.d., *Patriot*).

However, not all activist organizations took issue with the same sections. For example, the civil liberties organization, *Center for Democracy & Technology* [CDT], opposed the following sections of the "big sixteen":

- Section 203 - intelligence agency cooperation and information sharing
- Section 206 - the FISA court and the use of roving wiretaps
- Section 209 - the use of warrants for the purpose of capturing voice mail
- Section 212- the use of emergency e-mail disclosure not requiring a court order
- Section 214 - pen registers, trap and trace standards reduced
- Section 215 - library records collection under FISA
- Section 217 - warrantless interception of computer trespasser information
- Section 218 - the "significant purpose" provision
- Section 220 - extend limits for service of search warrants for electronic evidence (CDT, n.d., *Patriot*).

To this organization, the other sections of the "big sixteen" are benign. However, not unlike other activist groups, they also took issue with sections of the Patriot Act not allocated to sunset. These sections include:

- o Section 203(a) - includes the sharing of previously secret grand jury information
- o Section 213 - delayed notification of search warrant "sneak and peek" warrants
- o Section 216 - acquiring pen register for the internet
- o Section 358 - lower standards for financial privacy laws
- o Section 505 - the lowering of standards for privacy laws incorporating "National Security Letters"
- o Section 802 - expansion of definition of domestic terrorism (CDT, n.d., *Patriot*).

As with both the supporters and the opponents to the Patriot Act, the arguing points differed to a small degree. However, this gives the Patriot Act observer a fairly accurate look at the sections most likely to be fought over during the reauthorization period of the Patriot Act.

It is important to note that a historically important player in the Patriot Act saga was not present for the sequel. That player was Attorney General John Ashcroft. Following the presidential re-election of George W. Bush, John Ashcroft stepped down and was replaced by Alberto R. Gonzales (ABC News, n.d.). Gonzales was confirmed by the Senate on a vote of 60-36. While 35 of the 36 opposition votes came from Democrats, Gonzales fared much better than his predecessor, Ashcroft, who attained the position through a very close vote of 58-42 (ABC News, n.d.; Political News, 2005). Though Gonzales would be the first Hispanic attorney general, he was opposed by civil liberties groups like the ACLU and Human Rights Watch (Political News, 2005). It is possible that some of the tension among those who opposed Gonzales was spawned from Gonzales' involvement in memos related to prisoner abuse in Afghanistan, among other locations, in the war on terror (Political News, 2005). Although Gonzales was not as hard driven as Ashcroft, he still carried the Patriot Act banner for the administration. Gonzales involved himself in several speaking engagements which endorsed his support of the Patriot Act (Gyan, 2005). An example of this can be seen in the transcripts of an interview between Gonzales and Fox commentator Chris Wallace on July 24, 2005. When asked about the Patriot Act and the ensuing negotiations occurring for the sequel, Gonzales said,

> Well, what I've said is I would welcome clarifications and certain reforms in The Patriot Act. But I've always been very clear, very consistent in

saying that I could not support provisions or changes, amendments to the act that would weaken the act, that would make it more difficult to protect America against these kinds of threats and against these kinds of attacks. And so we now have... (Wallace, 2005)

As the House Representatives met to deliberate a possible new bill, there continued to be the echo of dissent to renewing sections of the Patriot Act. John Podesta, a visiting professor of law at Georgetown University Law Center, spoke to how Sections 203, 206, 217, and 218 of the "big sixteen," among others, had been controversial prior to the Patriot Act. In his article, "USA Patriot Act, The Good, the Bad, and the Sunset," Podesta stated:

> Many of the electronic surveillance provisions in the Patriot Act faced serious opposition prior to September 11 from a coalition of privacy advocates, computer users, and elements of high-tech industry. The events of September 11 convinced many in that coalition and overwhelming majorities in Congress that law enforcement and national security officials need new legal tools to fight terrorism. But we should not forget what gave rise to the original opposition... (2002)

Some signaled a welcome to Patriot Act change. Johnny Sutton, a United States Attorney for the Western District of Texas, spoke strongly for the renewal of section 203(b). Sutton believed that this section, which brought down the "wall" between information sharing between intelligence agencies, had been instrumental in taking down several terrorist cells inside the United States. One of the strongest testimonials for the need for continued information sharing came during the Patriot Act renewal process. This information came in the form of the revelation of government knowledge of al-Qaeda operatives within the U.S. pre-9/11.

Thomas Ryan brought forward several shocking but illuminating pieces of information in his article, "The Writing on 'The Wall'." One of the first elements of this article was the introduction to "Able Danger." Able Danger was a highly secretive army intelligence unit which operated from 1998-2001 (Ryan, 2005). The revelation that Able Danger brought to public light was that prior to the 9-11 attacks this secret unit, whose mission was to investigate al-Qaeda, had identified Mohamed Atta within the U.S. (Ryan, 2005). Mohamed Atta, an al-Qaeda operative, led four other terrorists in crashing American Airlines Flight 11 into the North Tower of the World Trade Center (Ryan, 2005). How the Able Danger story affected the fight over the Patriot Act was as follows: Intelligence agents were unable to give their information concerning Mohamed Atta to the FBI because of a pre-existing "wall" forbidding the exchange of information between agencies. This "wall," constructed during the Jimmy Carter administration and strengthened during the Bill Clinton presidency, limited the cooperation allowed between intelligence agencies and domestic agencies (Ryan, 2005). The Able Danger story has taken on a unique place within the historical context of events as one of the most relevant to the argument of information sharing while also receiving an uncommonly low amount of media coverage.

Viet Dinh, a recent assistant attorney general and major constructionist of the original Patriot Act, spoke of the law's ability to address inadequacies of the past:

> The Patriot Act, he [Dinh] says, 'does not enlarge the overall net of surveillance of criminal or terrorist conversations, rather it patches the holes in that net arising from new technology and inefficiencies within government. It doesn't matter how big your net is if the fish can get away through the holes.' (Curry, 2004)

The House Rules Committee scheduled several meetings in which amendments to, deletions from, and other various alterations of the Patriot Act took place. Representative Otter submitted H.R. 1526, known as The Security and Freedom Ensured Act of 2005 or "SAFE Act" on April 6, 2005 (H.R. 1526 I.H., 2005). This bill was full of civil liberty provisions designed to limit the Patriot Act's ability, in the minds of its creators, to violate citizen rights (CDT, n.d., *Security*).

During the House Committee's deliberations, Representative Bernie Sanders suffered a defeat in bringing forward his amendment, Freedom to Read Act, which would have made libraries and bookstores exempt from Sections 215 and 501 of the Patriot Act (ACLU, 2005). Although Sanders' amendment had won a funding vote earlier in the year, the House Committee would not let the amendment on the table for an up or down vote. Both the Freedom to Read Act and the SAFE Act were attempts to both ensure civil liberties, as well as create a piece of legislation that moderate, if not a few conservative, politicians would endorse. Past examples of attempts to curb the government's legal authority had met with little fanfare. The bill, H.R. 3171, known as the Benjamin Franklin True Patriot Act, had been submitted on September 24, 2003. This bill was championed by Representatives Dennis Kucinich (D-OH) and Ron Paul (R-TX), and was designed to gut more than 11 controversial sections of the Patriot Act 90 days after it went into effect (Answers.com, 2006). The large-scale eradication style of bill construction by Kucinich and associates went too far to be embraced by many.

More recent Patriot Act reductionists took great pains to temper Patriot Act limitations within their bills to avoid a perception of trying to overreach. Democrats specifically felt that bills such as the Freedom to Read and the SAFE Act were viable alterations to the Patriot Act, and a defeat on these bills would not be accepted lightly.

No one was angrier over the defeat of the Freedom to Read Act than co-sponsor Representative Anna Eshoo. Eshoo, on June 15, 2005, stood with 198 Democrats, 38 Republicans, and 1 Independent to pass an amendment on H.R. 2862 entitled, Science, State, Justice & Commerce Appropriations Act for FY 2006, which would limit the scope of the Patriot Act authority to access library records (Shapiro, 2005, June 15). This victory would be short lived when on July 21, 2005, her co-sponsored bill with Bernard Sanders was refused consideration by a Republican majority in the House (Shapiro, 2005, July 21). Eshoo, in anger, vented, "This is an outrageous use of procedural baloney to silence reasonable opposition." Eshoo continued, "There's bipartisan support for this amendment in the House and the majority knows it --- that's the only reason this amendment isn't being considered" (Shapiro 2005, July 21). Lisa Graves, Senior Counsel for the ACLU, commented on the defeat by saying,

> Sadly, the House leadership has continuously blocked efforts to allow fair-minded lawmakers to make meaningful changes to the Patriot Act. When the House Judiciary Committee considered this issue, partisan politics trumped a commitment to freedom. Yesterday, the Rules Committee showed deference not to the Constitution, but again to party politics. When it comes to protecting the Bill of Rights and our freedoms, lawmakers must engage in a full and open debate, and the leadership has effectively prevented that. (ACLU, 2005)

An opposing view to the Freedom to Read Act came from the trio of Alane Kochems, Paul Rosenzweig, and James Jay Carafano, all three well-known scholars in the area of national security. Their article, "Should Libraries Become Terrorist Sanctuaries?", challenges the Freedom to Read Act as a direct hindrance in the war on terror. Furthermore, they assert that the act would make places such as libraries havens for terrorists. The primary theme of the article is that the Freedom to Read Act plays off the false assumption that the Patriot Act is overly expansive and without safeguards. Included within the text is an attack on the credibility of alleged abuses of the Patriot Act cited by the ACLU (Kochems, Rosenzweig, & Carafano, 2005). Other articles have been forwarded that defend different sections of the Patriot Act on the similar basis that civil rights groups over-magnify the threat of potential government abuse via the Patriot Act (MacDonald, 2005).

House Democratic Leader Nancy Pelosi spoke on the final day of deliberations on the Patriot Act reauthorization. Pelosi stated that as far as she was concerned, the Patriot Act was law and only the sunsetting sections were up for debate before the House (Daly & Crider, 2005). Pelosi said that she had originally supported the Patriot Act in 2001 because of the sunset provisions and a promise of strict oversight. However, because she felt that due to the lack of oversight, in combination with a proposed 10-year extension of the sunset provisions, she stated she would be voting against the reauthorization bill (Daly & Crider, 2005).

Also speaking on July 21, 2005, was House Judiciary Chairman James Sensenbrenner who had authored a House bill known as H.R. 3199. This bill had previously passed the House Judiciary Committee on July 13, 2005, by a vote of 23-14 (Lungren & Shawn, 2005, July 13). The committee had listened to dozens of potential amendments before adopting some into the final product (H.R. 3199) during an 11-hour presentation session (Lungren & Shawn 2005, July 13). Now Sensenbrenner stood before the House of Representatives in an attempt to win final support for his bill. Sensenbrenner highlighted before the House that H.R. 3199 was the product of four years of rigorous oversight which included, but was not limited to, the following: hearing testimony, Inspector General reports, briefings, and oversight letters (Lungren & Shawn, 2005, July 21). After highlighting changes to Section 215 that would be likeable to civil liberties- conscious individuals, Sensenbrenner, in defense of the Patriot Act, concluded:

> ...for too long, opponents of the Patriot Act have transformed it into a grossly distorted caricature that bears no relation to the legislation itself. The Patriot Act has been misused by some as a spring board to launch limitless allegations that are not only unsubstantiated, but false and irresponsible. Our constituents expect and deserve substantive consideration on this vital issue, and I hope today's debate reflects the bipartisan seriousness the issue demands. (Lungren & Shawn, 2005, July 21)

Comments that struck at the heart of the argument proffered by many civil liberties groups came from Majority Leader Tom DeLay. DeLay, who also spoke on the final day of deliberations in the House, stated:

> I rise in strong support of the reauthorization and extension of the USA Patriot Act....Opponents of the Patriot Act suggest that we have an either/or choice when it comes to safety and civil liberties....To date, 4 years after Big brother supposedly imposed this draconian usurpation of liberty on the American people, no one has suggested a single instance of a single person's civil liberties being violated. This point bears repeating: no one, not the Justice Department, not the ACLU, not even moveon.org has produced evidence of a single, verifiable Patriot Act civil liberties abuse. It just hasn't happened. (151 Cong. Rec. 100)

Out of the smoke of the House debates, and on the heels of recent terrorist bombings in London (McMullan, 2005), on July 21, 2005, House Bill 3199 emerged victorious. The bill was passed by a vote of 257-171 (Barrett, 2005). In the end, 14 Republicans voted against the renewal in contrast to 43 Democrats who crossed party lines to vote for the act renewal (Barrett, 2005).

A pivotal component of H.R. 3199 was that it made permanent 14 of the "big sixteen" sections, and put 10-year sunset renewals on Section 206 and Section 215 (Barrett, 2005; Johnson, 2005). It is interesting to note that the decision to lengthen the life of the sunset provisions was a battle within itself. Working late into the night, lawmakers barely defeated a 4-year sunset package brought forth by Representative Rick Boucher. Supporting Boucher, Representative Dana Rohrabacher alluded that her support for the Patriot Act was not only based on necessity, but also on the ability to rein in the law in a safer time (Barrett, 2005).

Specifically, H.R. 3199, under its official title, USA Patriot and Terrorism Prevention Reauthorization Act of 2005, was introduced by Representative Sensenbrenner. Officially, Sections 3, 4, and 5 repeal the sunset provisions as stated in the Uniting and Strengthening America by Providing Appropriate Tools Required to Interpret and Obstruct Terrorism (USA Patriot) Act of 2001. Section 6 is an amendment of the original Section 203(b) and requires additional documentation of intelligence information sharing (H.R. 3199 I.H.). Section 7 amends the original Section 207 of the Patriot Act to make it pertain to people "who are not a United States person" (H.R. 3199 I.H.). Section 8 amends Section 215 and Section 501 of the Patriot Act. These amendments require the FBI director to personally approve requests for records, such as those kept by libraries and bookstores, of those individuals believed to be involved in terrorist activities (H.R. 3199 I.H.). This amendment was first sponsored by Representative Jeff Flake and passed by a vote of 402-26 (Barrett, 2005; Johnson, 2005). Democrat Committee Leader John Conyers was not content with the 10-year sunset on Sections 206 and 215 saying, "that while I support the majority of the 166 provisions of the Patriot Act," the extensions could lessen accountability. "Ten years is not a sunset; 10 years is semi-permanent" (Fox News, 2005).

The League of Women Voters, a civil rights organization established in the 1950s to oppose Senator Joseph McCarthy, voiced their dismay at the House of Representatives' refusal to give further debate to the Freedom to Read Act (Burnett & Skoglund, 2005). Others echoed the feeling of inadequacy with the House of Representatives' 10-year extension on Section 215, while also being disheartened that certain permanent sections of the Patriot Act were not altered. In fact, the 10-year sunset provision in the House bill would serve as an unrelenting albatross to future deliberations. For those who were dismayed over the House version, it was their hope that the Senate would be a saving grace in the battle over the Patriot Act.

References

151 Cong. Rec. 100, 6242 (2005). (remarks of Tom DeLay). Retrieved August 31, 2005, from http://frwebgate.access.gpo.gov/cgi-bin/getpage.cgi?dbname=2005_record&page= H6242&position=all

ABC News. (n.d.). *Profile: Attorney General Alberto Gonzales: From humble beginnings to Harvard to the White House.* Retrieved August 28, 2005, from http://abcnews.go.com/ Politics/Inauguration/story?id=241596

American Civil Liberties Union [ACLU]. (2005, July 21). *House Rules Committee shuts out needed Patriot Act reform, yet adds "smokeless tobacco" amendment.* Retrieved July 30, 2005, from http://www.aclu.org/safefree/general/20257prs20050721.html

Answers.com. (2006). *Benjamin Franklin True Patriot Act.* Retrieved March 25, 2006, from http://www.answers.com/Benjamin%20Franklin%20True%20Patriot%20Act

Barrett, T. (2005, July 22). *House approves renewal of Patriot Act*. Retrieved August 17, 2005, from http://www.cnn.com/2005/POLITICS/07/21/patriot.act/index.html

Burnett, J., & Skoglund, R. (2005, August 15). *The women's league of voters*. Retrieved August 25, 2005, from http://www.wiltonlwv.org/index_files/votersep.htm

Center for Democracy & Technology [CDT]. (n.d.). *Patriot Act overview*. Retrieved August 19, 2005, from http://www.cdt.org/security/usapatriot/overview2005.php

Center for Democracy & Technology. [CDT]. (n.d.). *Security & freedom legislation (109th)*. Retrieved March 24, 2006, from http://www.cdt.org/legislation/109/4

Curry, T. (2004, November 12). *Patriot Act renewal up to Congress*. Retrieved August 17, 2005, from http://msnbc.msn.com/id/6469357/

Daly, B., & Crider, J. (2005, July 21). *Pelosi statement on extension of USA Patriot Act*. Retrieved August 28, 2005, from http://www.democraticleader.house.gov/press/articles.cfm?pressReleaseID=1100

Gyan, J., Jr. (2005, August 1). *Gonzalez defends USA Patriot Act*. Retrieved September 2, 2005, from http://www.infowars.com/articles/ps/patriot_act_gonzales_defends_act.htm

H.R. 1526 I.H.: 1st Session 109th Congress. (2005, April 6). *Security and Freedom Ensured Act of 2005 (SAFE) Act*. Retrieved March 25, 2006, from http://thomas.loc.gov/cgi-bin/query/z?c109:H.R.1526:

H.R. 3199 I.H.: 1st Session 109th Congress. (2005, July 11). *USA PATRIOT and Terrorism Prevention Reauthorization Act of 2005 (Introduced in House)*. Retrieved August 19, 2005, from http://thomas.loc.gov/cgi-bin/query/z?c109:H.R.3199:

FOX News. (2005, July 22). House oks extending patriot act. Retrieved August 19, 2005, from http://www.foxnews.com/story/0,2933,163219,00.html

Johnson, G. (2005, July 22). *House votes to extend Patriot Act.* Retrieved August 19, 2005, from http://gwillard.home.att.net/patriotgames05.htm#extend

Kochems, A., Rosenzweig, P., & Carafano J. J. (2005, June 23). *Should libraries become terrorist sanctuaries?* Retrieved July 1, 2005, from http://www.heritage.org/Research/ HomelandDefense/wm772.cfm

Lungren, J., & Shawn, T. (2005, July 13). *House Judiciary Committee approves Patriot Act Reauthorization.* Retrieved August 28, 2005, from http://judiciary.house.gov/newscenter. aspx?A=533

Lungren, J., & Shawn, T. (2005, July 21). *Sensenbrenner House floor statement on USA Patriot Act Reauthorization legislation.* Retrieved July 22, 2005, from http://judiciary.house.gov/ media/pdfs/PatriotFJSfloorstate72105.pdf

MacDonald, H. (2005, April 8). *The Patriot Act is no slippery slope: Protecting ourselves doesn't lead to tyranny.* Retrieved April 8, 2005, from http://www.city-journal.org/ html/eon_04_08_05hm.html

McMullan, M. (2005, July 25). *Patriot Act provisions renewed in House.* Retrieved July 27, 2005, from http://www.idsnews.com/news/story.php?id=30346

Podesta, J. (2002). *USA Patriot Act: The good, the bad, and the sunset.* Retrieved August 17, 2005, from http://www.abanet.org/irr/hr/winter02/podesta.html

Political News. (2005, February 4). *Gonzales sworn in as US attorney general (AFP).* Retrieved August 28, 2005, from http://www.political-news.org/breaking/6057/gonzales-sworn-in-as-us-attorney-general

Ryan, T. (2005, August 22). *The writing on "the wall."* Retrieved August 23, 2005, from
http://www.frontpagemag.com/Articles/ReadArticle.asp?ID=19218

Shapiro, L. (2005, June 15). *Eshoo fights for freedom to read.* Retrieved August 28, 2005, from
http://eshoo.house.gov/index.php?option=com_content&task=view&id=79&Itemid=159

Shapiro, L. (2005, July 21). *Eshoo seeks constructive debate on Patriot Act.* Retrieved August 28, 2005, from http://eshoo.house.gov/index.php?option=com_content&task=view&id= 74&Itemid=159

Wallace, C. (2005, July 24). *Transcript: AG Alberto Gonzales on 'FOX News Sunday'.* Retrieved August 17, 2005, from http://www.foxnews.com/story/0,2933,163494,00. html

CHAPTER 15

The Senate

THE SECOND LEG OF THE journey to a Patriot Act sequel led to the Senate. More specifically, the committees within the Senate which heard and debated what form of the Patriot Act they wanted to represent this branch of the government.

The Senate deliberations were as colorful and controversial as anything seen in the House of Representatives; however, the game was the same. The Bush administration wanted a full authorization of the sunsetting provisions of the Patriot Act (Chen, 2005). The question was, would the Senate simply go along or break out with new limits on the Patriot Act? What effect would four years of the Patriot Act have on this branch of the government? Of the several committees that heard the Patriot Act bills and debate, a number of new and old faces emerged immediately. Senator Pat Roberts, a staunch conservative and Patriot Act supporter, chaired the Senate Intelligence Committee. It was this committee that had previously been fundamental in many of the surveillance provisions in the first Patriot Act (Abramson, 2005). Senator Arlen Specter replaced the senator from Utah, Orrin Hatch, who had been instrumental in hashing out a final resolution on the Patriot Act's first time around. Specter, seen as a moderate Republican and sometimes political lone wolf, had already alluded to his desire to limit the Patriot Act's power (Abramson, 2005).

In June of 2005, the Senate Intelligence Committee passed forward a bill for further Senate discussion which revised the Patriot Act to allow individuals to challenge administrative orders. The bill passed by a vote of 11-4 (Kellman, 2005). The legislation would renew almost all of the sunsetting provisions and expand government search powers. Senators Jay Rockefeller and Dianne Feinstein feared the extra powers and hoped for additional trimming of the bill when it was heard later on the Senate floor (Kellman, 2005).

The overriding concern within the Senate Intelligence bill was that the government would now have the power to issue their own subpoenas, minus permission from a judge to collect information and records (Corcoran, 2005). Civil liberties groups, such as the ACLU, saw the Roberts' bill as a deliberate attempt to alter what they believed was a growing movement to minimize the authority contained in the Patriot Act (Corcoran, 2005).

The Patriot Act was then heard in other committees, such as the Senate Select and Judiciary Committees. Scrutiny over the sunset provisions increased as the bill got closer to the finished product.

The Senate Judiciary Committee conducted hearings that looked at the SAFE Act. Other than the Freedom to Read Act, which had a short lived victory in the House of Representatives, the SAFE Act was considered the most comprehensive bill to reduce government power (Chen, 2005). While this was in no way meant to take away from other Senate bills that were presented during Senate deliberations, the SAFE Act was, for many, symbolic of the " hero on the white horse," coming to save the day. The SAFE Act (S. 737), whose counterpart in the House was H.R. 1526, was a bipartisan bill championed by Senators Dick Durbin, Larry Craig, Russ Feingold, and Ken Salazar. Based in part over concerns about contentious sections of the Patriot Act, the SAFE Act was advanced as a bill that would place more accountability on the Patriot Act while allowing the law to operate (Durbin, 2005, April 4). The Durbin group recognized that concerns over civil liberties had sparked 375 cities to pass resolutions showing concern in regard to the uncontrolled power of the Patriot Act (Durbin, 2005, April 4). Senator Larry Craig stated that the Justice Department had refused to converse with them on the subject of the SAFE Act, and had threatened to veto the bill (Pulliam, 2004). Craig observed that the SAFE Act had received the endorsement of a wide array of organizations including: American Conservative Union, the Gun Owners of America, the American Civil Liberties Union, the League of Women Voters, and the American Library Association [ALA] (Pulliam, 2004).

While pleas were being made for the consideration of the SAFE Act, a counterargument was made in testimony by Deputy Attorney General James B. Comey. While pointing out to committee members the need to reauthorize the Patriot Act, Comey emphasized the need to educate people on the law. Specifically, "People in this country don't understand the Patriot Act, and people who understand it don't oppose it" (Pulliam 2004). Comey stated that the SAFE Act was an unneeded piece of legislation as there had been no directly reported cases of abuse involving the Patriot Act (Pulliam, 2004).

James X. Dempsey, who had lobbied to include civil rights provisions in the original Patriot Act (Abramson, 2005), spoke before the Senate Judiciary Committee on May, 10, 2005, as a supporter of the SAFE Act. Relaying the focus of the SAFE Act, that is, the surveillance provisions of Section II, Dempsey laid out the traditional protections of the Fourth Amendment by saying,

> First, as a general rule, searches and seizures and access to private data should be subject to prior judicial approval. Second, a warrant or subpoena must describe with particularity the items to be seized or disclosed. Third, individuals should have notice when the government acquires their private data, either before, during or after the search. Finally, if the government overreaches or acts in bad faith, there should be consequences, including making sure the government does not use anything improperly seized. (Dempsey 2005)

While Dempsey admitted that at times there are exceptions to one of these rules, he did not agree that there should be a blanket exception for all four which is given in the Patriot Act (Dempsey, 2005). What Dempsey advocated in his support of the SAFE Act was what he felt was a middle ground. Under the SAFE Act, the government would retain all the provisional authority under the original Patriot Act, however higher standards would be put in place for allowing the implementation of many of the Title II provisions (Dempsey, 2005).

Other bills which were debated included:

> S. 316 - A bill submitted by Senator Feingold to limit authority on delay notice search warrants.

> S. 1266 - A bill forwarded by Senator Pat Roberts to clarify definitions in the FISA Act of 1978, and reauthorize a provision of the Intelligence Reform and Terrorism Prevention Act of 2001. This bill would ultimately give permanent authorization to certain provisions within the Patriot Act (CDT, n.d.).

S. 317 - A bill submitted by Senator Feingold to limit access by the government to library records (CDT, n.d.).

S. 1389 - A bill brought forth by Senator Arlen Specter to reauthorize and improve the USA Patriot Act (CDT, n.d.).

S. 2476 - A bill brought forth by Senator Jon Kyl meant to repeal the sunset provisions of the current USA Patriot Act (Pulliam, 2004).

Including the SAFE Act, Senator Russ Feingold had three bills out for consideration (Fisher, 2005). This time around, the senator was more prepared and, more importantly, not alone in his opposition to the Patriot Act. Robert O'Harrow, Jr. chronicled the 2001 plight of the senator he called "A liberal who routinely bucks pressure from his own party..." in his 2002 *Washington Post* article, "Six Weeks in Autumn." Following the terrorist attacks of 9-11, Feingold found himself overwhelmed by those who wished to legislate quickly and those who feared losing more civil rights by legislating too slowly (O'Harrow, 2002).

The landscape had changed for the better for Feingold, but would it be enough to bring about the fundamental changes that he and his colleagues wanted? Would the senator from Wisconsin, who had worked with senators like John McCain to bring about bipartisan landmark campaign finance reform law (Fisher, 2005), be able to persuade a Republican controlled Congress to temper the Patriot Act?

In the end, a little bit of everything happened. Officially, Senate bill S. 1389, entitled the USA Patriot Improvement and Reauthorization Act of 2005, was passed (Lilienthal, 2005). This bill, authored by Senators Arlen Specter, Dianne Feinstein, and Jon Kyl, was passed unanimously by a voice vote at the end of the final day of the Senate session on July 29, 2005 (Eggen, 2005; Schepers, 2005). The bill reauthorized 14 of 16 sunsetting provisions. However, the Senate version of the bill placed tighter restrictions on Section 206 and 215 by making them sunset in 4 years, instead of 10 years, as was the House's version (Eggen, 2005). The Senate version also raised the requirements for the seizure of business records and required that individuals must be notified of a search warrant within 7 days unless an extension is directly approved by a judge (Eggen, 2005).

While the SAFE Act failed to make it into law, Senator Feingold felt that a middle ground that he could subscribe to had been reached. On the Senate floor on the day of the passage of S. 1389, Feingold said:

> Mr. Chairman, I want to say a few words about this bill and about the compromise that was worked out last night…I believe the end result of the negotiations process has been a positive one—and one that I can support.…But I could not have supported your bill without additional changes on the key issues that I and others have been concerned about. (Feingold, 2005)

Specifically, Feingold alluded to restrictions placed on Section 215 by the implementation of higher standards, sneak and peek searches, and judicial review of National Security Letters. While the bill did not do everything the SAFE Act would have, Feingold was content (Feingold 2005).

SAFE Act co-author, Dick Durbin, while noting that he had not gotten everything that he wanted in the new bill, was generally happy with the end result, and praised Chairman Specter for his leadership (Durbin, 2005, July 21). A mixed review came from civil rights organizations. The League of Women Voters thought the failure of detailed analysis of the SAFE Act was tantamount to a rush to action (Skoglund & Burnett, 2005). Groups like the ACLU praised the efforts of the Senate while simultaneously condemning the end product (ALA, 2005). Tim Edgar, National Security Policy Counsel for the ACLU, following the passage of the Senate bill, stated:

> Senators worked hard, in good faith, to improve the Patriot Act and this bill takes some steps in the right direction, although significant flaws remain…Although we cannot endorse it, this bill is substantially better, from a civil liberties perspective, than the House bill. (Inouye, 2005)

With both branches of government having their prospective Patriot Act bills, the stage was set for the final act. For the moment, politicians enjoyed the fall session break, while the world waited for a future House/Senate conference and a final Patriot Act product. That moment would not last long as a new storm was brewing.

References

Abramson, L. (2005, July 18). *The Patriot Act: Political players*. Retrieved September 1, 2005, from http://www.npr.org/templates/story/story.php?storyId=4754492&sourceCode=RSS

American Library Association [ALA]. (2005, August 5). *Senate passes Patriot Act Reauthorization.* Retrieved August 29, 2005, from http://www.lita.org/ala/alonline/ currentnews/newsarchive/2005abc/august2005abc/senateusapa.htm

Center for Democracy & Technology. [CDT]. (n.d.). *Security & freedom legislation (109th).* Retrieved March 24, 2006, from http://www.cdt.org/legislation/109/4

Chen, M. (2005, July 15). *Patriot Act reforms clash in Congress, public.* Retrieved August 29, 2005, from http://newstandardnews.net/content/index.cfm/items/2102

Corcoran, M. (2005, June 14). *Battle over Patriot Act set to take place in Boston.* Retrieved August 29, 2005, from http://www.jsons.org/media/storage/paper139/news/2005/06/03/ EmersonNews/Battle.Over.Patriot.Act.Set.To.Take.Place.In.Boston-957803.shtml? nore write200610032253&sourcedomain=www.jsons.org

Dempsey, J. X. (2005, May 10). *Statement of James X. Dempsey, executive director, Center for Democracy & Technology before the Senate Committee of the Judiciary.* Retrieved June 25, 2005, from http://www.cdt.org/testimony/ 20050510dempsey.pdf

Durbin, D. (2005, April 4). *Bipartisan group of senators introduce "safe act" to remedy problems in Patriot Act.* Retrieved August 30, 3005, from http://durbin.scnate.gov/ record.cfm?id=236435

Durbin, D. (2005, July 21). *Patriot Act bill includes reforms proposed by Senators Durbin and Craig.* Retrieved August 30, 2005, from http://durbin.senate.gov/record.cfm?id=241192

Eggen, D. (2005, July 30). Senate approves partial renewal of Patriot Act. [Electronic Version]. *The Washington Post,* p. A03. Retrieved August 17, 2005, from http://www. washingtonpost.com

Feingold, R. (2005, July 21). *Statement of U.S. Senator Russ Feingold at the Senate Judiciary Committee markup on the Patriot Act Reautho-*

rization. Retrieved August 30, 2005, from http://feingold.senate. gov/~feingold/statements/05/07/2005721526.html

Fisher, W. (2005, February 25). *Senator seeks to curb controversial "Patriot Act."* Retrieved August 30, 2005, from http://www.commondreams.org/cgi-bin/print.cgi?file=/ headlines05/0225-10.htm

Inouye, S. (2005, July 21). *Senate committee's positive steps on Patriot Act welcome, but flaws remain.* Retrieved August 31, 2005, from http://libertycoalition.net/aclu_on_senate_judiciarys_usa_patriot_reauthorization_bill

Kellman, L. (2005, June 8). *Senate gives FBI more Patriot Act power.* Retrieved July 4, 2005, from http://www.sfgate.com/cgi-bin/article.cgi?file=/n/a/2005/06/07/national/ w162204D49. DTL&type=printable

Lilienthal, S. (2005, September 2). *Reauthorization the USA Patriot Act: The battle moves to conference.* Retrieved September 2, 2005, from http://www.aim.org/guest_column_ print/3982_0_6_0/

O'Harrow, R., Jr. (2002, October 27). Six weeks in Autumn. [Electronic Version]. *The Washington Post,* p. W06. Retrieved January 1, 2005, from http://www. washingtonpost.com

Pulliam, D. (2004, September 22). *Justice official defends Patriot Act.* Retrieved August 29, 2005, from http://www.govexec.com/dailyfed/ 0904/092204dp2.htm

Schepers, E. (2005, August 20). *Good news, bad news on Patriot Act.* Retrieved August 27, 2005, from http://www.pww.org/article/articleview/7574/0/

Skoglund, R. & Burnett, J. (2005, August 30). *Patriot Act needs open evaluation.* Retrieved October 13, 2006, from http://www.wiltonlwv.org/index_files/votersep.htm

CHAPTER 16

The Creation of the "Coalition of Opposition"

THE STORM WAS HURRICANE KATRINA. This storm reeked tremendous devastation on the southeast part of the United States and forced Congress out of recess to deal with the allocation of emergency funds for victims and infrastructure. However another storm, a political storm, was brewing over the reauthorization of the Patriot Act, and this storm would last much longer than the winds of Katrina. In early November, a conference committee was formed to begin the difficult task of reconciling S. 1389 and H.R. 3199 into one bill that not only could the committee agree on, but also the majority of House and Senate members. Finally, the collective bill from Congress would be passed on for a signature by the President to make the renewal complete. The list of the probable members, called "conferees," included the following:

Senators

Arlen Specter (R-PA)	Orrin Hatch (R-UT)
Jon Kyl (R-TX)	Jeff Sessions (R-AL)
Mike DeWine (R-OH)	Pat Roberts (R-KS)
Pat Leahy (D-VT)	John Rockefeller (D-WV)
Carl Levin (D-MI)	Ted Kennedy (D-MA)

Representatives

James Sensenbrenner (R-5th, WI)	Peter Hoekstra (R-2nd, MI)
Howard Coble (R-6th, NC)	Lamar Smith (R-21st, TX)
Elton Gallegly (R-24th, CA)	Bob Goodlatte (R-6th, VA)
Steve Chabot (R-1st, OH)	John Conyers (D-14th, MI)
Howard Berman (D-28th, CA)	Rick Boucher (D-9th, VA)
Jerry Nadler (D-8th, NY)	

(Bill of Rights Defense Committee, 2005).

It was evident that an agreement would have to be struck between the House and Senate bills. Of particular interest was whether a new version of the Patriot Act would require sunset provision limitations and, if so, could everyone agree on a specific amount of time?

On November 9, 2005, the House voted unanimously to request conferees to place 4-year sunsets on certain sections of the Patriot Act (Glasstetter, 2005). This was considered a large concession to the 10-year sunsets that had previously been in H.R. 3199. It could be argued that a series of articles released on November 6, 2005, which chronicled the FBI's use of an excess of 30,000 National Security Letters yearly (Glasstetter, 2005), may have had an effect in the House decision to tighten the sunset provision time period. Democratic Representative John Conyers echoed concern over the reported 30,000 National Security Letters issued yearly since the creation of the Patriot Act, saying, "Unless the government believes there have been over 100,000 terrorists in our borders over the last 4 years, we have a serious civil liberties problem" (Conyers, 2005). The Representative from Michigan, who had criticized the Patriot Act, also warned against pet projects being placed in the Patriot Act renewal bill during the reauthorization process (Conyers, 2005).

A simplistic, but illuminating analogy on the potential damages of National Security Letters was forwarded by Jane Ahlin in her article, "USA Patriot Act Needs Revision and Oversight." In this article Ahlin (2005) presented a scenario she felt embodied the potential problems with National Security Letters and their usage through the Patriot Act as follows:

> Here's how it works. Let's say I call Ole's Fine Dry Cleaning and Tanning Salon to see how much it would cost to get my living room drapes

> cleaned. In the meantime, the FBI decides that Ole needs investigating because his cousin Sven called him from a hotel in Lebanon -- suspected of being a hangout for terrorists -- and Ole wired Sven some money. The FBI issues a national security letter to investigate Ole's telephone, Internet, and email records. No judge or court has to give the FBI permission....By issuing the national security letter for Ole, the FBI also has the right to investigate the telephone, Internet, and e-mail records of every citizen who has done business with Ole, or, like me, simply called his business on the phone....The information on hundreds or perhaps thousands of innocent Americans is in the FBI data bank. And it stays there. (¶ 4-5)

On November 10, 2005, the conference committee officially convened to begin the deliberation process. With the House's new agreement to a shorter sunset period for provocative sections of the law, some felt that the reauthorization could take place within a week (Lichtblau, 2005, November 11); however, this would not be the case. By November 16, 2005, the prospect of a speedy reauthorization appeared possible. The conference committee had reached an unofficial deal that would make the majority of the sunsetting sections permanent and would place added restrictions on Sections 206 and 215, pertaining to FISA court National Security Letters, and standards for monitoring "lone wolf" terrorists to a 7-year sunset (Kellman, L., 2005, November 16). One major factor did not go the way many civil liberties advocates would expect. Even though the House of Representatives had endorsed a 4-year sunset, the conference committee went with a 7-year sunset provision (ACLU, 2005). Representative James Sensenbrenner (R-5th, WI), had called the 7-year sunset of the conference agreement a compromise between the original 10-year sunset of the House bill (H.R. 3199) and the 4-year sunset of the Senate Bill (S. 1389) (Lungren & Shawn, 2005). However, within a short amount of time the bill began to fall apart. House Democrats presiding on the conference committee challenged the 7-year sunsets in the bill, as the entire House had already endorsed 4-year sunsets days previously (Kellman, L., 2005, November 16). Another bone of contention was the many "add-on" bills that Democrats were against, which included: measures to lower the number of federal appeals in state court decisions, 20-year prison sentences for sex offenders who failed to properly register, and adding additional security to courthouses (Kellman, L., 2005, November 16).

The ACLU scorned the tentative deal, officially titled as the "Patriot Reauthorization Act Conference Report," by saying that it was renewing almost all the sunsetting provisions without making adequate modifications. Within the litany of complaints on the law by the civil liberties organization was highlighted the disparity of the House and Senate support for a 4-year sunset provision and the 7-year sunset provision constructed by the conference committee (ACLU, 2005).

It would be naïve to say that the Patriot Reauthorization Act Conference Report was the only factor that divided the conference panel. During the conference committee process, six Senators initially stepped forward threatening to halt the process. The dissenting congressional members included Sen. Russ Feingold D-WI, Sen. Larry Craig R-ID, Sen. Dick Durbin D-IL, Sen. John Sununu R-NH, Sen. Ken Salazar D-CO, and Sen. Lisa Murkowski R-AK (Holland, 2005, November 17). Working together, these politicians would comprise the inner core of the "Coalition of Opposition" to the renewal process. These members had unsuccessfully attempted to pass bills such as the SAFE Act, and had already voiced strong opinions that the Patriot Act needed to be tempered (CBS, 2005).

While differing ideologies within the conference committee existed from the onset, certain provisions that had originally been in the Senate version of the renewal bill were now missing in the conference committee draft. Most notably, the compromise bill had removed the mandated judicial review for officials who used the Patriot Act to collect sensitive records. Additionally, the 7 to 30-day notification of sneak and peek warrants usage was also missing (CBS, 2005). Seeing that an impasse was likely to occur on a conference committee report, which, at that point in time, did not have a single signature, Committee Chairman Arlen Specter vowed to try and deal with the problem (Holland, 2005, November 17). The Thanksgiving holiday threatened to slow the legislative process more, and although senators like Senate Majority Leader Bill Frist, R-TN, had urged the committee to take action before the break, it was not to be. With the conference committee in recess for the holiday, in what was termed by some as, "…a mid-November rebellion in both houses" (Schepers, 2005, ¶ 9), time continued to tick away. The conference committee would officially reconvene on December 12, 2005, with a mere 15 working days to reach a compromise (Hudson, 2005; Schepers, 2005). Would this be enough time? For those who opposed the Patriot Act, the clock would now be another ally in the fight to see the sun set on portions of this confrontational law (Hudson, 2005).

As time wound down on the renewal of the Patriot Act, professionals and academics alike weighed in on issues related to the law. James J. Carafano, Senior Research Fellow for National Security and Homeland Security, along with Alane Kochems, Policy Analyst for National Security and Defense, reported on some deficiencies of the Patriot Act in their Heritage Foundation article titled, "Congress Poised to Pass Patriot Act Provisions." Specifically, they reaffirmed the 9-11 Commission's report which warned of pork barrel spending and flawed disbursements of homeland security grants (Carafano & Kochems, 2005). However, even with the weak points within the law, they felt for the sake of national security that procrastination at the legislative level on the Patriot Act was not prudent.-

> Congress needs to act now. As we speak, terrorism investigations are ongoing. The last thing law enforcement agents need is an "authority gap" when they don't know what they can legally do until new legislation is passed. The terrorists are not going to take a break over the holidays. We shouldn't have to either. (2005)

On December 8, 2005, Senate Judiciary Chairman Arlen Specter announced that there had been an agreement to change Sections 215 and 206 to 4-year sunsets to push the process forward (Holland, 2005, December 8). In addition, the compromise got rid of previous proposals that would have put into effect punishments for private individuals publicly disclosing government requests for records. The compromise also lacked some previously included penalties for terrorism-related crimes which would have expanded death penalty qualification in certain cases (Lichtblau, 2005, December 9). While Senator Feingold had been publicly expressing his intent to filibuster the renewal, Democratic Leader Harry Reid of Nevada stated his intent to vote against the law as it stood. (Holland, 2005, December 8). Feingold's strategy was that if at least 41 senators were convinced to oppose the renewal, a filibuster could not be stopped (Holland, 2005, December 8). Senator Patrick Leahy, D-VT, a major Senate contributor to the original law, stated that he would oppose the renewal of the Patriot Act as well, despite the addition of the 4-year sunset provisions (McCullagh & Broache, 2005). Senate Judiciary Chairman Arlen Specter, who stated that he also wished for more civil liberties guarantees in the law (Lichtblau, 2005, December 9), was still attempting to get the law passed, in what was now quickly approaching the eleventh hour. Specter said that a filibuster would most likely not succeed.

As time wound down without a resolution to the dilemma of how to get a majority of the conference committee to agree on a Patriot Act renewal

Living Under The Patriot Act: Educating A Society | 223

deal, House Democrat Nancy Pelosi further endorsed a stalemate by announcing her disapproval of the conference report and proposing that a 3-month extension might be necessary to allow conference members to come to a consensus (Riechmann, 2005). During the same time, the president was strongly urging a resolution to the Patriot Act renewal. In his weekly radio address, the president said, "In the war on terror, we cannot afford to be without this vital law for a single moment" (Riechmann, 2005, ¶ 2). The need to renew the Patriot Act was echoed by former FBI Director Louis Freeh. Freeh, now Vice Chairman and General Counsel for MBNA Corp., told listeners that people are more worried about issues such as identity theft, than they are about the Patriot Act. Specifically Freeh said, "For all the talk and concerns about the Patriot Act, the No. 1 privacy concern people have is about identity theft because of the tremendous damage it can do to their lives," (Jackson, 2005, ¶ 2). While stressing the need to protect civil liberties in times of war, Freeh called for the renewal of the Patriot Act to allow the government the ability to perform electronic searches in the name of national security (Jackson, 2005).

As the Able Danger story, even with its limited coverage, bolstered the need for a Patriot Act that allowed for the sharing of intelligence information, court rulings in the Sami al-Arian case threatened to create more questions about the viability of the Patriot Act. On December 6, 2005, a federal jury acquitted former Florida professor of computer engineering, Sami al-Arian, of conspiracy to commit murder.

The case, started in 2003 involving al-Arian and several alleged co-conspirators, was one of the first criminal terrorism cases to fundamentally hinge on the Patriot Act and its usage of the FISA Act (Dahlburg, 2005; Hsu & Eggen, 2005). After the jury had been presented evidence, which included 20,000 hours of phone conversations and hundreds of monitored faxes, the prosecutions' allegations that al-Arian was a ring leader of the Palestinian Islamic Jihad, orchestrating killings under cover as a university professor in the U.S., was not accepted by a jury (Dahlburg 2005; Hsu & Eggen, 2005). The terrorist group Palestinian Islamic Jihad has taken credit for the deaths of more than 100 individuals from Israel, as well as other occupied territories (Dahlburg, 2005).

In the al-Arian trial, jurors were presented with evidence by the prosecution in which Sami al-Arian conversed, by several means of communication, with other alleged conspirators about the mission and future of the terrorist group, and appeared to rejoice over completed suicide bombings that had killed Israelis (Stacy, 2005). At one point in the trial, a videotape of al-Arian publicly calling for "death to Israel" was presented (Dahlburg, 2005). Although the lawyer for al-Arian stated that his client lied about having ties to the terrorist group (Dahlburg, 2005), of the 17 counts that had been presented against al-Arian, 8 charges having to do with conspiracy to maim and murder were dismissed. However, jurors deadlocked on 9 charges having to do with money-laundering and aiding terrorists (Hsu & Eggen, 2005). Another charge leveled at al-Arian that jurists deadlocked on was the charge of illegally attempting to obtain citizenship in the United States (Dahlburg, 2005). Jurors in the case said that there was lots of evidence but not enough to directly link the defendant to the violent acts (Stacy, 2005). While Sami al-Arian would later plead guilty to conspiring to aid the Palestinian Islamic Jihad terrorist group, a charge that would entail a 46-57 month prison sentence and later deportation from the United States (Hsu, 2006), these events would not transpire until after the Patriot Act renewal. For the critical period in which decisions would be made on the Patriot Act renewal, the Sami al-Arian case, the case that had been exclaimed as an early triumph for the Patriot Act, was now tarnished.

On December 13, 2005, Attorney General Alberto Gonzales placed pressure on legislators to move the renewal process forward. Gonzales warned conference committee members that allowing the sunset provisions of the Patriot Act to expire would be detrimental to the war on terror (Cowan, 2005). At this point the House was expected to pass a compromise version; however, the Senate was strained over concerns with civil liberties. Again, the topic of a short extension to the Patriot Act was brought up as an option by the ever growing "Coalition of Opposition" which consisted of the additional Democratic senators: Patrick Leahy, Carl Levin, Edward Kennedy, John Rockefeller, and Debbie Stabenow. Three Republicans joined in opposition to accepting the 219-page conference report, including: John Sununu, Lisa Murkowski, and Larry Craig (McCullagh, 2005, December 12, *Patriot*). Gonzales and many members of the House rejected the temporary extension idea. Senator Russ Feingold was preparing to block the compromise bill in the Senate (Cowan, 2005). One of the many concerns that were raised about the compromise bill was that it was heavy laden with additional, if not unnecessary, pet projects (McCullagh, 2005, December 12, *Perspective*). Some of the additions to the Patriot Act renewal bill were: a reduction in the amount of illegal cigarettes that qualify as a federal crime, and new federal crimes for taking photos or videoing bridges, garages, tracks, warehouses, etc., if done with the intent to do harm. Another addition to the law included increased penalties for methamphetamine distribution to a minor. Under this law, individuals found guilty of selling meth to a minor could be put in prison for up to 20 years. The compromise bill would also expand the FBI's ability to obtain information using the Foreign Intelligence Surveillance Court (FISC) by making the person served with the warrant in a legal position where they must, "divulge any temporarily assigned network address or associated routing or transmission information" (McCullagh, 2005, December 12, *Perspective*). Also included in the bill were limitations on the amount of pseudoephedrine a person could buy, and government allocations of millions in funds for use in drug courts

On December 14, 2005, a group of civil liberties organizations spoke to legislators on Capitol Hill requesting an extension of the Patriot Act for the purpose of adding further civil liberties safeguards to the law. Speaking for the Electronic Privacy Information Center (EPIC), Marc Rotenburg presented investigative information, through the use of the Freedom of Information Act, to alleged reporting violations and poor oversight in the usage of the Patriot Act to date. From his presentation Rotenburg concluded, "Congress should not reauthorize the Patriot Act until these questions are resolved" (Chaddock, 2005, December 14, ¶ 3-4).

With the possibility of a House vote happening on the same day, and a Senate vote the following day, lead dissenter Senator Feingold reiterated his plan to stymie the renewal process in the Senate. Feingold stated that prior to Thanksgiving there was in excess of 50 votes to stop the bill; however, he was unsure if the dissension votes were still in place (Chaddock, 2005, December 14). Senate Minority Leader Harry Reid officially stated that he would vote against the Patriot Act renewal in the Senate. Technically, Reid stated that he would vote against "cloture," which is a Senate procedure requiring that 60 senators support a bill before it is allowed to be brought before the Senate for an up or down vote. In reality, a vote against "cloture" is the same as supporting a filibuster (Byrne, 2005).

If there was one thing about the Patriot Act renewal process, it was that the unexpected would be commonplace. Thursday, December 15, 2005, did see the House of Representatives pass the Patriot Act renewal bill. The vote in the House for renewal was 251-174 (Bonjean & Miller, 2005; Ferraro, 2005). Only 18 Republicans voted in opposition, while 44 Democrats voted for renewal.

Like history repeating itself, the House was the first to deal with the renewal of the Patriot Act. For those versed in the Patriot Act history, that may have been expected. It may have also been expected that civil liberty dissent would come primarily from the Senate, as it had the last time. What wasn't known was if a Feingold-led "Coalition of Opposition" would be strong enough to alter the events in the Senate from what had happened the first time around in the creation of the Patriot Act.

On December 16, 2005, the Senate voted on renewing the Patriot Act and, once again, a new piece of theatre in the ongoing saga of this law's renewal was seen. In contrast to the events of 2001, Feingold had found a literal army of 41 Democrats to follow his banner of opposition to the Patriot Act renewal. The opposition to the law's renewal in the Senate crossed political parties, if only marginally, as now 4 Republicans and 1 Independent also voted against renewal. The 4 dissenting Republicans were Chuck Hagel R-NE, Lisa Murkowski R-AK, Jon Sununu R-NH, and Larry Craig R- ID (Babington, 2005) In the end, the vote was 52-47 and against cloture (CNN.com, 2005; Daly, 2005).

For all intents and purposes, the Patriot Act had been defeated by not allowing the law to come up for a vote. In a parliamentary maneuver to allow for a possible future roll call, and possible salvation of the Senate portion of the Patriot Act renewal, Majority Leader Bill Frist purposely changed his vote from yes to no (Babington, 2005). The Patriot Act renewal defeat in the Senate was extremely devastating as time was rapidly running out. Repeated offers by Democrats for a 3-month temporary extension of the law, sponsored by Senator John Sununu and Patrick Leahy, to weed out alleged civil liberty shortcomings, was flatly refused by the president (Hunter, 2005). In fact, President Bush stated that he would veto any short term Patriot Act extension bills that came to his desk (CNN.com, 2005).

Further exacerbating the political landscape was the Senate delay to take final action on a $453.5 billion defense spending bill which covered items from Pentagon funding to possible Katrina relief (Chaddock, 2005, December 20). The defense spending bill was reportedly stalled because of issues dealing with the highly controversial subject of Alaska oil and gas exploration (Chaddock, 2005, December 20).

The fact was that the dissension over the Patriot Act was now spilling into other matters of government. Senator Russ Feingold, emboldened by his newfound support in opposition to the Patriot Act, now boldly challenged the president's authority on the topic of the Patriot Act by saying,

Living Under The Patriot Act: Educating A Society | 227

"He is the president, not a king" (Hunter, 2005, ¶ 11). Even the ever optimistic Judiciary Chairman Arlen Specter, R-PA, appeared to be acknowledging that a true impasse between senators had been established when he said, "I'm not going to make any allusions to changing any minds by additional debate" (Babington, 2005, ¶ 9). If Republicans had been banking on Patriot Act deadlines to pressure Democrats to cease obstruction tactics (Chaddock, 2005, December 20), they were sorely mistaken.

As with the 2001 creation of the Patriot Act, the entire period of the reauthorization of the law was denoted by several strong and unique impacting events that served, at times, to push legislation forward and, at other times, to slow the legislative process. It has been documented within this book how the 9-11 attacks served to stimulate legislators to act. It has also been documented how events during the first Patriot Act deliberations, such as the anthrax scare that temporarily shut down Congress, served to stimulate a need for not only enhanced national security, but also a need to hurry the legislative process. When the reauthorization of the Patriot Act four years later was undertaken, several key events have been documented as well. At the risk of being redundant, it is too important for readers to understand how specific factors fell into place in the reauthorization process not to reiterate them once again. These factors are listed in chronological order and represent the major pivotal moments of the Patriot Act renewal process that brought events to the Senate defeat of December 16, 2005.

1. In the 2004 presidential election, George Bush defeats John Kerry placing a pro-Patriot Act president in office during reauthorization period.
2. U.S. Ally Great Britain suffers subway bombing during House deliberations on the Patriot Act renewal process.
3. Able Danger story breaks detailing need for the sharing of intelligence information.
4. Story breaks that government has issued approximately 30,000 National Security Letters a year since the creation of the Patriot Act.
5. The Sami al-Arian verdict is announced. Prosecutors were unable to secure murder conspiracy charges.

The December 16, 2005, defeat of the Patriot Act in the Senate was not without its own specific event that would serve to fuel the passions of the moment. This event was the *New York Times* story that President Bush had secretly authorized the National Security Agency (NSA) to listen in on conversations of individuals, including Americans, without a court order or search warrant. Some civil liberties groups were also disturbed that the NSA, a group constructed to do surveillance on foreign soil, would be charged with conducting surveillance within the U.S. (Glasstetter & Berning, 2005). The timing of the *New York Times* article was advantageous to anti-Patriot Act factions. The *New York Times*, a left leaning, anti-Bush newspaper, had reportedly been keeping the NSA story under wraps for a year by request of the government. It was not until the pivotal vote on the Patriot Act renewal in the Senate that the story was released to the public. The article, which had included reflections of alleged Vietnam era surveillance violations, included an account of the secret program: initiated by the president in 2002, used the NSA in place of the FBI to monitor various forms of communications on possibly thousands of individuals in the U.S. without a warrant, and while some congressional leaders had been briefed about the program by the vice-president, it was left unclear within the article if proper disclosure of the secret program had been given by the administration to members of Congress (Risen & Lichtblau, 2005). The article had ample examples of specialists in the field who attested to having concerns with the secret eavesdropping program (Risen & Lichtblau, 2005).

The president was quick and thorough in his negative response to the actions of the Senate. In a year-end news conference, the president called the Senate's failure to renew the Patriot Act "inexcusable" and a "shameful act" (Branigin, 2005, ¶ 1). In voicing his frustration at the actions of a "minority of senators," President Bush stated:

> I happen to know there's an enemy there. And the enemy wants to attack us. That is why I hope you can feel my passion about the Patriot Act. It is inexcusable to say to the American people..."We're going to be tough on terror," but take away the very tools necessary to help fight these people. (Branigin, 2005, ¶ 9)

The president was unequivocal in placing Congress responsible for maintaining the Patriot Act as a tool to safeguard the nation from terrorism. In a stern admonishment to senators, the president warned:

> The terrorists want to attack America again and kill the innocent and inflict even greater damage than they did on September 11th -- and the Congress has a responsibility not to take away this vital tool that law

Living Under The Patriot Act: Educating A Society | 229

enforcement and intelligence officials have used to protect the American people. (Babington, 2005, ¶ 3)

The president also weighed in on the issue of the NSA wiretap program. Specifically, the president stated that the program looked at individuals with known links to al Qaeda, and that he had authorized the wiretaps 30 times for national security purposes (Epstein, 2005, December 19). The president stated that the NSA wiretap program is not only set up to be reviewed every 45 days; but also must be repetitiously renewed at the same time as the review takes place. The president also voiced his disapproval of the intelligence leak to the *New York Times* and said that an investigation by the Justice Department would be forthcoming (Epstein, 2005, December 19). Once again, the president spoke plainly about the seriousness of information leaks during wartime by saying, "My personal opinion is it was a shameful act for someone to disclose this very important program in a time of war. The fact that we're discussing this program is helping the enemy" (Epstein, 2005, December 19, ¶ 8).

While senators like John E. Sununu attempted to legitimize their opposition to the Patriot Act by saying that they really did not want the law to expire, but to just additionally alter it (Tirrell-Wysocki, 2005), senators like John Cornyn of Texas, spoke about the Patriot Act and American principles. Specifically Senator Cornyn said,

> The Patriot Act has served our national security in a way that is both consistent with our national values and with the protection of civil liberties -- in fact, the war on terror must be waged in a manner consistent with American principles. The hysteria over this legislation (and the fact that people have in too many instances not focused on the hard-fought attempts to balance security with civil-liberty concerns) is a disservice to the American people....The failure to reauthorize the Patriot Act returns Americans to the protections of September 10th tools. (Cornyn, 2005, ¶ 3-4)

The senator also spoke of the practicality and unobtrusiveness of the law by saying,

> The legislation enjoys a successful track record. In addition to helping prevent any terrorist attacks on American soil since September 11 and playing a crucial role in the dismantling of several terrorist cells within the United States, the Department of Justice inspector-general

has consistently found no systematic abuses of any of the act's provisions. (Cornyn, 2005, ¶ 8)

The topic of accountability and the lack of evidence of Patriot Act abuses were echoed by Frances Townsend, the assistant to the president for homeland security. In a prepared speech following the failure of the Senate to pass the renewal of the Patriot Act, Townsend said,

> The Patriot Act has been one of the most debated measures on Capitol Hill this year. Members of Congress have heard from 60 witnesses in 23 hearings. Extensive oversight has demonstrated conclusively that the act has played a vital role in the War on Terror, and there has never been a single verified abuse under the act. (Townsend, 2005)

Senator Larry Craig, R-ID, went straight to the radio airwaves to defend his Democratic collaboration to strike down the Patriot Act in the Senate. Speaking in an interview with conservative guru and radio specialist Rush Limbaugh, Craig stated the same response as his compatriot, Republican Senator John Sununu, in that he did not actually want to strike down the law, but to additionally alter it. Under examination from the seasoned Limbaugh, Craig alluded to his present dissatisfaction with the law and its ties to the political failure of his co-sponsored SAFE Act amendment (Limbaugh, 2005).

On December 21, 2005, the coalition of dissenting senators agreed to extend the Patriot Act for 6 months to allow for the law to remain active but still open for further alterations (Holland, 2005, December 21). Later the same day, a vote took place and the Senate passed a temporary extension of the Patriot Act for 6 months (Kellman, R., 2005). The Senate decision caused several ramifications. First, it changed the landscape completely as the compromise package created by the conference committee was for all intents and purposes made irrelevant. For the Patriot Act to be extended for 6 months, the House would have to pass a vote for the temporary extension, thus capitulating to Senate demands. While less than exuberant, the president was reported as expected to sign the extension (Kellman, R., 2005).

While the final grains of sand fell from the hourglass, the murkiness caused by the possibility of the temporary extension began to abound. Would Congress start from scratch on a renewal package? Would a temporary extension inevitably involve a new House and Senate bill, with possibly a newly created conference committee to create a compromise upon which both the House and Senate could agree? Probably the most looming question was, after 6 more months of debate, would the Patriot Act renewal still be in the same quagmire?

While questions floated about on the ramifications of a 6-month renewal, the Patriot Act timetable took another unexpected twist. This time, the change came from the House of Representatives; more specifically, from House Judiciary Committee Chairman Sensenbrenner. Sensenbrenner, a key player in the original Patriot Act, refused the Senate's 6- month extension (Forster, 2005; Kellman, L., 2005, December 23). Sensenbrenner put forth the proposal for a 1-month extension, stating that a shorter time period would force the Senate to deal with the renewal in a more timely matter (Kellman, L., 2005, December 23). This shorter extension period placed the president in an uncomfortable position of having to accept a 6-month extension he didn't want or a 1-month extension that was closer to an extension period he had previously stated he would veto. However, on December 26, 2005, the president relented, as well as the House and Senate, to Sensenbrenner's 1-month extension. Congress passed Senate Bill 2167, which extended the Patriot Act to February 3, 2006 (Pike, 2005).

While the extension kept the law alive, it failed to answer any long-term questions. In fact, the 6-month scenarios involving many challenges for the Patriot Act were still there, but now compacted into a 5-week period. Temporarily, if not permanently, the methamphetamine crime fighting supplemental rider had been eliminated. Law enforcement officials were saddened to see the potential funding that the legislation would have provided law enforcement stopped by the partisan politics over the renewal. The renewal bill rider would have placed additional regulations on ephedrine and pseudoephedrine production (Furber, 2005). In addition, if the original House-Senate compromise bill had passed, it would have restricted the amount of medicines containing ephedrine, a key component in the production of the illegal drug "meth," to 120 pills per day. Retailers of products such as Sudafed, NyQuil, and Benadryl, would have had to store the product behind a counter (Furber, 2005). The fate of the crime fighting and methamphetamine abuse assistance rider was taken from probable reality to possible theory, or worse, the scrap heap.

The year's end of political dealings was most eloquently stated by Robert Novak who called it "...a case study in poor gambling" (2005). This time around, under strict time constraints, Democrats refused to capitulate from opposition tactics and were willing to kill the Patriot Act in the face of future personal political fall-out, and it was the Republicans and the administration who found themselves making deals outside their initial desires. While Democrats were successful in curbing the Patriot Act renewal, the media's mantra of a bipartisan effort was more propaganda than reality. In reality, out of 48 Senate votes to deny an up or down vote on the compromise package, only 4 votes came from Republican Senators. In fact, even without the support of what has been labeled by some conservatives as the "four Republican defectors," (Lowry, 2005), there would have not been enough votes to stop the Senate Democratic filibuster. The truth of the matter was that Democrats had won the battle and the day.

As the dust settled, the victors began verbal celebrations. Senate Minority Leader Harry Reid shouted to friends, "We killed the Patriot Act" (Lowry, 2005). Senator Russ Feingold, with his newfound political muscle, was already alluding that the Patriot Act extension period would be inadequate, stating that coming off the congressional New Year's break, the Senate would not convene to begin deliberating until January 18th, nor the House until January 26th (Forster, 2005). In fact, a gloomy vision of 2006 was beginning to form around the Patriot Act.

In the wake of the Patriot Act extension, which was for all intents and purposes the same as a postponement, the legislation was at risk of being caught in the middle of several political storms. Most notably was the likelihood of extended congressional hearings into the warrantless surveillance authorized by the president that had been leaked to the *New York Times* during the critical Senate vote on the compromise package. To exacerbate the surveillance issue, a FISA court judge had resigned, reportedly over the issue of the presidential authorized eavesdropping (Epstein, 2005, December 24). With the recent news story released by the *New York Times* came a revitalization of a possible presidential impeachment (Epstein, 2005, December 24), which had been circling amongst Democrats since the Bush 2004 presidential victory.

In addition to looking at who had endorsed the Patriot Act and who was vacillating, or worse, playing politics with national security, conservative analysis was being made on the controversial statements of Democratic politicians. In a scathing analogy to the "We killed the Patriot Act" statement made by Senate Minority Leader Harry Reid, Rich Lowry, a National Review contributor, said Reid's statement was the same as saying, "I've got great news. I just set law enforcement back years and reinstated the arbitrary constraints that kept us from having any chance of preventing 9/11. Drinks are on me!" (Lowry, 2005).

It would be direct challenges to the Democratic opposition that would be needed to turn the tide. The question was, would there be enough time to rouse public support for national security to a level anywhere near the early post 9-11 levels? Would the throng of allegations of improprieties leveled at the administration by Democrats suffocate the Patriot Act? Would the president's slow rise in public opinion give him the clout to sway moderates to join Republican ranks? Of course, always looming, always possible, would another major terrorist attack on U.S. soil jolt the entire country back together, and could we pay that price?

References

Ahlin, J. (2005, November 13). *USA Patriot Act needs revisions and oversight.* Retrieved December 11, 2005, from http://www.in-forum.com/articles/printer.cfm?id=108393

American Civil Liberties Union [ACLU]. (2005, November 16). *Summary of Patriot Reauthorization Act conference report.* Retrieved November 21, 2005, from the ACLU Web site: http://www.aclu.org/safefree/patriot/21582res20051116.html

Babington, C. (2005, December 17). Renewal of Patriot Act is blocked in Senate. [Electronic Version]. *The Washington Post,* p. A01. Retrieved December 21, 2005, from http://www.washingtonpost.com

Bill of Rights Defense Committee. (2005, November 3). *Support Senate PATRIOT Act reauthorization bill.* Retrieved November 12, 2005, from http://www.bordc.org/ newsletter/bordc-act-alert43.php

Bonjean, R., & Miller, L. C. (2005). *House speaker Dennis Hastert applauds passage of the Patriot Act.* Retrieved December 15, 2005, from http://releases.usnewswire.com/ GetRelease.asp?id=58161

Branigin, W. (2005, December 15). Bush calls blockage of Patriot Act 'inexcusable'. [Electronic Version]. *The Washington Post.* Retrieved December 20, 2005, from http://www. washingtonpost.com/wp-dyn/content/article/2005/12/19/AR2005121900447.html

Byrne, J. (2005). *Reid to oppose Patriot Act, will join efforts to block bill.* Retrieved December 14, 2005, from http://rawstory.com/news/2005/Reid_to_oppose_Patriot_Act_will_ 1214.html

Carafano, J. J., & Kochems, A. (2005, December 2). *Congress poised to pass Patriot Act provisions.* Retrieved December 5, 2005, from the Heritage Foundation Web site: http://www.heritage.org/Research/HomelandDefense/wm930.cfm?renderfor print=1

CBS News. (2005, November 17). *Senators vow to block Patriot Act.* Retrieved December 5, 2005, from http://www.cbsnews.com/stories/2005/11/17/politics/main1054934.shtml

Chaddock, G. R. (2005, December 14). *An 11th hour drive to amend Patriot Act.* Retrieved December 14, 2005, from http://www.csmonitor.com/2005/1214/p03s02-uspo.htm

Chaddock, G. R. (2005, December 20). *Patriot Act, drilling in Arctic roil Senate.* Retrieved December 20, 2005, from http://www.csmonitor.com/2005/1220/p03s03-uspo.html? s=widep

CNN.com. (2005, December 16). *Patriot Act renewal fails in Senate.* Retrieved December 20, 2005, from http://www.cnn.com/2005/POLITICS/12/16/patriot.act/index.html

Conyers, J. (2005, November 11). *Conyers calls for changes in Patriot Act to protect nation's civil liberties.* Retrieved November 12, 2005, from http://www.commondreams.org/ news2005/1110-16.htm

Cornyn, J. (2005, December 20). Targeting the Patriot Act. [Electronic Version]. *The Washington Times.* Retrieved December 21, 2005, from http://www.washingtontimes. com/op-ed/20051219-093818-5234r.htm

Cowan, R. (2005, December 13). *Gonzalez pushes for Patriot Act renewal.* Retrieved December 14, 2005, from http://www.populistamerica.com/gonzalez_pushes_for_patriot_act_ renewal

Dahlburg, J. (2005, December 7). *Ex-professor acquitted in Patriot Act test case.* Retrieved December 20, 2005, from http://www.populistamerica.com/ex_professor_acquitted_in_ patriot_act_test_case

Daly, M. (2005, December 16). NW democrats hail Senate rejection of USA Patriot Act. [Electronic Version]. *Seattle Post-Intelligencer.* Retrieved December 20, 2005, from http://seattlepi.nwsource.com-

Epstein, E. (2005, December 19). *Bush defends eavesdropping, blasts senators on Patriot Act.* Retrieved December 21, 2005, from http://www.sfgate.com/cgi-bin/article.cgi?f=/c/a/ 2005/12/19/MNG9JGAFEV10.DTL

Epstein, E. (2005, December 24). *Bush to face tough questions over Patriot Act, spy orders.* Retrieved December 29, 2005, from http://www.sfgate.com/cgi-bin/article.cgi?f=/c/a/ 2005/12/24/MNGBOGD4FF1.DTL

Ferraro, T. (2005, December 14). *House votes to renew anti-terrorism Patriot Act.* Retrieved December 15, 2005, from http://www.redorbit.com/news/display/?id=330313

Forster, S. (2005, December 23). *Patriot Act deadline poses a challenge, Feingold says.* Retrieved December 29, 2005, from http://www.jsonline.com/story/index.aspx?id= 380215

Furber, M. (2005, December 28). *Feds' anti-meth bill dies with Patriot Act extension.* Retrieved December 29, 2005, from http://www.mtexpress.com/index2.php?ID=2005107130

Glasstetter, J. (2005, November 10). *Patriot Act: Conference committee can protect Americans' rights.* Retrieved November 12, 2005, from http://www.pfaw.org/pfaw/general/default. aspx?oid=19961

Glasstetter, J., & Berning, N. (2005, December 16). *Patriot Act stopped in Senate.* Retrieved December 20, 2005, from http://www.pfaw.org/pfaw/general/default.aspx?oid=20183

Holland, J. (2005, December 8). *House, Senate to extend Patriot Act*. Retrieved December 12, 2005, from http://www.news14charlotte.com/content/top_stories/nationalworld_news/?SecID=334&ArID=108544

Holland, J. J. (2005, November 17). Legislation renewing Patriot Act stalls. [Electronic Version]. *The Washington Post*. Retrieved November 21, 2005, from http://www.washingtonpost.com/wp-dyn/content/article/2005/11/17/AR2005111700844.html

Holland, J. J. (2005, December 21). *Senators near deal to extend Patriot Act*. Retrieved December 22, 2005, from http://abcnews.go.com/Politics/wireStory?id=1431210

Hunter, M. (2005, December 19). *Democrats aim to 'mend,' not end Patriot Act*. Retrieved December 20, 2005, from http://www.cnsnews.com/ViewPolitics.asp?Page=%5CPolitics%5Carchive%5C200512%5CPOL20051219b.html

Hsu, S. S. (2006, April 18). Former Fla. Professor to be deported. [Electronic Version]. *The Washington Post*, p. A03. Retrieved May 14, 2006, from http://www.washingtonpost.com

Hsu, S. S., & Eggen, D. (2005, December 6). Fla. Professor is acquitted in case seen as Patriot Act test. *The Washington Post*, p. A01. Retrieved December 13, 2005, from http://www.washingtonpost.com

Hudson, A. (2005, November 26). Time favors foes of Patriot Act. [Electronic Version]. *The Washington Times*. Retrieved December 5, 2005, from http://www.washingtontimes.com/national/20051125-113235-3982r.htm

Jackson, P. (2005, December 3). *Ex-FBI chief Freeh backs Patriot Act renewal*. Retrieved December 5, 2005, from http://www.populistamerica.com/ex_fbi_chief_freeh_backs_patriot_act_renewal

Kellman, L. (2005, November 16). *Tentative deal on Patriot Act, sources say.* Retrieved November 16, 2005, from http://www.sfgate.com/cgi-bin/article.cgi?f=/n/a/2005/11/16/ national/w115802S58.DTL

Kellman, L. (2005, December 23). *Congress extends Patriot Act 1 month.* Retrieved December 29, 2005, from http://www.findarticles.com/p/articles/mi_qn4155/is_20051223/ ai_n15963362

Kellman, R. (2005, December 21). *Patriot Act: Temporary extension.* Retrieved December 22, 2005, from http://www.wgrz.com/printfullstory.aspx?storyid=34024

Lichtblau, E. (2005, November 11). Lawmakers meet to settle differences on Patriot Act. [Electronic Version]. *The New York Times,* p. A.20. Retrieved November 11, 2005, from http://www.nytimes.com

Lichtblau, E. (2005, December 9). Congress reaches Patriot Act deal. [Electronic Version]. *International Herald Tribune.* Retrieved December 12, 2005, from http://www.iht.com/bin/print_ipub.php?file=/articles/2005/12/09/news/patriot.php

Limbaugh, R. (2005, December 21). *Senator Larry Craig defends his Patriot Act vote.* Retrieved December 22, 2005, from http://www.ruptured-duck.com/sixties/shockhorror/node/82/

Lowry, R. (2005, December 28). *Patriot misses: Demagoguery and the Patriot Act.* Retrieved December 29, 2005, from http://www.nationalreview.com/lowry/lowry200512280854. asp

Lungren, J., & Shawn, T. (2005, November 18). *Sensenbrenner statement on status of Patriot Act conference agreement.* Retrieved November 21, 2005, from http://releases. usnewswire.com/printing.asp?id=56979

McCullagh, D. (2005, December 12). *Patriot Act critics propose temporary extension.* Retrieved December 14, 2005, from http://news.com.com/Patriot+Act+critics+propose+ temporary+extension/2100-1028_3-5992347.html

McCullagh, D. (2005, December 12). *Perspective: Must we renew the Patriot Act?* Retrieved December 14, 2005, from http://news.com.com/Must+we+renew+the+Patriot+Act/2010-1028_3-5989887.html

McCullagh, D., & Broache, A. (2005, December 8). *Patriot Act renewal draws filibuster threat.* Retrieved December 12, 2005, from http://news.zdnet.com/2100-1009_22-5987892.html

Novak, R. (2005, December 27). *Bush, Congress set themselves up to fail on Patriot Act, anwr.* Retrieved December 29, 2005, from http://www.humaneventsonline.com/article.php?id=11141

Pike, G. H. (2005, December 26). *Congress extends USA Patriot Act by 1 month.* Retrieved December 29, 2005, from http://www.infotoday.com/newsbreaks/nb051226-1.shtml

Riechmann, D. (2005, December 11). Bush urges Congress to renew Patriot Act. [Electronic Version]. *Kilgore New Herald.* Retrieved December 12, 2005, from http://www.kilgorenewsherald.com/news/2005/1211/Front_Page/004.html

Risen, J., & Lichtblau, E. (2005, December 16). Bush lets U.S. spy on callers without courts. [Electronic Version]. *The New York Times,* p. A1. Retrieved December 21, 2005, from http://www.nytimes.com

Schepers, E. (2005, December 1). Renewal of Patriot Act runs into trouble. [Electronic Version]. *People's Weekly World.* Retrieved December 5, 2005, from http://www.pww.org/article/articleprint/8196/

Stacy, M. (2005, December 9). Terror case result casts shadow on Patriot Act. [Electronic Version]. *The Star Ledger.* Retrieved December 12, 2005, from http://www.nj.com–

Tirrell-Wysocki, D. (2005, December 19). *Bush blasts Patriot Act critics, including Sununu.* Retrieved December 20, 2005, from http://www.fosters.com/apps/pbcs.dll/article?AID=/20051219/NEWS0202/112190116/-1/services0510

Townsend, F. F. (2005, December 20). Pass the Patriot Act. [Electronic Version]. *The Salt Lake Tribune.* Retrieved December 22, 2005, from http://www.sltrib.com/opinion/ci_3327614

CHAPTER 17

The Second Extension of the Patriot Act

THE PATRIOT ACT RENEWAL PROCESS had been struck a severe blow by the failure of a renewal package on December 31, 2005. However, like a prizefighter who gets caught with that "lucky punch," what happens next usually tells the tale definitively. For those wishing to see the Patriot Act renewed in short order, they were to be disappointed. For those looking to curb or quash the Patriot Act's extended provisions, victory was closer with each passing day. Either way, the Patriot Act renewal would be an "extra rounds" event.

The president started 2006 with a heavy public campaign for the Patriot Act renewal. However, several events within the political arena would cause the Patriot Act to be just one of many items on his plate. These events, which would have the effect of diluting a more focused effort by the president on the Patriot Act, included, but were not limited to, the following: the Samuel Alito confirmation to the Supreme Court, the Jack Abramoff scandal, the Katrina event, and the aftermath of the Tom Delay resignation as majority leader (Vlahos, 2006). These events, combined with the domestic spying scandal that had been launched at the original renewal deadline, would force supporting members of the administration to step front and center. While this is commonplace in politics, at times the president's support staff would have a mixed effect on turning the tide against a "Coalition of Opposition" that was firmly ensconced.

As has been stated previously, the issues of contention surrounding the Patriot Act were numerous and shifted in importance depending on which particular daily event was center stage. What we do know is that concessions by both the House and Senate committee members to a shortened 4-year sunset for a reauthorized Patriot Act was not enough for the bill to make the December 31, 2005, deadline. What remained to hold up a renewal was debatable; however, most certainly the following issues were hotly contested starting in early 2006:

1. The matter of National Security Letters which allow the government to access records without a search warrant. Arguments were raging over whether people should be able to challenge the order and limitations to when these orders could be used (Vlahos, 2006).
2. Section 215 remained a front issue in which the argument still centered on the government's authority to get records from institutions. Specifically, could these searches be challenged in court, and could the government continue to implement gag orders on targeted subjects (Vlahos, 2006)?
3. The notification period for "sneak and peek" orders remained a controversy as Senate members wanted to reduce the current 90-day average time before notification to 7 days (Vlahos, 2006).

As the new year began, and the Patriot Act began living on the "borrowed time" of the February 3rd extension, the legislative process simply started as it had before December 31, 2005. That is, the original House and Senate Committee bills still stood, as well as the un-renewed compromise package. While legislators would not have to start over at square one per se, they were still no closer to a consensus.

One of the front-runners of the Republican Party's renewal brigade was House Judiciary Committee Chairman James Sensenbrenner. Sensenbrenner went on a daily campaign to educate the public on the upgraded safeguards found within the Patriot Act Conference report (Lungren & Shawn, 2006, January 5). Starting with the highly contested Section 215, Sensenbrenner stated that as of April 2005 the section had not been used for the collection of library records (Lungren & Shawn, 2006, January 5), which had been a voice of concern to many civil liberties groups. Additionally, Sensenbrenner stated that sensitive records, such as those found in libraries, bookstores, tax returns, firearm sales and so on, could only be collected by an application from either the FBI Director, Deputy Director, or an official in charge of intelligence made directly to the FISA court. These legislative upgrades would represent additional civil liberties safeguards that at current did not exist (Lungren & Shawn, 2006, January 5). This particular safeguard was originally requested by Democrat Patrick Leahy (Broache, 2006), and might be seen as an inroad toward a final resolution. Sensenbrenner vowed to continue educating the public on civil liberties safeguards found in the reauthorization package (Broache, 2006). However, this single bipartisan agreement on Section 215 would not sway the "Coalition of Opposition" which articulated a resolve to maintain their opposition to renewal via a letter sent to Senate Judiciary Chairman Arlen Specter during the same time period (Broache, 2006).

At a final stop in Fort Leavenworth, Kansas, Vice President Dick Cheney reinforced the need to renew the Patriot Act. Speaking before nearly 1,000 soldiers, Cheney said, "That law has done exactly what it was intended to do and this country cannot afford to be without its protections" (Burke, 2006, ¶ 13). Of the soldiers who listened to the vice president's call for a Patriot Act renewal, nearly one-third had served at least one year in Iraq or Afghanistan (Burke, 2006). A fundamental question that could be asked was whether speeches, such as the one given by the vice president, were simply an act of preaching to the converted or seeking to bring new believers into the fold? Where did the average American, if there is such a thing, stand on the Patriot Act in 2006? With such a narrow timeline for renewal, set by Republicans no less, support would be needed from all sides.

To get another glimpse at the perception of Americans on the Patriot Act, in January 2006 a *USA Today*/CNN Gallup Poll was conducted. The strengths and weaknesses of polls in general were covered in Chapter 11. With that said, in 2006 do we see radical changes in people's perceptions of the Patriot Act? The *USA Today*/CNN Gallup Poll consisted of 1,003 adults and was conducted on January 6-8, 2006. Among a myriad of political related questions, respondents were asked if they thought the Bush administration had gone "too far," "about right," or "not far enough" in restricting civil liberties in order to fight terrorism (*USA Today*, 2006). Of those polled, 38% responded that the government had gone "too far," while 40% said "about right," with 19% saying "not far enough" (*USA Today*, 2006). Only 3% of respondents had no opinion on the matter.

While it would not be accurate to assume that the Patriot Act embodies all aspects of civil liberties in the war on terror, it has been one of the administration's most publicized tools for that effort. From this poll, it can be seen that while the largest percentage of respondents still think the president has gone about right in restricting people's civil liberties in order to fight terrorism, there has been a consistent drop in that support. The next question would be, after four years, has the public come to be familiar with this law? If so, to what extent do they want it modified? Further, poll results give a perspective of this. From the same January 6-8, 2006, *USA Today*/CNN/Gallup Poll, 59% of respondents claimed to be somewhat familiar with the law, which was a large increase from 46% who made the same claim in February 16-17, 2004. A reduction from 27% to 18% of respondents who claimed that they were not too familiar with the law was seen as well (*USA Today*, 2006). Those claiming to be very familiar rose 4% from February 16-17, 2004, to January 6-8, 2006, from 13% to 17%. While there is little doubt that these are subjective questions, the results are promising. This poll, with all its inherent limitations, would say that people have taken increased interest in the Patriot Act issue over time. This growing interest appears to have increased familiarity progressively over time despite the laws enactment difficulties.

If the public in general is not totally out of touch on the Patriot Act renewal debate, what degree of change did they want in the renewed version? When people were asked in the same study about degree of changes they would like to see in the Patriot Act, 24% wanted major changes, 50% requested minor changes, 13% would have left the law as it stood, and 7% favored getting rid of the Patriot Act altogether (*USA Today*, 2006).

For Democrats, polls such as this one could be argued as the desire in line with the "Coalition of Opposition's" mantra, that they just want to improve the Act and not destroy it. Regardless, if destroying the Patriot Act was a conscious desire of the Feingold group, continued resistance to the renewal process was putting the Patriot Act's sunset sections at risk of becoming a part of history and not the future.

Democrats incorporated a brilliant tactic during early 2006 to oppose the Patriot Act renewal. Using the few Republican Party members who joined the opposition, Democrats framed the Patriot Act debate as a bipartisan concern. Edward Epstein of the Chronicle Washington Bureau alluded to the war hawk versus doves tightrope that Democrats were walking on national security issues when he said, "Not wanting to be painted as obstructionists in the terrorism fight, the Democrats have been only too happy to let a handful of Senate Republicans take the lead in fighting for more changes to the act" (Epstein, 2006, ¶ 21).

An example of "bipartisan presentation" is seen in the Fox News interview between Mike Wallace and Dick Durbin. Wallace interviewed

Durbin, the Senate's number two Democratic leader, on January 22, 2006. When asked about the Patriot Act, Durbin quickly took the bipartisan defense. Specifically he said, "Now, when it gets to issues—specific issues like the Patriot Act, take a look at the coalition that is trying to talk to the White House and Republican leadership about change. It is a bipartisan coalition" (Wallace, 2006). Durbin was quick to mention his recent communications with one of the four Republican opposition members, Senator John Sununu (Wallace, 2006). Later in the interview, as the conversation entered topics such as laws as they pertain to the FISA court, the issue of the Patriot Act came up again. When Wallace reiterated the fact of Democratic obstruction involving the Patriot Act, Durbin reacted quickly to hide behind the bipartisan shield. The exchange was as follows:

> Wallace: I know, but you're fighting the Patriot Act, Senator.
> Durbin: No, no, Chris, don't take this further than it goes. We overwhelmingly support the Patriot Act. There are three or four sections with modifications which passed the Senate, incidentally, on a bipartisan basis, unanimously -- three or four sections that we're talking about, and they can be modified and it wouldn't compromise our security." (Wallace, 2006)

Democrats reproduced three themes during the first extension period that included the following: 1) the efforts to oppose the Patriot Act renewal were bipartisan, 2) the requested changes to the renewal package were small and easily fixable, and 3) an agreement was around the corner. Democrat Ken Salazar was confident in early January 2006 that an agreement was around the corner (Roper, 2006).

In an attempt to rally support for the complex issues surrounding the war on terror, on January 23, 2006, President Bush spoke at Kansas State University. The focus of the visit was, in part, to speak about national security concerns. During the president's presentation, which included a question and answer session, he addressed the domestic spying program and the renewal of the Patriot Act. Uncharacteristic of presidential speeches, the president conversed with the audience for over an hour and a half. The president attempted to squelch concerns that he had acted covertly, if not also outside his legal authority, by his domestic spying program by telling listeners, "If I had wanted to break the law, why was I briefing Congress" (Bush, 2006)? With great urgency the president called on Congress to renew the Patriot Act before the February 3rd deadline. Highlighting the need for the Patriot Act to fight terrorism, the president emphasized the lack of any documented cases of civil rights violations and its constant review (Bush, 2006). The president framed his lengthy discussion on the war against terrorism as a war on ideologies in which those who would do harm to America cannot be appeased and will not stop. Under this reality, listeners were advised that America must actively confront threats, using tools such as the Patriot Act, before a future attack takes place (Bush, 2006).

Earlier in the same month, Robert Spencer released his article on the domestic spying program titled, "How the Patriot Act Saves Lives," and its relation to the Noel Exinia case. Exinia was in the process of transporting approximately 500 pounds of cocaine from Mexico to the U.S. when government officials intercepted one of his phone calls. Within this January 5th, 2005, intercepted phone call, Exinia was attempting to smuggle, for $8,000, 20 Iraqis through the Mexican border into the U.S. (Spencer, 2006). These individuals, termed by Exinia as *la gente de Osama,* or Osama's people, frightened even the drug runner (Spencer, 2006). Spencer, who took issue with the tactics of civil rights organizations such as the ACLU on national security matters, gave a sterling example of the usefulness of the Patriot Act.

It has been stated that 2006 brought many obstacles to the renewal process. It would be accurate to say that some of the president's own personnel may have inadvertently been detrimental to the renewal process at times. At the very least, confusion was added to the renewal process by the 42-page memo released by Attorney General Alberto Gonzales on January 25, 2006. The memo's purpose was to explain and legitimize the president's domestic spying program; however, it was reported to allude to the fact that the president did not need Congress to renew the Patriot Act for him to have the authority to investigate terrorists (Savage, 2006). Specifically, Gonzales asserted in a footnote within the memo that Congress had already given the president this authority when authorizing him to use force against groups such as al Qaeda (Savage, 2006). Gonzales had previously been taken to task over memos that pertained to torture. Those highly controversial "torture" memos had been a focal point of Democratic debate during his appointment phase to the position of U.S. Attorney General.

Now, a new debate over another legal analysis by Gonzales would muddy the waters over the renewal of the Patriot Act. The fundamental question raised by the Gonzales memo was whether the president had the authority to continue exercising investigative powers regardless of how Congress would act on the Patriot Act renewal. Presidential power and the scope of that power was again drawn into hot debate. When pressed by reporters, Scott McClellan, the official White House spokesman, refused to give a definitive answer to whether Patriot Act based actions would continue if the renewal sections were to sunset (Savage, 2006). Unintentionally, administrational staff for the president had fueled the fire for dissent. At the same time the administration was attempting damage control, civil liberties groups were busy rallying support for the Senate's version of the Patriot Act Reauthorization.

January 25, 2006, was designated as National Patriot Act Call-In Day (LibraryJournal.com, 2006). The goal was to inspire library advocates to contact Senators and Representatives and support the Senate package, which was believed to comprise more civil liberty safeguards (LibraryJournal.com, 2006).

Patriot Act scholar Amitai Etzioni, author of the book *How Patriotic is the Patriot Act?: Freedom vs. Security in the Age of Terrorism,* summarized the highly contentious and unproductive environment of the renewal process in a *USA Today* editorial/opinion. Specifically, Etzioni denoted the Patriot Act/President Bush drama.

> A steady stream of revelations, and the ensuing news media reports, have portrayed a president hungry for power, doing whatever is necessary—legal or not—to protect this country. In the wake of such news, some lawmakers in Congress see weakness and an opportunity to gut one of President Bush's vital weapons in the war on terror: the USA Patriot Act. (2006, ¶1).

Etzioni prognosticated a possible February 3rd deadline failure due to, among other things, the current political feasibility of opposing the Patriot Act (Etzioni, 2006). To Etzioni, the Patriot Act was more victim than culprit. In fact, Etzioni stated that current media issues such as torture, secret prisons, and spying were nothing more than red herrings for holding a vital law hostage (Etzioni, 2006).

By January 30, 2006, it was inevitable that the extension was in big trouble. Sensenbrenner stated that he had originally felt the first extension would probably not serve to break the deadlock (Orr, 2006). Specifically, Sensenbrenner alluded to an inability to timely engage the topic as the problem by saying, "They never take up anything until a week before the deadline" (Orr, 2006). It appeared that both sides were firmly dug in and unwillingly to negotiate. The House was no longer willing to make further concessions of the conference report and the "Coalition of Opposition" would not accept the package as it stood. While Specter debated an attempt to try and block a filibuster (Orr, 2006), this did not work. In the end, a second extension introduced by House Judiciary Committee Chairman James Sensenbrenner, entitled H.R. 4659, which would extend the Patriot Act until March 10, 2006 (Deans, 2006; Leahy, 2006; Lungren & Shawn, 2006, February 1), was the only option left. For all the media revelations, political maneuvers, and scholarly observations, the Patriot Act renewal process had not moved an inch.

References

Broache, A. (2006, January 9). *Patriot Act defender touts 'safeguards'*. Retrieved January 11, 2006, from http://news.com.com/Patriot+Act+defender+touts+safeguards/2100-1028_3-6024917.html

Burke, G. (2006, January 7). "Cheney touts economy in visit." [Electronic Version]. *The Kansas City Star*. Retrieved January 11, 2006, from the Infotrac Web database.

Bush, G. W. (2006, January 23). *President discusses global war on terror at Kansas State University*. Retrieved October 3, 2006, from http://www.whitehouse.gov/news/ releases/2006/01/20060123-4.html

Deans, B. (2006, February 3). *House approves temporary extension of Patriot Act*. Retrieved August 17, 2006, from http://www.cox-washington.com/reporters/content/reporters/ stories/2006/02/03/BC_PATRIOT_ACT02_COX.html

Epstein, E. (2006, January 31). *Spying in U.S. strains debate on Patriot Act: Congress no closer to renewal after 5-week extension*. Retrieved May 2, 2006, from http://www.mindfully. org/Reform/2006/Spying-Patriot-Act31jan06.htm

Etzioni, A. (2006, January 11). *Patriot Act is convenient target*. Retrieved May 2, 2006, from http://www.usatoday.com/news/opinion/editorials/2006-01-11-patriot-act-edit_x.htm -

Leahy, P. (2006, February 2). *Statement of Senator Patrick Leahy ranking member, Judiciary Committee improving the Patriot Act (in support of the extension), Senate floor statement Thursday, February 2, 2006.* Retrieved August 17, 2006, from http://leahy.senate.gov/press/200602/020206c.html

LibraryJournal.com. (2006, January 19). *January 25 National Patriot Act Call-In Day.* Retrieved May 2, 2006, from http://www.libraryjournal.com/article/CA6300505.html

Lungren, J., & Shawn, T. (2006, January 5). *Sensenbrenner to highlight civil liberty safeguards in Patriot Act conference report.* Retrieved May 1, 2006, from http://releases.usnewswire.com/GetRelease.asp?id=58911

Lungren, J., & Shawn, T. (2006, February 1). *Sensenbrenner: House passes legislation extending Patriot Act until March 10th.* Retrieved February 15, 2006, http://judiciary.house.gov/ media/pdfs/patriotextension2106.pdf

Orr, J. S. (2006, January 30). *Patriot Act nears the wire - again.* Retrieved February 2, 2006, from http://www.populistamerica.com/patriot_act_nears_the_wire_again

Roper, P. (2006, January 6). *Salazar expects compromise on Patriot Act.* Retrieved January 11, 2006, from http://www.chieftain.com/print.php?article=/metro/1136538450/3

Savage, C. (2006, January 25). *AG's memo raises questions on Patriot Act: Suggests it's not needed for domestic spying.* Retrieved October 3, 2006, from http://www.truthout.org/ cgi-bin/artman/exec/view.cgi/48/17214

Spencer, R. (2006, January 18). *How the Patriot Act saves lives.* Retrieved May 2, 2006, from http://www.frontpagemag.com/Articles/ReadArticle.asp?ID=20953

USA Today. (2006, January 9). *USA Today/CNN Gallup Poll.* Retrieved May 2, 2006, from http://www.usatoday.com/news/polls/2006-01-09-poll.htm#patriot

Vlahos, K. B. (2006, January 23). *Patriot Act fix wedged among many priorities.* Retrieved May 2, 2006, from http://www.foxnews.com/story/0,2933,182451,00.html

Wallace, C. (2006, January 22). *Transcript: Sen. Dick Durbin on 'FOX News Sunday'.* Retrieved May 2, 2006, from http://www.foxnews.com/story/0,2933,182436,00.html

CHAPTER 18

The Renewal of the Patriot Act

THE DEADLOCK BETWEEN THE HOUSE and the Senate was a bitterly contested battle. By February 3, 2006, neither party appeared ready to budge and a second extension, which would expire March 10, 2006, showed no more likelihood of being met than the previous extension. If the Patriot Act were to break from an endless cycle of short term extensions, it would require that both sides find a middle ground. The protracted stalemate over the Patriot Act renewal had received media saturation and, eventually, one side would have to make a move.

By February 9, 2006, the winds of change began to blow. Word of a secret agreement between Senate Republicans began to surface. Lacking specific details, the agreement was reported to be the brainchild of Republican Senators John Sununu, Larry Craig, Lisa Murkowski, and Chuck Hagel (Espo, 2006). This secret agreement labeled as "tentative," was not a direct road to victory for Republicans as Democrats in the Senate could still block the bill with another vote against cloture (Espo, 2006). What separated S. 2271, officially titled the "USA Patriot Act Additional Reauthorizing Act of 2006," and coined by the media as the "Sununu Compromise," was that it was a Senate Republican creation and had the blessing of the White House going in (CBS News, 2006, February 10). The term "compromise" was strategically avoided by the Senate Republicans (Bishop, 2006). Previously, a fundamental component of the Feingold "Coalition of Opposition" was not only that an army of Democrats (over 40) in the Senate had opposed renewal, but also a handful of Republicans had crossed the line and joined what was trumpeted by Democrats as a "bipartisan" cause. As previously stated, these Senate Republican dissenters had served as the front line soldiers for Senate Democrats. However, with the Sununu Compromise (S. 2271), Feingold was losing a vital field asset in the war against the Patriot Act renewal. The next question would be if Senate Democrats would subscribe to the Sununu Compromise and take steps toward a Patriot Act renewal, or would they stand firm in the Feingold camp?

By February 10, 2006, as the Sununu Compromise became more expanded upon in the media, the level of Democratic support to step toward renewal became more prevalent. The Sununu Compromise basically comprised three fundamental alterations from pervious proposals:

1. People served with a subpoena in a terrorist related investigation would be allowed to contest a gag order.
2. The Sununu compromise struck the previous wording that required an individual provide the FBI with the name of an attorney consulted on a National Security Letter.
3. A clarification that would state that most libraries would not be subject to National Security Letter requests for terrorist information (Abrams, 2006; Shawl, 2006).

While giving a general highlight of his compromise package on February 12, 2006, Senator John Sununu included these new changes, in conjunction with past agreed upon changes, that would also be seen H.R. 3199, entitled the "USA Patriot Improvement and Reauthorization Act of 2005." Sununu elaborated some of these additional safeguards as the following:

1. The mandate for the destruction of accidental information collected on innocent citizens.
2. Enhanced judicial review for Section 215.
3. A 4-year sunset on Section 215.
4. A reduced time of notification of sneak and peek warrants to 30 days.
5. Higher standards for the use of roving wiretaps (Sununu, 2006).

Senator Lisa Murkowski, R-AK, stated, "It has always been my intention to work to improve the legislation to offer greater protections...I believe we have accomplished that and what we see today is a better Patriot Act" (Bishop, 2006, ¶ 4). House Speaker Dennis Hastert was reported to give his blessing to the compromise. Furthermore, Senate Democrat Harry Reid praised the compromise and pledged his support (Abrams, 2006). Senator Dianne Feinstein also stated that the compromise was workable and that she would vote for it (Abrams, 2006).

Within the Patriot Act reauthorization would be a law enforcement package that was feared lost when the renewal had failed its original deadline. The law enforcement methamphetamine package was a collaboration between Feinstein and Republican Senator Jim Talent of Missouri (Talent & Feinstein, 2006). Democratic Senator Dick Durbin stated that he would vote for the compromise, but intended to work for further changes (LibraryJournal.com, 2006). A more skeptical James Sensenbrenner had been briefed on the compromise but withheld comment (Abrams, 2006).

As Democrats began to flock to the Sununu Compromise, Senator Russ Feingold weighed in. In reliable form, Feingold rejected the compromise in an official statement on the Sununu Compromise (S. 2271).

> While I greatly respect the Senators who negotiated this deal, I am gravely disappointed in the outcome. The White House would agree to only a few minor changes to the same Patriot Act conference report that could not get through the Senate back in December. These changes do not address the major problems with the Patriot Act that a bipartisan coalition has been trying to fix for the past several years. They are, quite frankly a fig leaf to allow those who were fighting hard to improve the Act to now step down, claim victory, and move on....We've come too far and fought too hard to agree to reauthorize the Patriot Act without fixing any of the major problems with the Act. A few insignificant, face-saving changes just don't cut it. I cannot support this deal, and I strongly oppose proceeding to legislation that will implement it. (Feingold, 2006, February 15, ¶ 2)

Feingold was not alone in his opposition. Civil liberties groups joined the Senator from Wisconsin in condemning the compromise. Specifically, they objected to the time limit for challenging gag orders for National Security Letters. The Sununu Compromise, while allowing for challenges of gag orders, allowed for a 1-year period to pass before a challenge could be made. This was a much lengthier period than the Senate's 90-day version (LibraryJournal.com, 2006). Furthermore, while National Security Letter service would not be able to blanket libraries in toto, libraries that serve as Internet Service Providers, that is, e-mail communication services, could still be petitioned for records (Bishop, 2006; LibraryJournal.com, 2006).

Living Under The Patriot Act: Educating A Society | 253

On a lighter note, the push for Patriot Act renewal by the Senate brought forth additional media coverage of civil rights awareness initiates, such as the Patriot Act board game. This Monopoly style board game, created in 2004 by Michael Kabbash, an Arab civil rights activist, featured changes such as "Go to Guantanamo Bay," with winners retaining their civil rights (Parry, 2006). Kabbash's board game, which uses humor to illustrate the creator's belief in government abuses brought forth by the Patriot Act, is available via Internet download (Parry, 2006).

Feingold would attempt to see that a Senate vote never happened (Associated Press, 2006). It was unknown just how many Democrats would agree to stop the Patriot Act renewal process once again. When reflected against Feingold's lone struggles in the 2001 Patriot Act creation period, he had built vast support to oppose the renewal. While it appeared that Feingold was going to lose Democratic support, he would not be alone. Senator Robert Byrd, the eldest statesman in the Senate with 48 years of service, vowed to oppose the renewal (Kellman, 2006, February 28). In fact, Byrd counted his support of Patriot Act legislation as one of a handful of career mistakes which included the following: the 1964 Civil Rights Act filibuster, a Vietnam War expansion vote, and deregulating airlines (Kellman, 2006, February 28).

On February 16, 2006, at 10:31 a.m., a filibuster vote on S. 2771, entitled the "USA Patriot Act Additional Reauthorization Amendments Act of 2006," went to the Senate and a new consensus was illuminated. The final vote was 96-3 in favor of letting the Sununu agreement proceed for an official vote in the Senate. The three lone dissenting votes were Russ Feingold, D-WI, Robert Byrd, D-WV, and Jeff Jeffords, I-VT (Kellman, 2006, February 16; U.S. Senate, 2006, February 16).

On March 1, 2006, at 12:02 p.m., the Senate officially voted on S. 2271. The final tally was in favor of the Sununu agreement 95-4 with one nonvoting member. Senators Byrd, Feingold, Harkin, and Jeffords were the 4 dissenting votes (U.S. Senate, 2006, March 1). At this point it was obvious that Feingold was no longer the king of the "Coalition of Opposition," but the caretaker of a house of cards that had truly fallen.

The Senate would move forward to its last hurdle, the reauthorization of H.R. 3199, the USA Patriot Improvement and Reauthorization Act of 2005. Democrat Senator Patrick Leahy, a key negotiator in the original Patriot Act version, stated that he applauded the Sununu Compromise. However, while he thought the Sununu Compromise was a good thing, Leahy stated that he would not be voting to reauthorize H.R. 3199 as it had not reached a level of civil liberty safeguards that he could support (Leahy, 2006).

As the cool winds of March 2, 2006, blew past Washington, the Senate convened at 3:01 p.m. and the votes were cast. The matter at hand was the passage of H.R. 3199, titled the "USA Patriot Improvement and Reauthorization Act of 2005" (U.S. Senate, 2006, March 2). Senator Feingold asserted a final warning to his colleagues prior to the vote by saying, "Without freedom, we are not America. If we don't preserve our liberties, we cannot win this war, no matter how many terrorists we capture or kill" (Feingold, 2006, March 2). The final tally was 89 yea votes to 10 votes dissenting, with one Senator not voting (U.S. Senate, 2006, March 2). Specifically, the votes went as follows:

Votes in Favor of Reauthorization

Alexander (R-TN)	Allard (R-CO)	Allen (R-VA)	Baucus (D-MT)
Bayh (D-IN)	Bennett (R-UT)	Biden (D-DE)	Bond (R-MO)
Boxer (D-CA)	Brownback (R-KS)	Bunning (R-KY)	Burns (R-MT)
Burr (R-NC)	Cantwell (D-WA)	Carper (D-DE)	Chafee (R-RI)
Chambliss (R-GA)	Clinton (D-NY)	Coburn (R-OK)	Cochran (R-MS)
Coleman (R-MN)	Collins (R-ME)	Conrad (D-ND)	Cornyn (R-TX)
Craig (R-ID)	Crapo (R-ID)	Dayton (D-MN)	DeMint (R-SC)
DeWine (R-OH)	Dodd (D-CT)	Dole (R-NC)	Domenici (R-NM)
Dorgan (D-ND)	Durbin (D-IL)	Ensign (R-NV)	Enzi (R-WY)
Feinstein (D-CA)	Frist (R-TN)	Graham (R-SC)	Grassley (R-IA)
Gregg (R-NH)	Hagel (R-NE)	Hatch (R-UT)	Hutchison (R-TX)
Inhofe (R-OK)	Isakson (R-GA)	Johnson (D-SD)	Kennedy (D-MA)
Kerry (D-MA)	Kohl (D-WI)	Kyl (R-AZ)	Landrieu (D-LA)
Lieberman (D-CT)	Lincoln (D-AR)	Lott (R-MS)	Lugar (R-IN)
Martinez (R-FL)	McCain (R-AZ)	McConnell (R-KY)	Menendez (D-NY)
Mikulski (D-MD)	Murkowski (R-AK)	Nelson (D-FL)	Nelson (D-NE)
Obama (D-IL)	Pryor (D-AR)	Reed (D-RI)	Reid (D-NV)
Roberts (R-KS)	Rockefeller (D-WV)	Salazar (D-CO)	Santorum (R-PA)
Sarbanes (D-MD)	Schumer (D-NY)	Sessions (R-AL)	Shelby (R-AL)
Smith (R-OR)	Snowe (R-ME)	Specter (R-PA)	Stabenow (D-MI)
Stevens (R-AK)	Sununu (R-NH)	Talent (R-MO)	Thomas (R-WY)
Thune (R-SD)	Vitter (R-LA)	Voinovich (R-OH)	Warner (R-VA)

Dissenting Votes

Akaka (D-HI)	Bingaman (D-NM)	Byrd (D-WV)	Feingold (D-WI)
Harkin (D-IA)	Jeffords (I-VT)	Leahy (D-VT)	Levin (D-MI)
Murray (D-WA)	Wyden (D-OR)		

Not Voting: Inouye (D-HI) (U.S. Senate, 2006, March 2).

With the Senate concluding procedures it may have seemed that it would be smooth sailing for the Patriot Act renewal. After all, the House of Representatives had already approved H.R. 3199 on December 14, 2005, several days before the original December 31, 2005, deadline. If not for obstructions in the Senate, the law would have already been renewed. The only matter left for the House of Representatives was to pass the Sununu Compromise, S. 2271, and the president would have the Patriot Act reauthorization in the form of S. 2771 and H.R. 3199 on his desk to sign into law. However, as with all matters involving the Patriot Act, this perceived last step formality would be full of drama.

Originally, the House was scheduled to take its final vote to accept the Sununu Compromise on March 2, 2006. However, due to possible division among members of the House Judiciary Committee, Chairman James Sensenbrenner was forced to postpone the vote until March 7, 2006 (Raw Story, 2006). This delay brought the process again dangerously close to the March 10, 2006, extension deadline. The contention among House members was mild compared to the ongoing verbal battle between James Sensenbrenner and Russ Feingold. Sensenbrenner had sometimes been at vicious odds with Feingold, reported as a potential presidential candidate for 2008 (Hudson, 2006), during the entire reauthorization process (Frommer, 2006). Sensenbrenner was vocal publicly about his frustration with the Feingold crusade saying, "'The Patriot Act has made America safer,...and Russ Feingold doesn't want that'" (Frommer, 2006, ¶ 3). Sensenbrenner was specifically angered with Feingold's perceived attitude toward compromise in the Patriot Act alterations toward answering the questions over civil liberties. "'He can't have it both ways,' Sensenbrenner said. 'He can't complain about civil liberties violations in the Patriot Act that don't exist, and then try to defeat an amendment to the Patriot Act that provides civil liberties protections'" (Frommer, 2006, ¶ 12).

It was within this ongoing air of animosity that the House of Representatives made its final vote on March 7, 2006, at 7:16 p.m., on S. 2271. When the dust settled, the final vote was 280-138 in favor of accepting S. 2271. The vote breakdown by political parties was as follows: 214 Republicans and 66 Democrats voted in favor, and 13 Republicans, 124 Democrats and 1 Independent voted against S. 2271. Representatives who did not vote included 3 Republicans and 11 Democrats. While a 280-138 vote might appear lopsided, that was not the case. In fact, due to the necessity of a two-thirds majority for passage, S. 2271 was passed by only two votes. The closeness of the vote was nothing short of a shock (Kellman, 2006, March 8) to a drama that had been full of such last minute surprises.

On March 9, 2006, less than 48 hours after final congressional approval, and one day before the extension deadline, President George W. Bush signed the USA Patriot Act Improvement and Reauthorization Act of 2005,

Living Under The Patriot Act: Educating A Society | 257

P. L. 109-177, 120 Stat. 192 (2006) and the USA Patriot Act Additional Reauthorization Amendments Act of 2006, P. L. 109-178, 120 Stat. 278 (2006) into law (Yeh & Doyle, 2006). The signing ceremony, which took place in the White House East Room, marked a unique chapter in U.S. history in the war on terror.

While various politicians and new media outlets gave small summaries of what changes would take place in a Patriot Act renewal, a more detailed summary will be given now. This summary will focus mainly on the changes made to the Patriot Act by the USA Patriot Act Improvement and Reauthorization Act of 2005 and, when applicable, some of the modifications brought about by the USA Patriot Act Additional Reauthorization Amendments Act of 2006. The USA Patriot Act Improvement and Reauthorization Act of 2005 consist of the following seven titles:

I. USA Patriot Improvement and Reauthorization Act
II. Terrorist Death Penalty Enhancement Act of 2005
III. Reducing Crime and Terrorism at America's Seaports Act of 2005
IV. Combating Terrorism Financing Act of 2005
V. Miscellaneous Provisions
VI. Secret Service Authorization and Technical Modification Act of 2005
VII. Combat Methamphetamine Epidemic Act of 2005

The greatest majority of changes that served as the crux of the Patriot Act renewal debates are found in Title I. With the signature of the president, 14 of the 16 sunsetting provisions of the Patriot Act were made permanent. Specifically, Section 102(a) of Title I repealed the sunset provisions found in Section 224 of the original law and made permanent the following 14 sections:

Section 201 - terrorism wiretapping authority
Section 202 - computer fraud and abuse wiretapping authority
Section 203(b) - wiretap information sharing by law enforcement agencies
Section 203(d) - foreign intelligence information sharing by law enforcement agencies
Section 204 - pen register and trap device usage
Section 207 - FISA wiretap and search order time limits

Section 209 - stored voice mail seizures by warrant
Section 212 - disclosure of communication content by communication providers
Section 214 - FISA pen register order amendments for electronic communications
Section 217 - computer trespassers
Section 218 - FISA wiretap and search orders and the removal of the "wall" for information sharing
Section 220 - nationwide service of court orders
Section 223 - civil liability for FISA violations
Section 225 - civil immunity for giving assistance in the execution of a FISA order (Yeh & Doyle, 2006)

In addition to making these sections permanent, a new 4-year sunset was placed on Sections 215 and 206. These sections will be up for review on December 31, 2009 (Grier, 2006).

When looking at the highly contentious Section 215, several modifications were put into place by renewal legislation. Section 106(h) of the USA Patriot Act Improvement and Reauthorization Act of 2005 orders a report about the usage of Section 215 to be submitted every April, by the attorney general, to multiple government committees including the following: House and Senate Committee on the Judiciary, the House Permanent Select Committee on Intelligence, as well as the Senate Select Committee on Intelligence (Yeh & Doyle, 2006). Included in this yearly report is a requirement to disclose the total number of applications made, those granted as requested, as well as those granted with modification. Furthermore, the actual addition made by the renewal was the requirement to disclose the number of orders either granted, modified, or refused for the production of library circulation records, firearm sales records, education records, tax return records, and certain medical records (Yeh & Doyle, 2006).

Section 106(a) of the renewal would add U.S.C. 1861(a)(3), which requires that Section 215 orders could only be approved by the FBI Director, FBI Deputy Director, or the Executive Assistant Director for National Security (Yeh & Doyle, 2006). Prior to the renewal, Section 215 orders could be brought to the FISA court with only the standard that the records being sought were part of an "authorized investigation." The renewal would amend 50 U.S.C. 1861(b)(2) to require that any application for orders under Section 215 be accompanied by a lengthy "statement of facts" stating that

Living Under The Patriot Act: Educating A Society | 259

the records sought were relevant to an investigation for the purpose of protection from international terrorism or espionage.

Section 106(b)(A) of Title I gives certain items a presumptive relevance if the statement of facts can show that the items sought by the Section 215 order pertain to the following: a foreign power or agent thereof, activities of an individual of the same status previously described who is subject to an authorized investigation, and an individual who is in contact with, or known to, or a suspected agent of, a foreign power and a subject of an authorized investigation (Yeh & Doyle, 2006).

Section 106(f) establishes a lengthy review process in which individuals who receive a Section 215 order may challenge the legality of the order in a FISA court. Section 215 was also amended to allow an individual, who is normally bound by a gag order, to disclose that he or she was the recipient of a Section 215 order to contact a lawyer, in addition to other individuals, authorized by the FBI (Yeh & Doyle, 2006). In addition, the recipient of a Section 215 order does not have to disclose to the FBI their reason for contacting a lawyer. To further safeguard the process of recipients of Section 215 orders in contacting legal counsel, Section 4 of the USA Patriot Act Additional Reauthorization Amendments Act of 2006 removes the requirement for FBI disclosure of the name of any lawyer who was contacted for legal advice (Yeh & Doyle, 2006). Furthermore, Section 3 of the USA Patriot Act Additional Reauthorization Amendments Act of 2006 allows a petition to take place after one year before the FISA to ease or remove nondisclosure requirements (Yeh & Doyle, 2006).

The USA Patriot Act Improvement and Reauthorization Act of 2005 would have an effect on the highly contentious topic of the usage of National Security Letters (NSLs). It is important to note some of the differences between NSLs and Section 215 orders. NSLs are not requests for tangible items as is the case with Section 215 orders (Yeh & Doyle, 2006). NSLs are used to collect non-content information on telephone communications, as well as e-mail communications. Examples of non-content information are things such as lists of phone numbers dialed and e-mail addresses (Yeh & Doyle, 2006). In similar fashion, five federal statutes; 12 U.S.C. 3414, 15 U.S.C. 1681u, 15 U.S.C. 1618v, 18U.S.C. 2709, and 50 U.S.C. 436 allow federal intelligence agencies to seek out communication providers to provide non-content records (Doyle, 2005; Yeh & Doyle, 2006). Because NSLs do not collect tangible items, they do not require prior approval from a judge as do Section 215 production orders (Yeh & Doyle, 2006). Like Section 215 orders, NSLs come with some disclosure limitations.

Section 115 of the Patriot Act Improvement and Reauthorization Act of 2005 allows not only for the challenging of a NSL, but also for the modification, or a total release, from the non-disclosure agreement for those who receive the NSL request (Yeh & Doyle, 2006; Pickler, 2006).

Section 116 amends all five federal statutes on NSLs to limit mandatory non-disclosure agreements. Under Section 116, before non-disclosure of a NSL becomes mandatory, the investigative agency must certify that disclosure of the NSL would place at risk any of the following: an individual, national security, diplomatic relations, a criminal or intelligence investigation (Yeh & Doyle, 2006). In addition, like Section 215 orders, recipients of an NSL may contact a lawyer for legal advice without disclosing their intent for seeking counsel. Section 4 of the USA Patriot Act Additional Reauthorization Amendments Act of 2006 exempts the recipient from having to disclose the identity of their lawyer (Yeh & Doyle; CBS News 2006, March 10).

Section 5 of the USA Patriot Act Additional Reauthorization Amendments Act of 2006 entitled, "Privacy Protections for Library Patrons," removes much of the previous ambiguity concerning when libraries will be subject to NSLs. Under this section, libraries operating in their standard role of loaning out books and supplying basic Internet without electronic communication service, as defined in 2510(15), are not subject to NSLs (Grier, 2006). However, if libraries provide Internet service that allows for the ability to send or receive electronic or wire communications, they would still be subject to NSL requests (Yeh & Doyle, 2006).

Section 118 of the Patriot Act Improvement and Reauthorization Act of 2005 requires that the attorney general provide an annual report to Congress on the total number of NSL requests submitted. This report is to be made available to the public (Yeh & Doyle, 2006).

Prior to the Patriot Act Improvement and Reauthorization Act of 2005, an order for a roving wiretap (Section 206) simply had to state, if possible, the identity of the subject of interest for a multipoint wiretap. Section 108 would require that intelligence agencies fully describe the individual of interest and, if that information is not possible, the FISA court must decide, based on supplied facts by the petitioner, that there is merit in the issuance of a roving wiretap. In addition, if authorities wish to use surveillance at a location not previously disclosed to the FISA court, the court must be notified within 10 days of the different location, as well as the facts in the case, that would lead the petitioner to believe that this new location is being used by the individual(s) under investigation (Yeh & Doyle, 2006).

Section 114 would require Section 213 searches, those commonly known as the "sneak and peek" search, to give a notification within 30 days instead of a "reasonable period" which could last as long as a year (Salazar, 2006). Under Section 114, 90-day extensions could be granted if petitioners could supply evidence supporting the need for an extension (Yeh & Doyle, 2006). Furthermore, Section 114 removes "unduly delaying a trial" as an adverse consequence that can be articulated to the court as a reason for a delayed notification warrant (Yeh & Doyle, 2006). Finally, Section 114 requires that 30 days after a delayed notification warrant expires or is denied, the judge that issued or denied the warrant must notify the Administrative Office of the U.S. Courts with a detailed list of the facts pertaining to the delayed notification warrant request (Yeh & Doyle, 2006).

Section 112 of the Patriot Act Improvement and Reauthorization Act of 2005 adds receiving military-type training from a foreign terrorist organization and drug trafficking for the purpose of supporting terrorism to the definition of federal crimes of terrorism (Yeh & Doyle, 2006).

Section 121 lowers the threshold for the definition of contraband cigarettes from an excess of 60,000 cigarettes to 10,000 cigarettes.

Section 124 states that the government should not conduct investigations on individuals based only on their membership in non-violent political organizations.

Title II sections deal primarily with modifications to federal death penalty law.

Title III sections deal extensively with seaport security and, among others, the following issues: transportation of dangerous materials, transportation of terrorists, and smuggling (Yeh & Doyle, 2006). Title III sections would address port security by imposing strict punishments for individuals who impede law enforcement officers conducting maritime inspections of ships (CBS NEWS, 2006, March 10).

Title IV makes modifications to Racketeer Influenced and Corrupt Organizations (RICO) statutes for the purpose of thwarting money laundering in regard to terrorist activity (Yeh & Doyle, 2006)

Under Title V, Section 503 adds the Secretary of the Department of Homeland Security into the presidential line of succession behind the Secretary of Veterans Affairs (Yeh & Doyle, 2006). While there were discussions in Congress as late as June, 2005, concerning placing the Secretary of Homeland Security in the 8th position of presidential succession behind the Attorney General (Neale, 2005), the current seating places the position as 18th in the line of succession.

Section 506 creates a new National Security Division that will be run by a new Assistant Attorney General (Bush, 2006). This new department will work within the Department of Justice.

Section 602 creates a new federal crime for misconduct related to special events of national significance. This section makes it a federal crime for an individual to enter into a posted or cordoned off area during an event of national significance (Yeh & Doyle, 2006).

The USA Patriot Act Improvement and Reauthorization Act of 2005 would also contain an extensive law enforcement methamphetamine package (Grier, 2006). Under Title VII, entitled Combat Methamphetamine Epidemic Act of 2005, a large part of the title's sections would deal with retailers who sale ephedrine, pseudoephedrine, and phenlypropanolamine (EPP) based products. While EPP based products are commonly found in over-the-counter cold and allergy medicines, before the Patriot Act renewal they were also purchased in bulk for their EPP content as a precursor for the creation of the illegal drug methamphetamine. Title VII of the USA Patriot Act Improvement and Reauthorization Act of 2005 is an extensive attempt to curb this activity. Pertaining to retail vendors, Title VII limits vendors such as drugstores, convenience stores, grocery stores, as well as other vendors, to the sale of only 3.6 grams of EPP based products per person per day (Yeh & Doyle, 2006). Furthermore, EPP products would no longer be placed in open areas in stores. Vendors selling EPP based products will have to log the name of the product and quantity sold, as well as time and date of the sale. In addition to product information, a physical log will be maintained by all vendors of the name and address of the purchaser (Yeh & Doyle, 2006). Photo I.D. will also be required by all patrons wishing to buy EPP based products. Title VII also affords civil immunity to vendors who disclose EPP logbook information to law enforcement agencies as long as the disclosure is done in good faith. The 3.6 gram limit on EPP sales is to go into effect within 30 days after enactment, while the entire regulatory scheme is to be in place no later than September 30, 2006 (Yeh & Doyle, 2006).

Title VII also brought about additional changes to international regulations of precursors, enhanced penalties for methamphetamine production and trafficking, as well as changes to drug courts and grant programs (Yeh & Doyle, 2006). Section 736 of Title VII requires the attorney general to submit reports twice a year to the Judiciary Committees; Science and Transportation Committee; the Senate Committee; the House Energy and Commerce Committee; the House Government Reform Committee; and the Senate Caucus on International Narcotics Control about the uses of resources by the FBI and DEA in investigations and prosecutions of methamphetamine related offenses (Yeh & Doyle, 2006).

After the historical Patriot Act reauthorization signing, President Bush re-emphasized the global context of the war on terror in which the Patriot Act would continue to play a significant part by stating:

> America remains a Nation at war. The war reached our shores on September 11th, 2001. On that morning, we saw clearly the violence and hatred of a new enemy. We saw the terrorists' destructive vision for us when they killed nearly 3,000 men, women, and children. In the face of this ruthless threat, our nation made a clear choice: We will confront this mortal danger, we will stay on the offensive, and we're not going to wait to be attacked again....As we wage the war on terror overseas, we're also going after the terrorists here at home, and one of the most important tools we have used to protect the American people is the Patriot Act. (Bush, 2006, ¶ 7-10)

References

Abrams, J. (2006, February 10). *Hastert backs compromise on Patriot Act*. Retrieved March 20, 2006, from http://www.usatoday.com/news/washington/2006-02-10-hastert-patriot_x.htm

Associated Press. (2006). *Feingold launches another lonely effort to block the Patriot Act*. Retrieved March 3, 2006, from http://www.wbay.com/global/story.asp?s= 4507134&ClientType=printable

Bishop, S. (2006, February 26). *Patriot Act revisions get senator's support*. Retrieved March 20, 2006, from http://www.populistamerica.com/patriot_act_revisions_get_senator_s_ support

Bush, G. W. (2006, March 9). *President signs USA Patriot Improvement and Reauthorization Act.* Retrieved March 15, 2006, from http://www.whitehouse.gov/news/releases/2006/03/ 20060309-4.html

CBS News. (2006, February 10). *Patriot Act renewal gets green light.* Retrieved March 20, 2006, from http://www.cbsnews.com/stories/2006/02/10/politics/main1307635.shtml

CBS News. (2006, March 10). *Bush signs renewal of Patriot Act.* Retrieved March 20, 2006, from http://www.cbsnews.com/stories/2006/03/10/ap/politics/mainD8G8HIM07.shtml

Doyle, C. (2005, April 15). *Administrative subpoenas and national security letters in criminal and foreign intelligence investigations: Background & proposed adjustments.* The Library of Congress, Congressional Research Service. Retrieved June 5, 2006, from http://www.fas.org/sgp/crs/natsec/RL32880.pdf

Espo, D. (2006, February 9). *Tentative deal is reached on Patriot Act.* Retrieved March 20, 2006, from http://www.political-news.org/breaking/22476/tentative-deal-is-reached-on-patriot-act.html

Feingold, R. (2006, February 15). *Statement of U.S. Senator Russ Feingold on the Patriot Act deal.* Retrieved March 21, 2006, from http://feingold.senate.gov/~feingold/statements/ 06/02/2006215.html

Feingold, R. (2006, March 2). *Statement of U.S. Senator Russ Feingold on final passage of the Patriot Act Reauthorization.* Retrieved April 5, 2006, from http://feingold.senate.gov/ ~feingold/statements/06/03/2006302PA.html

Frommer, F. J. (2006, March 3). Patriot Act passage will cap long Feingold-Sensenbrenner battle. *The Associated Press State & Local Wire.* Retrieved March 21, 2006, from LexisNexis Academic database.

Grier, P. (2006, March 3). *How the Patriot Act came in from the cold.* Retrieved March 3, 2006, from http://www.csmonitor.com/2006/0303/p01s03-uspo.htm

Hudson, A. (2006, March 13). *Feingold pushes for Bush censure.* Retrieved March 13, 2006, from http://www.washingtontimes.com/national/20060313-123143-3992r.htm

Kellman, L. (2006, February 16). *Patriot Act moves closer to renewal.* Retrieved March 3, 2006, from http://www.lwvweston.org/patriotact.html

Kellman, L. (2006, February 28). *Sen. Byrd regrets voting for the Patriot Act.* Retrieved June 22, 2006, from http://www.sfgate.com/cgi-bin/article.cgi?file=/news/archive/2006/02/28/ national/w083721S89.DTL

Kellman, L. (2006, March 8). *US Congress renews Patriot Act; Bush to sign.* Retrieved March 3, 2006, from http://sify.com/printer_friendly.php?id=14157731&ctid=2&lid=1

Leahy, P. (2006, March 3). *"I will vote no on Patriot Act."* Retrieved March 3, 2006, from http://www.opednews.com/articles/opedne_senator__060303__22i_will_vote_no_on_p. htm

LibraryJournal.com. (2006, February 13). *ALA criticizes Patriot Act compromise.* Retrieved March 20, 2006, from http://www.libraryjournal.com/article/CA6306777.html

Neale, T. H. (2005, June 29). *Presidential succession: An overview with analysis of legislation proposed in the 109th Congress.* The Library of Congress, Congressional Research Service. Retrieved June 12, 2006, from http://www.fas.org/sgp/crs/misc/RL32969.pdf

Parry, W. (2006, March 18). *Patriot Act game pokes fun at government.* Retrieved June 22, 2006, from http://www.breitbart.com/news/2006/03/18/D8GEA4PG0.html

Pickler, N. (2006, March 9). *Bush signs renewal of Patriot Act.* Retrieved June 21, 2006, from http://www.newsvine.com/_news/2006/03/09/127173-bush-signs-renewal-of-patriot-act

Raw Story. (2006, March 1). *House pulls Patriot Act compromise vote; delays until Tuesday.* Retrieved March 3, 2006, from http://rawstory.com/news/2006/Patriot_Act_compromise_ may_be_ in_ 0301.html

Salazar, K. (2006, March 12). *New Patriot Act is an improvement.* Retrieved March 3, 2006, from http://www.chieftain.com/print. php?article=/editorial/1142150458/4

Shawl, J. (2006, February 10). *Senate approval of long-term Patriot Act renewal now likely.* Retrieved March 20, 2006, from http://jurist. law.pitt.edu/paperchase/2006/02/senate-approval-of-long-term-patriot.php

Sununu, J. E. (2006, February 12). Patriot Act deal balances liberty, security. [Electronic Version]. *Concord Monitor,* p. D01. Retrieved March 20, 2006, from http://nl.newsbank. com

Talent J., & Feinstein, D. (2006, February 10). *Talent-Feinstein combat meth legislation included in Patriot Act reauthorization compromise.* Retrieved March 10, 2006, from http://feinstein.senate.gov/06releases/r-meth-patriot.htm

United States Senate. (2006, February 16). *U.S. Senate roll call votes 109th Congress - 2nd session.* Retrieved February 19, 2006, from http://www.senate.gov/legislative/LIS/ roll_call_lists/roll_call_ vote_cfm.cfm?congress=109&session=2&vote=00022

United States Senate. (2006, March 1). *U.S. Senate roll call votes 109th Congress - 2nd session.* Retrieved March 2, 2006, from http:// www.senate.gov/legislative/LIS/ roll_call_lists/roll_call_vote_ cfm.cfm?congress=109&session=2&vote=00025

United States Senate. (2006, March 2). *U.S. Senate roll call votes 109th Congress - 2nd session.* Retrieved March 3, 2006, from http:// www.senate.gov/legislative/LIS/ roll_call_lists/roll_call_vote_ cfm.cfm?congress=109&session=2&vote=00029

Yeh, B. T., & Doyle, C. (2006, March 24). *USA Patriot Act improvement & Reauthorization Act of 2005: A legal analysis.* The Library of Congress, Congressional Research Service. Retrieved May 25, 2006, from http://www.fas.org/sgp/crs/intel/RL33332.pdf

CHAPTER 19

Conclusion

THE PATRIOT ACT RENEWAL PROCESS was a unique glimpse at how the government works and, at times, fails to work efficiently in making legislation. There are several reflections that come to mind but are in no way meant to be a complete list. First, we revisit the encompassing purpose of this book. Foremost, the purpose of bringing together this work was to expand public knowledge on a complex piece of legislation we know as the Patriot Act. As stated previously, in acquiring a rounded knowledge it was of the utmost importance to start at the beginning and take the full ride. Along the way, counting the flaws and strengths of the Patriot Act, it is hoped that readers have also received a strong flavor for the unique historical events that contributed to the legislative process.

Some people will see the Patriot Act renewal as a victory for the Bush administration and the war on terror. Others see the reauthorization as another governmental attempt to encroach further on individuals' civil rights. Without a doubt, the reauthorization process gave individuals and organizations the opportunity to debate where lines should be drawn between civil liberties and national security. While the protracted battle over renewal may have been frustrating to some, it defined the character and concerns of politicians, organizations, and the country in ways that might never have been focused upon otherwise. Peter Grier (2006) gives a poignant example of this in his article, "How the Patriot Act Came in From the Cold," when he said, "Even supporters of the Patriot Act acknowledged that the image of plucky librarians standing up to the Bush administration and refusing requests for information about their users was a politically powerful one" (¶ 15).

Senator Feingold, the determined Senator from Wisconsin, will most certainly have dug a niche in history for himself in both his lone oppositional stand on the Patriot Act in 2001, and his ability to create a "Coalition of Opposition" to the Patriot Act renewal. Feingold, whose current quests include a censorship movement against President Bush (Babington, 2006), will most certainly reap the benefits and detriments of being "the man who opposed the Patriot Act" if he runs for president in 2008.

Another salient belief that drove the creation of this book was the undying conviction that people are not only interested in the Patriot Act, but also are smart enough to process the information if it is just presented in a reader-friendly format. Hopefully this has been done. At this point a caveat is forwarded. While this book is believed to be one of the most comprehensive Patriot Act compilations to date, it should not be seen as the end-all resource. It is hoped that this book will serve as a tool for future exploration.

By its reauthorization alone, it is certain that the myriad of issues that the Patriot Act covers will be re-addressed in the future. When sections of the Patriot Act again face renewal, the history of its effect on both civil liberties and the war on terror, from now until then, will again be paramount to proper decision making.

On a personal level, it would be false to say that it is not tempting to insert a section where my own beliefs on the Patriot Act are presented to readers. I do so, and refuse to do so, at the same time. To qualify this statement, I go back to what was hoped readers would take from this book. From the beginning I stated that this book was not intended to sway people's thinking on the validity or non-validity of the Patriot Act, but rather to expand a level of knowledge beyond what is commonplace. While striving to stay true to this endeavor, there are no illusions that the personality of the author is inevitably reflected within the pages of this book. With the perceptiveness that I believe is often under-acknowledged of the public in certain circles, I am confident that many readers have already placed me in one of many political or ideological boxes. This is fine, and I accept it with a smile, as I know that this is a sign that people are thinking hard and trying to read between the lines. This, my friends, is the goal. With that said, a detailed account of my own philosophy on the Patriot Act would only detract from this book.

For Americans, the Patriot Act represents one of many crucial issues during a unique period in U.S. history. What makes the Patriot Act unique is its tremendous scope of influence. The many faces of the Patriot Act will continue to spark debate beyond national security matters and into a virtual plethora of ongoing moral debates (Hood, 2005) in which people attempt to define, by action, the true character of what it means to be an "American." The world audience, which inevitably includes allies and enemies, watches on as Americans continue to engage in a theatrical display for national identity in which the Patriot Act has played a recent part. The future shows no sign of being any less unpredictable or exciting.

I would like to thank readers for taking this journey of exploration through the Patriot Act. I firmly believe that readers of this book leave with a superior knowledge of the Patriot Act and, it is my hope, that it will be one of many ventures into a further understanding of this complex and dynamic law.

References

Babington, C. (2006, March 14). Feingold pushes to censure president. [Electronic Version]. *The Washington Post,* p. A08. Retrieved March 23, 2006, from http://www.washingtonpost.com

Grier, P. (2006, March 3). *How the Patriot Act came in from the cold.* Retrieved March 3, 2006, from http://www.csmonitor.com/2006/0303/p01s03-uspo.htm

Hood, R. (2005). *Issues that matter: America's moral battleground.* (M. Evans, Ed.). New York: iUniverse, Inc.

BIBLIOGRAPHY

BOOKS:

Berelson, B. (1971). *Content analysis in communication research.* New York: Hafner Publishing Co.

Crockatt, R. (2003). *America embattled: September 11, anti-Americanism, and the global order.* New York: Routledge.

Crotty, W. (2004). On the home front: Institutional mobilization to fight the threat of international terrorism. In W. Crotty (Ed.), *The politics of terror: The U.S. response to 9/11* (pp. 191-234). Boston: Northeastern University Press.

DeBecker, G. (2002). *Fear less: Real truth about risk, safety, and security in a time of terrorism.* New York: Little, Brown and Company.

Denzin, N. K., & Lincoln, Y. S. (2003). Appendix A. In N. K. Denzin & Y. S. Lincoln (Eds.), *9/11 in American culture* (pp. 277-279). Lanham, MD: AltaMira Press.

Domke, D. (2004). *God willing? Political fundamentalism in the White House, the "war on terror," and the echoing press.* Ann Arbor, MI: Pluto Press.

Farganis, J. (Ed.). (2004). *Readings in social theory: The classical tradition to post-modernism* (4th ed.). New York: McGraw-Hill.

Foerstel, H. N. (2004). *Refuge of a scoundrel: The Patriot Act in libraries.* Westport, CT: Libraries Unlimited.

Frankfort-Nachmias, C., & Leon-Guerrero, A. (2006). *Social statistics for a diverse society* (4th ed.). Thousand Oaks, CA: Pine Forge Press.

Freeh, L. J. (2000). Expanding the FBI's powers is a necessary response to terrorism. In L. K. Egendorf (Ed.), *Terrorism: opposing viewpoints* (pp. 173-178). San Diego, CA: Greenhaven Press.

Giddens, A. (1977). *Studies in social and political theory.* New York: Basic Books Inc.

Gorz, A. (1976). The tyranny of the factory: Today and tomorrow. In A. Gorz (Ed.), *The division of labour: The labour process and class-struggle in modern capitalism* (pp. 55-62). Atlantic Highlands, NJ: Harvester Press.

Holsti, O. R. (1969). *Content analysis for the social sciences and humanities.* Reading, MA: Addison-Wesley Publishing Co.

Hood, R. (2005). *Issues that matter: America's moral battleground.* (M. Evans, Ed.). New York: iUniverse, Inc.

Kessler, R. (2004). *A matter of character: Inside the white house of George W. Bush.* New York: Penguin Group (USA) Inc.

Kettl, D. F. (2004). *System under stress: Homeland security and American politics.* Washington, DC: CQ Press.

Krippendorff, K. (1980). *Content analysis: An introduction to its methodology.* Beverly Hills, CA: Sage Publications.

Krippendorff, K. (2004). *Content analysis: An introduction to its methodology* (2nd ed.). Thousand Oaks, CA: Sage Publications.

Krislov, D. (2004). Civil liberties and the judiciary in the aftermath of 9/11. In W. Crotty (Ed.), *The politics of terror: The U.S. response to 9/11* (pp. 134-159). Boston: Northeastern University Press.

Lewis, J. (1972). *The Marxism of Marx.* London, England: Lawrence & Wishart.

Lithwick, D., & Turner, J. (2004). From a guide to the Patriot Act. In N. Smith & L. M. Messina (Eds.), *Homeland security* (pp. 94-103). Bronx, NY: H.W. Wilson Co.

Little, D. (1986). *The scientific Marx.* Minneapolis, MN: University of Minnesota Press.

Neuendorf, K.A. (2002). *The content analysis guidebook.* Thousand Oaks, CA: Sage Publications.

Nunn, S. (2000). Weapons of mass destruction pose a terrorist threat. In L. K. Egendorf (Ed.), *Terrorism: Opposing viewpoints* (pp. 35-41). San Diego, CA: Greenhaven Press.

O'Hanlon, M. E., Orszag, P. R., Daalder, I. H., Destler, I. M., Gunter, D. L., Lindsay, J. M., et al. (2002). *Protecting the American homeland: one year on.* Washington, DC: Brookings Institution.

Parsons, T. (1954). *Essays in sociological theory* (Rev. ed.). New York: Free Press.

Ritzer, R., & Goodman, D. J. (2004). *Sociological theory* (6th ed.). New York: McGraw-Hill.

Roberts, C. W. (1997). Text analysis for the social sciences: Methods for drawing statistical inferences from texts and transcripts. In C. W. Roberts (Ed.), *Introduction* (pp. 1-8). Mahwah, NJ: Lawrence Erlbaum Associates.

Rosenzweig, P., Kochems, A., & Carafano, J. J. (Eds.). (2004). *The Patriot Act: Understanding the law's role in the global war on terrorism.* Washington, DC: The Heritage Foundation.

Simon, J. D. (2001). *The terrorist trap: America's experience with terrorism* (2nd ed.). Bloomington, IN: Indiana University Press.

Sprinthall, R. C. (2003). *Basic statistical analysis* (7th ed.). Boston, MA: Pearson Education Group, Inc.

COURT CASES:

Crist v. Bretz, 437 U.S. 28, 98 S. Ct. 2156 (1978).

Debs v. United States, 249 U.S. 211 (1919).

Ex Parte Milligan, 71 U.S. 2 (4 Wall.); 18 L. Ed. 281 (1866).

Ex Parte Quirin, 317 U.S. 1; 63 S. Ct. 2; 87 L. Ed. 3 (1942).

Gherebi v. Bush, 352 F.3d 1278 (9th Cir. 2003).

Hamdi v. Rumsfeld, 542 U.S. 507; 124 S. Ct. 2633; 159 L. Ed. 2d 578 (2004).

Hanft v. Padilla, 546 U.S. _____ (2006). January 4, 2006 Order in Pending Case. Retrieved August 10, 2006, from http://www.supremecourtus.gov/orders/courtorders/010406pzr.pdf

Illinois v. Somerville, 410 U.S. 458, 93 S. Ct. 1066; 35 L. Ed. 2d 425 (1973).

Johnson v. Eisentrager, 339 U.S. 763; 70 S. Ct. 936; 94 L. Ed. 1255 (1950).

The Oyez Project. (n.d.). *Rumsfeld v. Padilla, 542 U.S. 426 (2004).* Retrieved August 10, 2006, from http://www.oyez.org/oyez/resource/case/1730/

Padilla v. Bush, 233 F. Supp.2d 564 (S.D.N.Y. 2002).

Padilla v. Hanft, No. 05-6396 (4th Cir., Sept. 9, 2005). Retrieved August 10, 2006, from http://pacer.ca4.uscourts.gov/opinion.pdf/056396.P.pdf

Padilla v. Rumsfeld, 352 F.3d 695 (2d Cir. 2003).

Rasul v. Bush, 542 U.S. 466; 124 S. Ct. 2686; 159 L. Ed. 2d 548 (2004).

United States v. Dinitz, 424 U.S. 600, 96 S. Ct. 1075; 47 L. Ed. 2d 267 (1976).

United States v. Truong Dinh Hung, 629 F.2d 908 (4th Cir. 1980).

United States v. United States District Court, 407 U.S. 297 (1972).

GOVERNMENT SOURCES:

151 Cong. Rec. 100, 6242 (2005). (remarks of Tom DeLay). Retrieved August 31, 2005, from http://frwebgate.access.gpo.gov/cgi-bin/getpage.cgi?dbname=2005_record&page= H6242&position=all

Brand, R. & Pistole, J. (n.d.). *The use and purpose of National Security Letters (NSLs)*. Retrieved July 7, 2005, from http://www.fbi.gov/page2/natsecurityletters.htm

Buchanan, M. B. (2006, January 3). *U.S. attorneys discuss Patriot Act meeting with the president.* Retrieved August 6, 2006, from http://www.whitehouse.gov/news/releases/ 2006/01/20060103-3.html

Bush, G. (2003, November 6). *President Bush discusses freedom in Iraq and Middle East.* Retrieved October 22, 2005, from http://www.whitehouse.gov/news/releases/2003/11/ 20031106-2.html

Bush, G. W. (2005, June 9). *Remarks by the president on the Patriot Act.* Retrieved August 6, 2006, from http://www.gop.com/NEWS/Read.aspx?ID=5533

Bush, G. W. (2006, January 23). *President discusses global war on terror at Kansas State University.* Retrieved October 3, 2006, from http://www.whitehouse.gov/news/ releases/2006/01/20060123-4.html

Bush, G. W. (2006, March 9). *President signs USA Patriot Improvement and Reauthorization Act.* Retrieved March 15, 2006, from http://www.whitehouse.gov/news/releases/2006/03/ 20060309-4.html

Child Abduction Prevention Act and the Child Obscenity and Pornography Prevention Act of 2003: Hearing before the Subcommittee on Crime, Terrorism, and Homeland Security of the Committee of the Judiciary of the House of Representatives, House of Representatives, 108th Cong., 1 (2003).

Comstock, B. (2003, February 7). *Statement of Barbara Comstock, Director of Public Affairs*. Retrieved January 2, 2006, from the Department of Justice Web site: http://www.usdoj.gov/opa/pr/2003/February/03_opa-082.htm

Daly, B., & Crider, J. (2005, July 21). *Pelosi statement on extension of USA Patriot Act*. Retrieved August 28, 2005, from http://www.democraticleader.house.gov/ press/articles.cfm?pressReleaseID=1100

Department of Justice. (n.d.). *Dispelling the myths: preserving life and liberty*. Retrieved September 20, 2004, from http://www.lifeandliberty.gov/subs/u_myths.htm

Department of Justice. (n.d.). *DOJ accomplishments in the war on terror: preserving life and liberty*. Retrieved September 20, 2004, from http://www.lifeandliberty.gov/subs/ a_terr.htm

Department of Justice. (n.d.). *Myth v. reality*. Retrieved April 24, 2005, from http:// www.lifeandliberty.gov/subs/add_myths.htm

Department of Justice. (n.d.). *Responding to Congress: preserving life and liberty*. Retrieved September 20, 2004, from http://www.lifeandliberty.gov/subs/r_congress.htm

Department of Justice. (n.d.). *Support of the people: preserving life and liberty*. Retrieved September 20, 2004, from http://www.lifeandliberty.gov/subs/s_people.htm

Department of Justice. (2003, September 15). *Prepared remarks of Attorney General John Ashcroft: the proven tactics in the fight against crime*. Retrieved September 20, 2004, from http://www.usdoj.gov/archive/ag/speeches/2003/091503nationalrestaurant.htm

Department of Justice. (2003, October 28). *Iyman Faris sentenced for providing material support to Al Qaeda.* Retrieved August 6, 2006, from http://www.usdoj.gov/opa/pr/2003/ October/03_crm_589.htm

Department of Justice. (2004, July). *Report from the field: the USA Patriot Act at work.* Retrieved September 20, 2004, from http://www.lifeandliberty.gov/docs/071304_report_ from_the_field.pdf

Doyle, C. (2001, December 10). *Terrorism: Section by section analysis of the USA Patriot Act.* The Library of Congress, Congressional Research Service. Retrieved April 15, 2005, from http://www.epic.org/privacy/terrorism/usapatriot/RL31200.pdf

Doyle, C. (2002, April 15). *The USA Patriot Act: a legal analysis.* The Library of Congress, Congressional Research Service. Retrieved November 16, 2004, from http://www.fas.org /irp/crs/RL31377.pdf

Doyle, C. (2005, April 15). *Administrative subpoenas and national security letters in criminal and foreign intelligence investigations: Background & proposed adjustments.* The Library of Congress, Congressional Research Service. Retrieved June 5, 2006, from http://www.fas.org/sgp/crs/natsec/RL32880.pdf

Durbin, D. (2005, April 4). *Bipartisan group of senators introduce "safe act" to remedy problems in Patriot Act.* Retrieved August 30, 3005, from http://durbin.senate.gov/ record.cfm?id=236435

Durbin, D. (2005, July 21). *Patriot Act bill includes reforms proposed by Senators Durbin and Craig.* Retrieved August 30, 2005, from http://durbin.senate.gov/record.cfm?id=241192

Feingold, R. (2005, July 21). *Statement of U.S. Senator Russ Feingold at the Senate Judiciary Committee markup on the Patriot Act Reauthorization.* Retrieved August 30, 2005, from http://feingold.senate.gov/~feingold/statements/05/07/2005721526.html

Feingold, R. (2006, February 15). *Statement of U.S. Senator Russ Feingold on the Patriot Act deal.* Retrieved March 21, 2006, from http://feingold.senate.gov/~feingold/statements/ 06/02/2006215.html

Feingold, R. (2006, March 2). *Statement of U.S. Senator Russ Feingold on final passage of the Patriot Act Reauthorization.* Retrieved April 5, 2006, from http://feingold.senate.gov/ ~feingold/statements/06/ 03/2006302PA.html

Foreign Intelligence Surveillance Act of 1978, 50 U.S.C. § 1805 (1978).

Foreign Intelligence Surveillance Act of 1978, 50 U.S.C. § 1805 (2005).

H.R. 1526 I.H.: 1st Session 109th Congress. (2005, April 6). *Security and Freedom Ensured Act of 2005 (SAFE) Act.* Retrieved March 25, 2006, from http://thomas.loc.gov/cgi-bin/query/z?c109:H.R.1526:

H.R. 3199 I.H.: 1st Session 109th Congress. (2005, July 11). *USA PATRIOT and Terrorism Prevention Reauthorization Act of 2005 (Introduced in House).* Retrieved August 19, 2005, from http://thomas.loc.gov/cgi-bin/query/z?c109:H.R.3199:

Leahy, P. (2001). *The Uniting and Strengthening America by Providing Appropriate Tools Required to Intercept and Obstruct Terrorism (USA Patriot) Act of 2001, H.R. 3162 section-by-section analysis.* Retrieved April 17, 2005, from http://leahy.senate.gov/press/200110/102401a.html

Leahy, P. (2006, February 2). *Statement of Senator Patrick Leahy ranking member, Judiciary Committee improving the Patriot Act (in support of the extension), Senate floor statement Thursday, February 2, 2006.* Retrieved August 17, 2006, from http://leahy. senate.gov/press/200602/020206c.html

Leahy, P. (2006, March 3). *"I will vote no on Patriot Act."* Retrieved March 3, 2006, from http://www.opednews.com/articles/opedne_senator__060303__22i_will_vote_no_on_p. htm

Lormel, D. (2002, October 9). *Testimony of Dennis Lormel, chief, terrorist financing operations section, counterterrorism division, FBI before the Senate Judiciary Committee, Subcommittee on Technology, Terrorism, and Government Information.* Retrieved January 1, 2005, from http://www.fbi.gov/congress/congress02/lormel100902.htm

Lungren, J., & Shawn, T. (2005, July 13). *House Judiciary Committee approves Patriot Act Reauthorization.* Retrieved August 28, 2005, from http://judiciary.house.gov/newscenter. aspx?A=533

Lungren, J., & Shawn, T. (2005, July 21). *Sensenbrenner House floor statement on USA Patriot Act Reauthorization legislation.* Retrieved July 22, 2005, from http://judiciary.house.gov/ media/pdfs/PatriotFJSfloorstate72105.pdf

Lungren, J., & Shawn, T. (2006, February 1). *Sensenbrenner: House passes legislation extending Patriot Act until March 10th.* Retrieved February 15, 2006, http://judiciary.house.gov/ media/pdfs/patriotextension2106.pdf

Neale, T. H. (2005, June 29). *Presidential succession: An overview with analysis of legislation proposed in the 109th Congress.* The Library of Congress, Congressional Research Service. Retrieved June 12, 2006, from http://www.fas.org/sgp/crs/misc/RL32969.pdf

Sabin, B. (2004). *Statement of Barry Sabin before the Committee on Financial Services, U.S. House of Representatives: August 23, 2004.* Retrieved August 6, 2006, from http://financialservices.house.gov/media/pdf/082304bs.pdf

Shapiro, L. (2005, June 15). *Eshoo fights for freedom to read.* Retrieved August 28, 2005, from
http://eshoo.house.gov/index.php?option=com_content&task=view&id=79&Itemid=159

Shapiro, L. (2005, July 21). *Eshoo seeks constructive debate on Patriot Act.* Retrieved August 28, 2005, from http://eshoo.house.gov/index. php?option=com_content&task=view&id= 74&Itemid=159

Smith, S. S., Seifert, J. W., McLoughlin, G. J., & Moteff, J. D. (2002, March 4). *The Internet and the USA Patriot Act: Potential implications for electronic privacy, security, commerce, and government.* The Library of Congress, Congressional Research Service. Retrieved April 16, 2005, from http://www.epic.org/privacy/terrorism/usa-patriot/RL31289.pdf

United States Code. (2001). Washington, DC: U.S. Government Printing Office.

United States Code. (2004). Retrieved April 24, 2005, from Cornell University Law School, Legal Information Institute Web site: http://straylight.law.cornell.edu/uscode

United States Senate. (2006, February 16). *U.S. Senate roll call votes 109th Congress - 2nd session.* Retrieved February 19, 2006, from http://www.senate.gov/legislative/LIS/ roll_call_lists/roll_call_vote_cfm.cfm?congress=109&session=2&vote=00022

United States Senate. (2006, March 1). *U.S. Senate roll call votes 109th Congress - 2nd session.* Retrieved March 2, 2006, from http://www.senate.gov/legislative/LIS/ roll_call_lists/roll_call_vote_cfm.cfm?congress=109&session=2&vote=00025

United States Senate. (2006, March 2). *U.S. Senate roll call votes 109th Congress - 2nd session.* Retrieved March 3, 2006, from http://www.senate.gov/legislative/LIS/ roll_call_lists/roll_call_vote_cfm.cfm?congress=109&session=2&vote=00029

U.S. Constitution, Amendment V.

The White House. (2006, January 3). *U.S. attorneys discuss Patriot Act meeting with the president.* Retrieved August 6, 2006, from http://www.whitehouse.gov/news/releases/ 2006/01/20060103-3.html

Yeh, B. T., & Doyle, C. (2006, March 24). *USA Patriot Act improvement & Reauthorization Act of 2005: A legal analysis.* The Library of

Congress, Congressional Research Service. Retrieved May 25, 2006, from http://www.fas.org/sgp/crs/intel/RL33332.pdf

INTERNET SOURCES:

109th United States Congress. (2005, August 3). In *Wikipedia, The Free Encyclopedia*. Retrieved August 8, 2005, from http://en.wikipedia.org/w/index.php?title=109th_United_States_Congress&oldid=20213103

Abramson, L. (2005, July 18). *The Patriot Act: Political players.* Retrieved September 1, 2005, from http://www.npr.org/templates/story/story.php?storyId=4754492&sourceCode=RSS

Ahlin, J. (2005, November 13). *USA Patriot Act needs revisions and oversight.* Retrieved December 11, 2005, from http://www.in-forum.com/articles/printer.cfm?id=108393

American Civil Liberties Union [ACLU]. (n.d.). *About us.* Retrieved August 13, 2005, from http://www.aclu.org/about/aboutmain.cfm

American Civil Liberties Union [ACLU]. (n.d.). *Freedomwire: The USA Patriot Act: It could happen to you.* Retrieved August 13, 2005, from http://www.aclu.org/freedomwire/ patriotact/it_could_happen.pdf

American Civil Liberties Union [ACLU]. (n.d.). *List of communities that have passed resolutions.* Retrieved October 6, 2006, from http://www.aclu.org/safefree/resources/ 17102res20040610.html

American Civil Liberties Union [ACLU]. (n.d.). *The USA Patriot Act and government actions that threaten our civil liberties.* Retrieved August 13, 2005, from http://action.aclu.org/ site/DocServer/patriotactflyer.pdf?

American Civil Liberties Union [ACLU]. (2003, July 7). *Detention.* Retrieved August 13, 2005, from http://www.aclu.org/safefree/resources/16828res20030707.html

American Civil Liberties Union [ACLU]. '(2005, July 21). *House Rules Committee shuts out needed Patriot Act reform, yet adds "smokeless tobacco" amendment.* Retrieved July 30, 2005, from http://www.aclu.org/safefree/general/20257prs20050721.html

American Civil Liberties Union [ACLU]. (2005, November 16). *Summary of Patriot Reauthorization Act conference report.* Retrieved November 21, 2005, from the ACLU Web site: http://www.aclu.org/safefree/patriot/21582res20051116.html

American Library Association [ALA]. (2005, August 5). *Senate passes Patriot Act Reauthorization.* Retrieved August 29, 2005, from http://www.lita.org/ala/alonline/ currentnews/newsarchive/2005abc/august2005abc/senateusapa.htm

Amster, S. E. (2003). *Patriot Act redux: A second anti-terroism proposal, further eroding Americans' civil liberties, comes under attack from both parties.* Retrieved August 12, 2005, from http://www.splcenter.org/intel/intelreport/article.jsp?pid=100

Answers.com. (2006). *Benjamin Franklin True Patriot Act.* Retrieved March 25, 2006, from http://www.answers.com/Benjamin%20Franklin%20True%20Patriot%20Act

Ash, R. W. (2002, June 11). *American Center for Law & Justice memo - Lawfulness of incarceration of al-Qaeda "dirty bomb" suspect.* Retrieved March 9, 2005, from http://www.aclj.org/Issues/Resources/Document.aspx?ID=138

Beeson, A., & Jaffer, J. (2003, July 30). *Unpatriotic acts: The FBI's power to rifle through your records and personal belongings without telling you.* Retrieved August 12, 2005, from http://www.aclu.org/safefree/resources/16813pub20030730.html

Best, S., & McDermott, M. (2005, August 26). *University of Connecticut releases new national poll on the USA Patriot Act.* Retrieved June 26, 2006, from http://www.csra.uconn.edu/ pdf/PATRIOTACT-PRESSRELEASE.pdf

Bill of Rights Defense Committee. (2005, November 3). *Support Senate PATRIOT Act reauthorization bill.* Retrieved November 12, 2005, from http://www.bordc.org/ newsletter/bordc-act-alert43.php

Bishop, S. (2006, February 26). *Patriot Act revisions get senator's support.* Retrieved March 20, 2006, from http://www.populistamerica.com/patriot_act_revisions_get_senator_s_ support

Burnett, J., & Skoglund, R. (2005, August 15). *The women's league of voters.* Retrieved August 25, 2005, from http://www.wiltonlwv.org/index_files/votersep.htm

Byrne, J. (2005). *Reid to oppose Patriot Act, will join efforts to block bill.* Retrieved December 14, 2005, from http://rawstory.com/news/2005/Reid_to_oppose_Patriot_Act_will_ 1214.html

Carafano, J. J., & Kochems, A. (2005, December 2). *Congress poised to pass Patriot Act provisions.* Retrieved December 5, 2005, from the Heritage Foundation Web site: http://www.heritage.org/Research/HomelandDefense/wm930.cfm?renderfor print=1

Center for Democracy & Technology [CDT]. (n.d.). *Patriot Act overview.* Retrieved August 19, 2005, from http://www.cdt.org/security/usa-patriot/overview2005.php

Center for Democracy & Technology. [CDT]. (n.d.). *Security & freedom legislation (109th).* Retrieved March 24, 2006, from http://www.cdt.org/legislation/109/4

Cole, D. (2003, February 10). *What Patriot II proposes to do.* Retrieved February 15, 2005, from http://www.cdt.org/security/usapatriot/030210cole.pdf

Cowan, R. (2005, December 13). *Gonzalez pushes for Patriot Act renewal.* Retrieved December 14, 2005, from http://www.populistamerica.com/gonzalez_pushes_for_patriot_act_ renewal

Dahlburg, J. (2005, December 7). *Ex-professor acquitted in Patriot Act test case.* Retrieved December 20, 2005, from http://www.populistamerica.com/ex_professor_acquitted_in_ patriot_act_test_case

Dempsey, J. X. (2005, May 10). *Statement of James X. Dempsey, executive director, Center for Democracy & Technology before the Senate Committee of the Judiciary.* Retrieved June 25, 2005, from http://www.cdt.org/testimony/ 20050510dempsey.pdf

Dinh, V. D. (2004, June 9). *How the USA Patriot Act defends democracy.* Retrieved August 25, 2004 from http://www.defenddemocracy.org/usr_doc/USA _Patriot_Act.pdf

Domestic Security Enhancement Act of 2003 [DSEA]. (2003, January 9). Retrieved February 15, 2005, from The Center For Public Integrity Web site: http://www.publicintegrity.org/ docs/PatriotAct/story_01_020703_doc_1.pdf

Domestic Security Enhancement Act of 2003 [DSEA]. (2004, December 5). In *Wikipedia, The Free Encyclopedia.* Retrieved February 15, 2005, from http://en.wikipedia.org/w/index. php?title=Domestic_Security_Enhancement_Act_of_2003&oldid=13993637

Edgar, T. H. (2003, February 14). *Interested persons memo: Section-by-section analysis of Justice Department draft "Domestic Security Enhancement Act of 2003," also known as "Patriot Act II".* Retrieved February 15, 2005, from the ACLU Web site: http://www.aclu.org/safefree/general/17203leg20030214.html

Electronic Frontier Foundation. (n.d.). *EFF analysis of "Patriot II," provisions of the Domestic Security Enhancement Act of 2003 that impact the Internet and surveillance.* Retrieved August 19, 2005, from http://www.eff.org/Censorship/Terrorism_militias/patriot-act-II-analysis.php

Electronic Frontier Foundation (2005). *Let the sun set on Patriot Section 505 - National Security Letters (NSLs).* Retrieved October 5, 2006, from http://www.eff.org/patriot/sunset/ 505.php

Electronic Privacy Information Center [EPIC]. (2001). *HR 3162 RDS: 107th Congress.* Retrieved September 25, 2004, from http://www.epic. org/privacy/terrorism/hr3162.html

Encarta World English Dictionary [North American Edition]. (2005). [Electronic Version]. Retrieved April 1, 2005, from http://Encarta. msn.com/dictionary_/indefinite.html

Epstein, E. (2006, January 31). *Spying in U.S. strains debate on Patriot Act: Congress no closer to renewal after 5-week extension.* Retrieved May 2, 2006, from http://www.mindfully. org/Reform/2006/ Spying-Patriot-Act31jan06.htm

Eugene V. Debs Internet Archive. (2001). Retrieved February 10, 2005, from http://www. marxists.org/archive/debs

The Federalist Patriot. (n.d.). The 2001 USA Patriot Act. Retrieved September 20, 2004, from http://patriotpost.us/papers/03-41_paper. asp

Free Congress Foundation (2004, February 27). *Commentary: Gun owner takes aim at the USA-Patriot Act.* Retrieved August 13, 2005, from http://www.freecongress.org/centers/tp/ ccl/2004/040227.asp

Furber, M. (2005, December 28). *Feds' anti-meth bill dies with Patriot Act extension.* Retrieved December 29, 2005, from http://www. mtexpress.com/index2.php?ID=2005107130

Glasstetter, J. (2005, November 10). *Patriot Act: Conference committee can protect Americans' rights.* Retrieved November 12, 2005, from http://www.pfaw.org/pfaw/general/default. aspx?oid=19961

Glasstetter, J., & Berning, N. (2005, December 16). *Patriot Act stopped in Senate.* Retrieved December 20, 2005, from http://www.pfaw. org/pfaw/general/default.aspx?oid=20183

Grunwald, M. (2004, March 3). *John Kerry's waffles: If you don't like the democratic nominee's views, just wait a week.* Retrieved August 8, 2005, from http://www.slate.com/id/ 2096540

Gun Owners of America. (2004, June 16). *Gun owners of America e-mail alert.* Retrieved August 13, 2005, from http://www.gunowners.org/statealerts/va061604.txt

Gyan, J., Jr. (2005, August 1). *Gonzalez defends USA Patriot Act.* Retrieved September 2, 2005, from http://www.infowars.com/articles/ps/patriot_act_gonzales_defends_ act.htm

Inouye, S. (2005, July 21). *Senate committee's positive steps on Patriot Act welcome, but flaws remain.* Retrieved August 31, 2005, from http://libertycoalition.net/aclu_on_senate_judiciarys_usa_patriot_reauthorization_bill

Jackson, P. (2005, December 3). *Ex-FBI chief Freeh backs Patriot Act renewal.* Retrieved December 5, 2005, from http://www.populistamerica.com/ex_fbi_chief_freeh_backs_ patriot_act_renewal

Jaffer, J. (2003, August 26). *Patriot propaganda: Justice Department's Patriot Act Website creates new myths about controversial law.* Retrieved August 12, 2005, from http://www.aclu.org/safefree/resources/16761pub20030826.html

Johnson, G. (2005, July 22). *House votes to extend Patriot Act.* Retrieved August 19, 2005, from http://gwillard.home.att.net/patriotgames05.htm#extend

Jones, A. (2003, February 10). *A brief analysis of the Domestic Security Enhancement Act 2003.* Retrieved January 30, 2004, from http: www.rickieleejones.com/political/patriotact.htm

Keene, D. A. (2003, September 16). *Ashcroft shows shortcomings with 'victory'.* Retrieved September 23, 2006, from http://www.conservative.org/columnists/keene/ 030916dk.asp

Kellman, L. (2006, February 16). *Patriot Act moves closer to renewal.* Retrieved March 3, 2006, from http://www.lwvweston.org/patriotact.html

Kellman, L. (2006, March 8). *US Congress renews Patriot Act; Bush to sign.* Retrieved March 3, 2006, from http://sify.com/printer_friendly.php?id=14157731&ctid=2&lid=1

Kellman, R. (2005, December 21). *Patriot Act: Temporary extension.* Retrieved December 22, 2005, from http://www.wgrz.com/printfullstory.aspx?storyid=34024

Kelly, M. (n.d.). *Terrorism through America's history.* Retrieved August 23, 2004, from http://Americanhistory.about.com/library/fastfacts/blffterrorism.htm

Kerry, J. (n.d.). *John Kerry's Senate record.* Retrieved January 1, 2005, from http://www.johnkerry.com/about/john_kerry/senate.html#safer

Kochems, A., Rosenzweig, P., & Carafano J. J. (2005, June 23). *Should libraries become terrorist sanctuaries?* Retrieved July 1, 2005, from http://www.heritage.org/Research/ HomelandDefense/wm772.cfm

Lessmann, K. (2004). *Bush negative ad against Kerry's "first 100 days."* Retrieved August 8, 2005, from http://www.gradfree.com/kevin/bushnegativeadagainstkerry.htm

Levin, B. (2001). *Freedom and dissent: The nation struggles to balance civil liberties and police power in the aftermath of the September horror.* Retrieved August 12, 2005, from http://www.splcenter.org/intel/intelreport/article.jsp?aid=173

Lewis, C., & Mayle, A. (2003, February 7). *Justice Dept. drafts sweeping expansion of anti-terrorism act.* Retrieved February 15, 2005, from The Center for Public Integrity Web site: http://www.publicintegrity.org/report.aspx?aid=94

LibraryJournal.com. (2006, January 19). *January 25 National Patriot Act Call-In Day.* Retrieved May 2, 2006, from http://www.libraryjournal.com/article/CA6300505.html

LibraryJournal.com. (2006, February 13). *ALA criticizes Patriot Act compromise.* Retrieved March 20, 2006, from http://www.libraryjournal.com/article/CA6306777.html

Lilienthal, S. (2005, September 2). *Reauthorization the USA Patriot Act: The battle moves to conference.* Retrieved September 2, 2005, from http://www.aim.org/guest_column_ print/3982_0_6_0/

Limbaugh, R. (2005, December 21). *Senator Larry Craig defends his Patriot Act vote.* Retrieved December 22, 2005, from http://www.ruptured-duck.com/sixties/shockhorror/node/82/

Lochhead, C. (2002, December 5). *Dick Armey leaves House with call for freedom.* Retrieved September 23, 2006, from http://www.mindfully.org/Reform/2002/Dick-Armey-Conservative-Liberty5dec02.htm

Lowry, R. (2005, December 28). *Patriot misses: Demagoguery and the Patriot Act.* Retrieved December 29, 2005, from http://www.nationalreview.com/lowry/lowry200512280854. asp

Lynch, T. (2003, August 21). *Patriotic questions.* Retrieved June 29, 2006, from http://cato.org/ research/articles/lynch-030821.html

Lynch, T. (2003, September 10). *More surveillance equals less liberty: Patriot Act reduces privacy, undercuts judicial review.* Retrieved September 23, 2006, from http://www.cato. org/research/articles/lynch-030910.html

Merrimack Mortgage Company, Inc. (2006). *USA Patriot Act of 2001, Section 326 Customer identification program (CIP) policy.* Retrieved October 5, 2006, from http://www.merrimackmortgage.com/Patriot_Act. asp

Minow, M. (2002, February 15). *The USA Patriot Act and patron privacy on library Internet terminals. Law Library Resource Xchange, LLC.* Retrieved August 13, 2005, from http://www.llrx.com/features/usapatriotact.htm

Neas, R. G. (2003, September 9). *Two years after 9/11: Ashcroft's assault on the Constitution.* Retrieved July 1, 2005, from http://www.pfaw.org/pfaw/dfiles/file_232.pdf

Neill, J. (2006, July 5). *Analysis of Professional Literature.* Retrieved January 1, 2006, from http://www.wilderdom.com/OEcourses/PROFLIT/Class8Qualitative3.htm#Content

Neznanski, M. (2003, December 2). *Kerry speaks against Patriot Act legislation.* Retrieved August 8, 2005, from http://www.archives2004.ghazali.net/html/kerry_on_patriot_act.html

Novak, R. (2005, December 27). *Bush, Congress set themselves up to fail on Patriot Act, anwr.* Retrieved December 29, 2005, from http://www.humaneventsonline.com/article.php? id=11141

Orr, J. S. (2006, January 30). *Patriot Act nears the wire - again.* Retrieved February 2, 2006, from http://www.populistamerica.com/patriot_act_nears_the_wire_again

Pike, J. (2003, October 22). *How the Bush family profits from the Patriot Act.* Retrieved October 18, 2005, from http://www.evote.com/?q=node/1630

Podesta, J. (2002). *USA Patriot Act: The good, the bad, and the sunset.* Retrieved August 17, 2005, from http://www.abanet.org/irr/hr/winter02/podesta.html

Quotes From Famous People. (2004). *Famous terrorism quotations.* Retrieved September 20, 2004, from http://home.att.net/~quotesexchange/terrorism.html

Raw Story. (2006, March 1). *House pulls Patriot Act compromise vote; delays until Tuesday.* Retrieved March 3, 2006, from http://rawstory.com/news/2006/Patriot_Act_compromise_ may_be_ in_ 0301.html

Riba, E. (2002). *The USA Patriot Act: The response and responsibility of library management.* Retrieved August 13, 2005, from http://www.osmond-riba.org/lis/usapatriot.htm

Rice, R. (2002). The USA Patriot Act and American libraries. *Information for Social Change, 16.* Retrieved August 13, 2005, from http://libr.org/isc/articles/16-Rice.html

Savage, C. (2006, January 25). *AG's memo raises questions on Patriot Act: Suggests it's not needed for domestic spying.* Retrieved October 3, 2006, from http://www.truthout.org/ cgi-bin/artman/exec/view.cgi/48/17214

Skoglund, R. & Burnett, J. (2005, August 30). *Patriot Act needs open evaluation.* Retrieved October 13, 2006, from http://www.wiltonlwv.org/index_files/votersep.htm

Streisand, B. (2001, December 11). *Rainbow/PUSH Coalition fourth annual awards dinner: Remarks by Barbra Streisand.* Retrieved August 13, 2005, from http://www. barbrastreisand.com/news_statementsArchives.html#rainbow

Vermont Library Association. (2002, October 21). *USA Patriot Act letter.* Retrieved August 13, 2005, from http://www.vermontlibraries.org/patriot.html

Weich, R. (2002, October 15). *Insatiable appetite: The government's demand for new and unnecessary powers after September 11.* Retrieved August 12, 2005, from http://www.aclu.org/safefree/resources/17042pub20021015.html

Welsh, S. C. (2004, June 30). *Law watch - detainees: Supreme Court Guantanamo decision*. Washington, DC: The Center for Defense Information. Retrieved March 11, 2005, from http://www.ciaonet.org/wps/wes07/

JOURNALS:

Ackerman, B. (2004). The emergency constitution. *Yale Law Journal, 113*, 1029-1091.

Amorosa, J. (2005). Dissecting in re D-J-: The attorney general, unchecked power, and the new national security threat posed by Haitian asylum seekers. *Cornell International Law Journal, 38*, 263-292.

Ashran, J. (2004). *Stogner v. California*: A collision between the *ex post facto* clause and California's interest in protecting child sex abuse victims. *Journal of Criminal Law and Criminology, 94*, 723-760.

Aziz, S. (2003). The laws on providing material support to terrorist organizations: The erosion of constitutional rights or a legitimate tool for preventing terrorism? *Texas Journal on Civil Liberties & Civil Rights, 9*, 45-92.

Banks, W. C. (2003). And the wall came tumbling down: Secret surveillance after the terror. *University of Miami Law Review, 57*, 1147-1194.

Barbour, A. (2004). Ready...aim...foia! A survey of the Freedom of Information Act in the post-9/11 United States. *Boston Public Interest Law Journal, 13*, 203-226.

Beale, S. S., & Felman, J. E. (2002). Responses to September 11 attacks: The consequences of enlisting federal grand juries in the war on terrorism: Assessing the USA Patriot Act's changes to grand jury secrecy. *Harvard Journal of Law & Public Policy, 25*, 699-718.

Becker, S. W. (2003). "Mirror, mirror on the wall...": Assessing the aftermath of September 11th. *Valparaiso Law Review, 37*, 563-626.

Berg, N., & Kelly, C. (2004). Racketeer-influenced and corrupt organizations. *American Criminal Law Review, 41,* 1027-1078.

Block, F. (2005). Civil liberties during national emergencies: The interactions between the three branches of government in coping with past and current threats to the nation's security. *New York University School of Law Review of Law and Social Change, 29,* 459-524.

Broxmeyer, E. (2004). The problems of security and freedom: Procedural due process and the designation of foreign terrorist organizations under the Anti-terrorism and Effective Death Penalty Act. *Berkeley Journal of International Law, 22,* 439-488.

Calica, A. J. (2004). Self-help is the best kind: The efficient breach justification for forcible abduction of terrorists. *Cornell International Law Journal, 37,* 389-492.

Chesney, R. M. (2005). The sleeper scenario: Terrorism-support laws and the demands of prevention. *Harvard Journal on Legislation, 42,* 1-89.

Cocheo, S. (2003). License to fool? *ABA Banking Journal, 95,* 44-50. Retrieved January 27, 2005, from OCLC FirstSearch database.

Cole, D. (2004). The priority of morality: The emergency constitution's blind spot. *Yale Law Journal, 113,* 1753-1800.

Collins, J. M. (2002). And the walls came tumbling down: Sharing grand jury information with the intelligence community under the USA Patriot Act. *American Criminal Law Review, 39,* 1261-1286.

Committee on Federal Courts. (2004). The indefinite detention of "enemy combatants": Balancing due process and national security in the context of the war on terror. *The Record of the Association of The Bar of the City of New York, 59,* 41-161.

Davis, D. H. (2002). The dark side to a just war: The USA Patriot Act and counterterrorism's potential threat to religious freedom. *Journal of*

Church & State, 44, 5-17. Retrieved January 27, 2005, from OCLC FirstSearch database.

Demleitner, N. V. (2004). Risk assessment: Methodologies and application: Editor's observations: Risk assessment: Promises and pitfalls. *Federal Sentencing Reporter, 16*, 161-177.

Dhooge, L. J. (2003). A previously unimaginable risk potential: September 11 and the insurance industry. *American Business Law Journal, 40*, 687-778.

Engle, K. (2004). Constructing good aliens and good citizens: Legitimizing the war on terror(ism). *University of Colorado Law Review, 75*, 59-114.

Essex, D. (2004). Opposing the USA Patriot Act: The best alternative for American librarians. *Public Libraries, 43*, 331-340. Retrieved January 27, 2005, from OCLC FirstSearch database.

Fisher, L. E. (2004). Guilt by expressive association: Political profiling, surveillance and the privacy of groups. *Arizona Law Review, 46*, 621-675.

Fletcher, G. P. (2002). The military tribunal order: On justice and war: Contradictions in the proposed military tribunals. *Harvard Journal of Law & Public Policy, 25*, 635-652.

Frei, R. D. (2004). Does time eclipse time? *Stogner v. California* and the court's determination of the *ex post facto* limitations on retroactive justice. *University of Richmond Law Review, 38*, 1001-1045.

Gardner, J. W. (2003). Halfway there: Zadvydas v. Davis reins in indefinite detentions, but leaves much unanswered. *Cornell International Law Journal, 36*, 177-206.

Glick, L. A. (2002). World trade after September 11, 2001: The U.S. response. *Cornell International Law Journal, 35*, 627-638.

Gross, E. (2004). The struggle of a democracy against terrorism—protection of human rights: The right to privacy versus the national interest—the proper balance. *Cornell International Law Journal, 37*, 27-93.

Hannigan, J. M. (2004). Playing patriot games: National security challenges civil liberties. *Houston Law Review, 41*, 1371-1406.

Harris, G. C. (2003). Terrorism and the Constitution: Sacrificing civil liberties in the name of national security. *Cornell International Law Journal, 36*, 135-150.

Harrison, D. L. (2004). The USA Patriot Act: A new way of thinking, an old way of reacting, higher education responds. *North Carolina Journal of Law & Technology, 5*, 177-211.

Hatch, O. G. (2004). Religious pluralism, difference, and social stability. *Brigham Young University Law Review, 2*, 317-323.

Heymann, P. B. (2002). Civil liberties and human rights in the aftermath of September 11. *Harvard Journal of Law & Public Policy, 25*, 441-456.

Hitz, F. P. (2002). Responses to the September 11 attacks: Unleashing the rogue elephant: September 11 and letting the CIA be the CIA. *Harvard Journal of Law & Public Policy, 25*, 765-780.

Hoffman, G. A. (2003). Litigating terrorism: The new FISA regime, the wall, and the Fourth Amendment. *American Criminal Law Review, 40*, 1655-1682.

Howell, B. A. (2004). The future of Internet surveillance law: A symposium to discuss Internet surveillance, privacy & the USA Patriot Act: Surveillance law: Reshaping the framework: Seven weeks: The making of the USA Patriot Act. *George Washington Law Review, 72*, 1145-1207.

Ibbetson, P. (2005). The Patriot Act: Title VII: Analyzing the quiet giants. *Illinois Law Enforcement Executive Forum, 5,* 83-96.

Iraola, R. (2003). Enemy combatants, the courts, and the Constitution. *Oklahoma Law Review, 56,* 565-619.

Jackola, A. T. (2004). A second bite at the apple: How the government's use of the doctrine of enemy combatants in the case of Zacarias Moussaoui threatens to upset the future of the criminal justice system. *Hamline Law Review, 27,* 101-132.

Johnson, K. R. (2003). Beyond belonging: Challenging the boundaries of nationality: September 11 and Mexican immigrants: Collateral damage comes home. *DePaul Law Review, 52,* 849-870.

Keith, D. (2004). In the name of national security or insecurity? The potential indefinite detention of noncitizen certified terrorists in the United States and the United Kingdom in the aftermath of September 11, 2001. *Florida Journal of International Law, 16,* 405-481.

Kendrick, L. N. (2004). Alienable rights and unalienable wrongs: Fighting the "war on terror" through the Fourth Amendment. *Howard Law Journal, 47,* 989-1035.

Kerr, O. S. (2003). Internet surveillance law after the USA Patriot Act: The big brother that isn't. *Northwestern University Law Review, 97,* 707-673.

Kollar, J. F. (2004). USA Patriot Act, the Fourth Amendment, and paranoia: Can they read this while I'm typing? *Journal of High Technology Law, 3,* 67-93.

Kreimer, S. F. (2004). Watching the watchers: Surveillance, transparency, and political freedom in the war on terror. *University of Pennsylvania Journal of Constitutional Law, 7,* 133-181.

Kubler, J. (2004). U.S. citizens as enemy combatants; indication of a rollback of civil liberties or a sign of our jurisprudential evolution? *St. John's Journal of Legal Commentary, 18,* 631-673.

La Fond, J. Q. (2003, March/June). Preventive outpatient commitment for persons with serious mental illness: Outpatient commitment's next frontier: Sexual predators. *Psychology, Public Policy and Law, 9,* 159-182.

Lee, L. T. (2003). The USA Patriot Act and telecommunications: Privacy under attack. *Rutgers Computer and Technology Law Journal, 29,* 371-403.

Legomsky, S. H. (2005). Immigration law and human rights: Legal line drawing post-September 11: Symposium article: The ethnic and religious profiling of noncitizens: National security and international human rights. *Boston College Third World Law Journal, 25,* 161-196.

Lewis, A. (2003). Civil liberties in a time of terror. *Wisconsin Law Review, 2003,* 257-272.

Lilly, J. R. (2003). National security at what price?: A look into civil liberty concerns in the information age under the USA Patriot Act of 2001 and a proposed constitutional test for future legislation. *Cornell Journal of Law and Public Policy, 12,* 447-471.

Lyden, G. A. (2003). The International Money Laundering Abatement and Anti-terrorist Financing Act of 2001: Congress wears a blindfold while giving money laundering legislation a facelift. *Fordham Journal of Corporate & Financial Law, 8,* 201-243.

Mantle, D. R. (2003). What foreign students fear: Homeland security measures and closed deportation hearings. *Brigham Young University Education and Law Journal, 2003,* 815-834.

Marshall, K. M. (2002). Finding time for federal habeas corpus: *Carey v. Saffold. Akron Law Review, 37,* 549-587.

Mart, S. N. (2004). Protecting the lady from Toledo: Post-USA Patriot Act electronic surveillance at the library. *Law Library Journal, 96,* 449-473.

Martin, R. S. (2003). Watch what you type: As the FBI records your keystrokes, the Fourth Amendment develops carpal tunnel syndrome. *American Criminal Law Review, 40,* 1271-1300.

McCarthy, A. C. (2004, June 14). The Patriot Act without tears. *National Review, 56,* 32-35.

McKenzie, A. (2004). A nation of immigrants or a nation of suspects? State and local enforcement of federal immigration laws since 9-11. *Alabama Law Review, 55,* 1149-1165.

Miller, T. (2005). Immigration law and human rights: Legal line drawing post-September 11: Symposium article: Blurring the boundaries between immigration and crime control after September 11th. *Boston College Third World Law Journal, 25,* 81-123.

Minami, D., Narasaki, K., Nimr, H., Chang, J., Ting, P. (2004). Sixty years after the internment: Civil rights, identity politics, and racial profiling. *Asian Law Journal, 11,* 151-176.

Mousin, C. B. (2003). Standing with the persecuted: Adjudicating religious asylum claims after the enactment of the International Freedom Act of 1998. *Brigham Young University Law Review, 2003,* 541-591.

Nappen, L. P. (2003). School safety v. free speech: The seesawing tolerance standards for students' sexual and violent expressions. *Texas Journal on Civil Liberties & Civil Rights, 9,* 93-127.

Orlova, A. V., & Moore, J. W. (2005). "Umbrellas" or "building blocks"?: Defining international terrorism and transnational organized crime in international law. *Houston Journal of International Law, 27,* 267-310.

Osler, M. (2003). Capone and Bin Laden: The failure of government at the cusp of war and crime. *Baylor Law Review, 55*, 603-615.

Perry, N. J. (2004). The numerous federal legal definitions of terrorism: The problem of too many grails. *Journal of Legislation, 30*, 249-274.

Rabinovitz, J. (2004). Taking the ACLU into the limelight: Can Anthony Romero '90 change the way Americans view civil liberties? *Stanford Lawyer, 68*, 14-18, 80. Retrieved September 23, 2006, from http://www.law.stanford.edu/publications/stanford_lawyer/issues/68/TakingTheACLU.pdf

Ravenell, T. E. (2002). Left, left, left, right left: The search for rights and remedies in juvenile boot camps. *Columbia University School of Law, 35*, 347-370.

Richman, D. C., & Stuntz, W. J. (2005). Al Capone's revenge: An essay on the political economy of pretextual prosecution. *Columbia Law Review, 105*, 583-639.

Rosenzweig, P. (2004). Civil liberty and the response to terrorism. *Duquesne University Law Review, 42*, 663-723.

Saito, N. T. (2004). For "our" security: Who is an "American" and what is protected by enhanced law enforcement and intelligence powers? *Seattle Journal for Social Justice, 2*, 23-62.

Seamon, R. H., & Gardner, W. D. (2005). The Patriot Act and the wall between foreign intelligence and law enforcement. *Harvard Journal of Law & Public Policy, 28*, 319-386.

Sekhon, V. (2003). The civil rights of "others": Antiterrorism, the Patriot Act, and Arab and South Asian American rights in post-9/11 American society. *Texas Forum on Civil Liberties & Civil Rights, 8*, 117-148.

Solove, D. J. (2004). The future of Internet surveillance law: A symposium to discuss Internet surveillance, privacy & the USA Patriot Act:

Surveillance law: Reshaping the framework: Electronic surveillance law. *George Washington Law Review, 72*, 1264-1305. -

Thomas, P. A. (2003). Emergency and anti-terrorist power: 9/11: USA and UK. *Fordham International Law Journal, 26*, 1193-1229.

Travalio, G., & Altenburg, J. (2003). State responsibility for sponsorship of terrorist and insurgent groups: Terrorism, state responsibility, and the use of military force. *Chicago Journal of International Law, 4*, 97-119.

Traynor, M. (2005). Citizenship in a time of repression. *Wisconsin Law Review, 2005*, 1-34.

Vandenberg, Q. H. (2004). How can the United States rectify its post-9/11 stance on noncitizens' rights? *Notre Dame Journal of Law, Ethics & Public Policy, 18*, 605-645.

NEWS SOURCES:

ABC News. (n.d.). *Profile: Attorney General Alberto Gonzales: From humble beginnings to Harvard to the White House.* Retrieved August 28, 2005, from http://abcnews.go.com/ Politics/Inauguration/story?id=241596

Abrams, J. (2006, February 10). *Hastert backs compromise on Patriot Act.* Retrieved March 20, 2006, from http://www.usatoday.com/news/washington/2006-02-10-hastert-patriot_x.htm

Arena, K., Frieden, T., & Hirschkorn, P. (2005, November 22). *Terror suspect Padilla charged.* Retrieved August 10, 2006, from http://www.cnn.com/2005/LAW/11/22/padilla.case/ index.html

Associated Press. (2006). *Feingold launches another lonely effort to block the Patriot Act.* Retrieved March 3, 2006, from http://www.wbay.com/global/story.asp?s= 4507134&ClientType=printable

Babington, C. (2005, December 17). Renewal of Patriot Act is blocked in Senate. [Electronic Version]. *The Washington Post,* p. A01. Retrieved December 21, 2005, from http://www.washingtonpost.com

Babington, C. (2006, March 14). Feingold pushes to censure president. [Electronic Version]. *The Washington Post,* p. A08. Retrieved March 23, 2006, from http://www.washingtonpost.com

Baker, P. (2005, March 12). Karen Hughes to work on the world's view of U.S. [Electronic Version]. *The Washington Post,* p. A03. Retrieved April 15, 2005, from http://www.washingtonpost.com

Barrett, T. (2005, July 22). *House approves renewal of Patriot Act.* Retrieved August 17, 2005, from http://www.cnn.com/2005/POLITICS/07/21/patriot.act/index.html

bin Laden, O. (1996). *Declaration of war against the Americans occupying the land of the two holy places.* Retrieved October 22, 2005, from http://www.pbs.org/newshour/ terrorism/international/fatwa_ 1996.html

Blanton, D. (2005, June 16). *Fox poll: Congress 'out of touch'; Majority supports renewing Patriot Act.* Retrieved June 28, 2006, from http://www.foxnews.com/story/ 0,2933,159790,00.html

Bohn, K. (2003, July 30). ACLU files lawsuit against Patriot Act. *CNN Washington Bureau.* Retrieved September 25, 2004, from http://www.cnn.com/2003/LAW/07/30/patriot.act

Bonjean, R., & Miller, L. C. (2005). *House speaker Dennis Hastert applauds passage of the Patriot Act.* Retrieved December 15, 2005, from http://releases.usnewswire.com/ GetRelease.asp?id=58161

Branigin, W. (2005, December 15). Bush calls blockage of Patriot Act 'inexcusable'. [Electronic Version]. *The Washington Post.* Retrieved December 20, 2005, from http://www. washingtonpost.com/wp-dyn/content/article/2005/12/19/AR2005121900447.html

Broache, A. (2006, January 9). *Patriot Act defender touts 'safeguards'*. Retrieved January 11, 2006, from http://news.com.com/Patriot+Act+defender+touts+safeguards/2100-1028_3-6024917.html

Burke, G. (2006, January 7). "Cheney touts economy in visit." [Electronic Version]. *The Kansas City Star*. Retrieved January 11, 2006, from the Infotrac Web database.

Carlson, D. K. (2004, January 20). *Far enough? Public wary of restricted liberties*. Retrieved August 15, 2005, from http://www.gallup.com

Carlson, D. K. (2005, March 1). *Would Americans fight terrorism by any means necessary? Two-thirds willing to let government assassinate terrorists*. Retrieved August 16, 2005, from http://www.gallup.com

Carlson, D. K. (2005, March 8). *Americans frown on interrogation techniques: Sleep deprivation most acceptable to Americans*. Retrieved August 16, 2005, from http://www.gallup.com

Carlson, D. K. (2005, July 19). *Liberty vs. security: Public mixed on Patriot Act: Majority familiar with the law*. Retrieved August 15, 2005, from http://www.gallup.com

Caruba, A. (2005, June 13). *Can patriots survive the Patriot Act?* Retrieved September 23, 2006, from http://www.canadafreepress.com/2005/caruba061305.htm

Carroll, J. (2005, April 19). *American public opinion about terrorism*. Retrieved August 16, 2005, from http://www.gallup.com

CBS News. (2005, November 17). *Senators vow to block Patriot Act*. Retrieved December 5, 2005, from http://www.cbsnews.com/stories/2005/11/17/politics/main1054934.shtml

CBS News. (2006, February 10). *Patriot Act renewal gets green light*. Retrieved March 20, 2006, from http://www.cbsnews.com/stories/2006/02/10/politics/main1307635.shtml

CBS News. (2006, March 10). *Bush signs renewal of Patriot Act.* Retrieved March 20, 2006, from http://www.cbsnews.com/stories/2006/03/10/ap/politics/mainD8G8HIM07.shtml

Chachere, V. (2004, January 25). Florida case puts Patriot Act to test, investigators use the law to convert years of surveillance into a criminal case, and defense attorneys attack the government's arguments [Electronic version]. *The Grand Rapids Press*, p. C5. Retrieved April 24, 2005, from the Infotrac Web database.

Chaddock, G. R. (2005, December 14). *An 11th hour drive to amend Patriot Act.* Retrieved December 14, 2005, from http://www.csmonitor.com/2005/1214/p03s02-uspo.htm

Chaddock, G. R. (2005, December 20). *Patriot Act, drilling in Arctic roil Senate.* Retrieved December 20, 2005, from http://www.csmonitor.com/2005/1220/p03s03-uspo.html? s=widep

Chen, M. (2005, July 15). *Patriot Act reforms clash in Congress, public.* Retrieved August 29, 2005, from http://newstandardnews.net/content/index.cfm/items/2102

CNN.com. (2005, December 16). *Patriot Act renewal fails in Senate.* Retrieved December 20, 2005, from http://www.cnn.com/2005/POLITICS/12/16/patriot.act/index.html

Conyers, J. (2005, November 11). *Conyers calls for changes in Patriot Act to protect nation's civil liberties.* Retrieved November 12, 2005, from http://www.commondreams.org/ news2005/1110-16.htm

Corcoran, M. (2005, June 14). *Battle over Patriot Act set to take place in Boston.* Retrieved August 29, 2005, from http://www.jsons.org/media/storage/paper139/news/2005/06/03/ EmersonNews/Battle.Over.Patriot.Act.Set.To.Take.Place.In.Boston-957803.shtml? nore write200610032253&sourcedomain=www.jsons.org

Cornyn, J. (2005, December 20). Targeting the Patriot Act. [Electronic Version]. *The Washington Times.* Retrieved December 21, 2005, from http://www.washingtontimes. com/op-ed/20051219-093818-5234r.htm

Curry, T. (2004, November 12). *Patriot Act renewal up to Congress.* Retrieved August 17, 2005, from http://msnbc.msn.com/id/6469357/

Daly, M. (2005, December 16). NW democrats hail Senate rejection of USA Patriot Act. [Electronic Version]. *Seattle Post-Intelligencer.* Retrieved December 20, 2005, from http://seattlepi.nwsource. com–

Deans, B. (2006, February 3). *House approves temporary extension of Patriot Act.* Retrieved August 17, 2006, from http://www.cox-washington.com/reporters/content/reporters/ stories/2006/02/03/BC_PATRIOT_ACT02_COX.html

Eggen, D. (2005, July 30). Senate approves partial renewal of Patriot Act. [Electronic Version]. *The Washington Post,* p. A03. Retrieved August 17, 2005, from http://www. washingtonpost.com

Eggen, D., & Tate, J. (2005, June 12). U.S. campaign produces few convictions on terrorism charges. [Electronic Version]. *The Washington Post*, p. A01. Retrieved July 25, 2006, from http://www.washingtonpost.com

Epstein, E. (2005, December 19). *Bush defends eavesdropping, blasts senators on Patriot Act.* Retrieved December 21, 2005, from http://www.sfgate.com/cgi-bin/article.cgi?f=/c/a/ 2005/12/19/MNG9JGAFEV10.DTL

Epstein, E. (2005, December 24). *Bush to face tough questions over Patriot Act, spy orders.* Retrieved December 29, 2005, from http://www.sfgate.com/cgi-bin/article.cgi?f=/c/a/ 2005/12/24/MNGBOGD4FF1.DTL

Espo, D. (2006, February 9). *Tentative deal is reached on Patriot Act.* Retrieved March 20, 2006, from http://www.political-news.org/breaking/22476/tentative-deal-is-reached-on-patriot-act.html

Etzioni, A. (2003, May 2). Patriot Act is needed, but so are revisions. [Electronic Version]. *The Christian Science Monitor,* p. 11. Retrieved June 7, 2003, from http://www.gwu.edu/ ~ccps/etzioni/B419.html

Etzioni, A. (2006, January 11). *Patriot Act is convenient target.* Retrieved May 2, 2006, from http://www.usatoday.com/news/opinion/editorials/2006-01-11-patriot-act-edit_x.htm -

Ferraro, T. (2005, December 14). *House votes to renew anti-terrorism Patriot Act.* Retrieved December 15, 2005, from http://www.redorbit.com/news/display/?id=330313

Fisher, W. (2005, February 25). *Senator seeks to curb controversial "Patriot Act."* Retrieved August 30, 2005, from http://www.commondreams.org/cgi-bin/print.cgi?file=/ headlines05/0225-10.htm

Forster, S. (2005, December 23). *Patriot Act deadline poses a challenge, Feingold says.* Retrieved December 29, 2005, from http://www.jsonline.com/story/index.aspx?id= 380215

FOX News. (2005, June 16). *FOX news/opinion dynamics poll, 16 June 05.* [Data File] Retrieved June 6, 2005, from www.foxnews.com/projects/pdf/poll_061605.pdf

FOX News. (2005, July 22). House oks extending patriot act. Retrieved August 19, 2005, from http://www.foxnews.com/story/0,2933,163219,00.html

Frommer, F. J. (2006, March 3). Patriot Act passage will cap long Feingold-Sensenbrenner battle. *The Associated Press State & Local Wire.* Retrieved March 21, 2006, from LexisNexis Academic database.

Daly, M. (2005, December 16). NW democrats hail Senate rejection of USA Patriot Act. [Electronic Version]. *Seattle Post-Intelligencer.* Retrieved December 20, 2005, from http://seattlepi.nwsource.com–

Deans, B. (2006, February 3). *House approves temporary extension of Patriot Act.* Retrieved August 17, 2006, from http://www.cox-washington.com/reporters/content/reporters/ stories/2006/02/03/BC_PATRIOT_ACT02_COX.html

Glendinning, M. (2005, July 7). *Timeline: Al Qaeda attacks on western targets.* Retrieved August 7, 2006, from http://www.npr.org/templates/story/story.php?storyId=4733944

Grier, P. (2006, March 3). *How the Patriot Act came in from the cold.* Retrieved March 3, 2006, from http://www.csmonitor.com/2006/0303/p01s03-uspo.htm

Hirschkorn, P. (2005, March 1). *Federal judge: Charge Padilla or release him.* Retrieved August 10, 2006, from http://www.cnn.com/2005/LAW/03/01/padilla.ruling/

Hirschkorn, P. (2006, May 5). *Moussaoui curses America but judge gets final word.* Retrieved August 10, 2006, from http://www.cnn.com/2006/LAW/05/04/moussaoui.verdict/ index.html

Holland, J. (2005, December 8). *House, Senate to extend Patriot Act.* Retrieved December 12, 2005, from http://www.news14charlotte.com/content/top_stories/nationalworld_news/?SecID=334&ArID=108544

Holland, J. J. (2005, November 17). Legislation renewing Patriot Act stalls. [Electronic Version]. *The Washington Post.* Retrieved November 21, 2005, from http://www.washingtonpost. com/wp-dyn/content/article/2005/11/17/AR2005111700844.html

Holland, J. J. (2005, December 21). *Senators near deal to extend Patriot Act.* Retrieved December 22, 2005, from http://abcnews.go.com/Politics/wireStory?id=1431210

Hunter, M. (2005, December 19). *Democrats aim to 'mend,' not end Patriot Act.* Retrieved December 20, 2005, from http://www.cnsnews.

com/ViewPolitics.asp?Page=% 5CPolitics%5Carchive%5C20051 2%5CPOL20051219b.html

Hsu, S. S. (2006, April 18). Former Fla. Professor to be deported. [Electronic Version]. *The Washington Post,* p. A03. Retrieved May 14, 2006, from http://www.washingtonpost. com

Hsu, S. S., & Eggen, D. (2005, December 6). Fla. Professor is acquitted in case seen as Patriot Act test. *The Washington Post,* p. A01. Retrieved December 13, 2005, from http://www. washingtonpost. com

Hudson, A. (2005, November 26). Time favors foes of Patriot Act. [Electronic Version]. *The Washington Times.* Retrieved December 5, 2005, from http://www.washingtontimes. com/national/20051125-113235-3982r.htm

Hudson, A. (2006, March 13). *Feingold pushes for Bush censure.* Retrieved March 13, 2006, from http://www.washingtontimes.com/national/20060313-123143-3992r.htm

Kellman, L. (2005, June 8). *Senate gives FBI more Patriot Act power.* Retrieved July 4, 2005, from http://www.sfgate.com/cgi-bin/article.cgi?file=/n/a/2005/06/07/national/ w162204D49. DTL&type=printable

Kellman, L. (2005, November 16). *Tentative deal on Patriot Act, sources say.* Retrieved November 16, 2005, from http://www.sfgate.com/cgi-bin/article.cgi?f=/n/a/2005/11/16/ national/w115802S58.DTL

Kellman, L. (2005, December 23). *Congress extends Patriot Act 1 month.* Retrieved December 29, 2005, from http://www.findarticles.com/p/articles/mi_qn4155/is_20051223/ ai_n15963362

Kellman, L. (2006, February 28). *Sen. Byrd regrets voting for the Patriot Act.* Retrieved June 22, 2006, from http://www.sfgate.com/cgi-bin/article.cgi?file=/news/archive/2006/02/28/ national/w083721S89. DTL

Kiefer, H. M. (2003, June 3). *Public's partisanship evident on terror issue.* Retrieved August 16, 2005, from http://www.gallup.com

Knight, P. (2005, April 8). *We must never let the terrorists win.* Retrieved September 23, 2006, from http://www.michnews.com/cgi-bin/artman/exec/view.cgi/141/7772

Langer, G. (2005, June 9). *Poll: Support seen for Patriot Act.* Retrieved June 28, 2006, from
http://abcnews.go.com/US/print?id=833703

Lebowitz, L. (2003, February 25). Federal case against Florida professor treads new ground under Patriot Act [Electronic version]. *The Miami Herald (Knight Ridder/Tribune News Service),* p. K2478. Retrieved April 24, 2005, from the Infotrac Web database.

Lester, W. (2005, August 29). *Poll: Info shrinks Patriot Act support.* Retrieved June 28, 2006, from http://www.sfgate.com/cgi-bin/article.cgi?file=/news/archive/2005/08/29/ national/w151949D27.DTL

Lichtblau, E. (2005, November 11). Lawmakers meet to settle differences on Patriot Act. [Electronic Version]. *The New York Times,* p. A.20. Retrieved November 11, 2005, from http://www.nytimes.com

Lichtblau, E. (2005, December 9). Congress reaches Patriot Act deal. [Electronic Version]. *International Herald Tribune.* Retrieved December 12, 2005, from http://www.iht. com/bin/print_ipub.php?file=/articles/2005/12/09/news/patriot.php

Lungren, J., & Shawn, T. (2005, November 18). *Sensenbrenner statement on status of Patriot Act conference agreement.* Retrieved November 21, 2005, from http://releases. usnewswire.com/printing.asp?id=56979

Lungren, J., & Shawn, T. (2006, January 5). *Sensenbrenner to highlight civil liberty safeguards in Patriot Act conference report.* Retrieved May 1, 2006, from http://releases. usnewswire.com/GetRelease.asp?id=58911

MacDonald, H. (2005, April 8). *The Patriot Act is no slippery slope: Protecting ourselves doesn't lead to tyranny.* Retrieved April 8, 2005, from http://www.city-journal.org/ html/eon_04_08_05hm.html

Madigan, M. (2002, October 16). ACLU campaign challenges Patriot Act. *P. C. World.* Retrieved September 20, 2004, from http://www.pcworld.com/article/id,106002-page,1/article.html

Markon, J. (2005, December 1). Appeals court balks at Padilla transfer. [Electronic Version.] *The Washington Post,* p. A02. Retrieved August 10, 2006, from http://www. washingtonpost.com

McCullagh, D. (2005, December 12). *Patriot Act critics propose temporary extension.* Retrieved December 14, 2005, from http://news.com.com/Patriot+Act+critics+propose+ temporary+extension/2100-1028_3-5992347.html

McCullagh, D. (2005, December 12). *Perspective: Must we renew the Patriot Act?* Retrieved December 14, 2005, from http://news.com.com/Must+we+renew+the+Patriot+Act/2010-1028_3-5989887.html

McCullagh, D., & Broache, A. (2005, December 8). *Patriot Act renewal draws filibuster threat.* Retrieved December 12, 2005, from http://news.zdnet.com/2100-1009_22-5987892.html

McMullan, M. (2005, July 25). *Patriot Act provisions renewed in House.* Retrieved July 27, 2005, from http://www.idsnews.com/news/story.php?id=30346

Mitchell, L. (2005, August 15). *Blood for oil: The only justification that makes sense.* Retrieved October 22, 2005, from http://harpers.org/BloodForOil.html

Moore, D. W. (2001, October 3). *Support for war on terrorism rivals support for WWII: Vietnam War received least support.* Retrieved August 16, 2005, from http://www.gallup.com

Moore, D. W. (2003, September 8). *Worry about terrorism increases: Fifty-four percent of Americans expect new acts of terrorism in the United States in the next several weeks.* Retrieved August 16, 2005, from http://www.gallup.com

Moore, D. W. (2003, September 9). *Public little concerned about Patriot Act: Wants civil liberties respected, but feels Bush administration has not gone "too far" in restricting liberties.* Retrieved August 15, 2005, from http://www.gallup.com

Murdock, D. (2006, February 1). *Let the numbers do the talking: Patriot Act successes.* Retrieved August 6, 2006, from http://www.nationalreview.com/murdock/ murdock200602011350.asp

Novak, V. (2003, October 27). How the Moussaoui case crumbled. [Electronic Version]. *Time, 162*(17).

Nyhan, P. (2005, April 27). *High gas prices really sting low-wage workers.* Retrieved October 21, 2005, from http://seattlepi.nwsource.com/local/221825_gasprices27.html

O'Harrow, R., Jr. (2002, October 27). Six weeks in Autumn. [Electronic Version]. *The Washington Post,* p. W06. Retrieved January 1, 2005, from http://www. washingtonpost.com

Parry, W. (2006, March 18). *Patriot Act game pokes fun at government.* Retrieved June 22, 2006, from http://www.breitbart.com/news/2006/03/18/D8GEA4PG0.html

Pickler, N. (2005, June 9). *Bush: Patriot Act helped to nab terrorists.* Retrieved August 8, 2006, from http://www.sfgate.com/cgi-bin/article.cgi?f=/n/a/2005/06/09/national/ w092105D91.DTL

Pickler, N. (2006, March 9). *Bush signs renewal of Patriot Act.* Retrieved June 21, 2006, from http://www.newsvine.com/_news/2006/03/09/127173-bush-signs-renewal-of-patriot-act

Pike, G. H. (2005, December 26). *Congress extends USA Patriot Act by 1 month*. Retrieved December 29, 2005, from http://www.infotoday.com/newsbreaks/nb051226-1.shtml

Political News. (2005, February 4). *Gonzales sworn in as US attorney general (AFP)*. Retrieved August 28, 2005, from http://www.political-news.org/breaking/6057/gonzales-sworn-in-as-us-attorney-general

Prager, D. (2004, July 6). *Michael Moore and American self-hatred*. Retrieved October 20, 2005, from http://www.wnd.com/news/printer-friendly.asp?ARTICLE_ID=39300

Preston, J. (2004, September 30). Judge strikes down section of Patriot Act allowing secret subpoenas of Internet data. [Electronic Version]. *The New York Times*, p. A26. Retrieved October 1, 2004, from http://www.nytimes.com

Pulliam, D. (2004, September 22). *Justice official defends Patriot Act*. Retrieved August 29, 2005, from http://www.govexec.com/dailyfed/0904/092204dp2.htm

Regan, T. (2005, June 6). 'Secret' Senate meeting on Patriot Act. [Electronic Version]. *The Christian Science Monitor*. Retrieved June 6, 2005, from http://www.csmonitor.com/ 2005/0606/dailyUpdate.html

Riechmann, D. (2005, December 11). Bush urges Congress to renew Patriot Act. [Electronic Version]. *Kilgore New Herald*. Retrieved December 12, 2005, from http:// www.kilgorenewsherald.com/news/2005/1211/Front_Page/004.html

Risen, J., & Lichtblau, E. (2005, December 16). Bush lets U.S. spy on callers without courts. [Electronic Version]. *The New York Times*, p. A1. Retrieved December 21, 2005, from http://www.nytimes.com

Roper, P. (2006, January 6). *Salazar expects compromise on Patriot Act.* Retrieved January 11, 2006, from http://www.chieftain.com/print. php?article=/metro/1136538450/3

Ryan, T. (2005, August 22). *The writing on "the wall."* Retrieved August 23, 2005, from http://www.frontpagemag.com/Articles/ReadArticle.asp?ID=19218

Saad, L. (2001, October 31). *Americans want tighter airport security at any cost: Majority supports every major proposal.* Retrieved August 16, 2005, from http://www.gallup.com

Saad, L. (2001, December 10). *Fear of terrorism subsides despite persistent concerns about nation's security: Only 29% are highly confident future attacks can be prevented.* Retrieved August 16, 2005, from http://www.gallup.com

Saad, L. (2002, June 7). *Fewer Americans perceive anti-terror war as successful: But Americans' fear of being a victim holds stead.* Retrieved August 16, 2005, from http://www.gallup.com

Saad, L. (2004, March 2). *Americans generally comfortable with patriot act: Few believe it goes too far in restricting civil liberties.* Retrieved August 15, 2005, from http://www.gallup.com

Salazar, K. (2006, March 12). *New Patriot Act is an improvement.* Retrieved March 3, 2006, from http://www.chieftain.com/print. php?article=/editorial/1142150458/4

Schepers, E. (2005, August 20). *Good news, bad news on Patriot Act.* Retrieved August 27, 2005, from http://www.pww.org/article/articleview/7574/0/

Schepers, E. (2005, December 1). Renewal of Patriot Act runs into trouble. [Electronic Version]. *People's Weekly World.* Retrieved December 5, 2005, from http://www.pww.org/ article/articleprint/8196/

Shawl, J. (2006, February 10). *Senate approval of long-term Patriot Act renewal now likely.* Retrieved March 20, 2006, from http://jurist.law.pitt.edu/paperchase/2006/02/senate-approval-of-long-term-patriot.php

Sherman, M. (2005, November 22). *Dirty bomb suspect Padilla indicted.* Retrieved August 10, 2006, from http://www.sfgate.com/cgi-bin/article.cgi?f=/n/a/2005/11/22/national/ w080854S36.DTL

Sniffen, M. J. (2006, May 12). Moussaoui appeals judgment and sentence. [Electronic Version]. *The Washington Post.* Retrieved May 14, 2006, from http://www.washingtonpost.com/ wp-dyn/content/article/ 2006/05/12/AR2006051200367.html

Spencer, R. (2006, January 18). *How the Patriot Act saves lives.* Retrieved May 2, 2006, from http://www.frontpagemag.com/Articles/ReadArticle.asp?ID=20953

Stacy, M. (2005, December 9). Terror case result casts shadow on Patriot Act. [Electronic Version]. *The Star Ledger.* Retrieved December 12, 2005, from http://www.nj.com−

Sununu, J. E. (2006, February 12). Patriot Act deal balances liberty, security. [Electronic Version]. *Concord Monitor,* p. D01. Retrieved March 20, 2006, from http://nl.newsbank. com

Talent J., & Feinstein, D. (2006, February 10). *Talent-Feinstein combat meth legislation included in Patriot Act reauthorization compromise.* Retrieved March 10, 2006, from http://feinstein.senate.gov/06releases/r-meth-patriot.htm

Tirrell-Wysocki, D. (2005, December 19). *Bush blasts Patriot Act critics, including Sununu.* Retrieved December 20, 2005, from http://www.fosters.com/apps/pbcs.dll/article? AID=/20051219/NEWS0202/112190116/-1/services0510

Townsend, F. F. (2005, December 20). Pass the Patriot Act. [Electronic Version]. *The Salt Lake Tribune.* Retrieved December 22, 2005, from http://www.sltrib.com/opinion/ci_3327614

USA Today. (2006, January 9). *USA Today/CNN Gallup Poll.* Retrieved May 2, 2006, from http://www.usatoday.com/news/polls/2006-01-09-poll.htm#patriot

Vlahos, K. B. (2006, January 23). *Patriot Act fix wedged among many priorities.* Retrieved May 2, 2006, from http://www.foxnews.com/story/0,2933,182451,00.html

Wallace, C. (2005, July 24). *Transcript: AG Alberto Gonzales on 'FOX News Sunday'.* Retrieved August 17, 2005, from http://www.foxnews.com/story/0,2933,163494,00. html

Wallace, C. (2006, January 22). *Transcript: Sen. Dick Durbin on 'FOX News Sunday'.* Retrieved May 2, 2006, from http://www.foxnews.com/story/0,2933,182436,00.html

Windrem, R. (n.d.). *Hunt for Al-Qaida: Al-Qaida timeline: Plots and attacks.* Retrieved August 7, 2006, from http://www.msnbc.msn.com/id/4677978/

INDEX

A

Able Danger 202, 223, 227
Adams, John 117, 160
Afghanistan 19, 27, 61, 63, 64, 81, 82, 170, 201, 242
al-Arian, Sami 51, 223, 224, 227
al-Qaeda 81, 82, 156, 202
al-Qaida 81
Alien and Sedition Act 108, 114, 117
Alien Enemy Act 108, 114
American Civil Liberties Union 93
  ACLU 12, 83, 84, 92, 93, 94, 95, 96, 97, 102, 118, 164, 201, 204, 205, 212, 215, 220, 245
anthrax 17, 19, 108, 169, 227
Anti-Terrorism and Effective Death Penalty Act 58
Antiterrorism Enhancement Act of 2003 99
Ashcroft, John 15, 83, 92, 98, 101, 102, 162, 163, 164, 179, 187, 188, 201
Atta, Mohamed 202, 203

B

Benjamin Franklin True Patriot Act 99, 203
Bin Laden, Osama 46, 50, 51, 78
biological weapons 42, 49, 86
Bush, George 18, 76, 77, 114, 135, 150, 151, 152, 154, 163, 168, 187, 188, 201, 226, 227, 228, 244, 246, 256, 263, 269
Byrd, Robert 253

C

Capone, Al 46, 50, 51
Carter, David 76

Carter, Jimmy 203
CHAOS 111
Cheney, Dick 16, 179, 242
Chinese Act 114
Chinese Exclusion Act 109
Clinton, Bill 92, 113, 203
COINTELPRO 111
Communications Act of 1934 25
Congressional Research Service 14
Conyers, John 194, 207, 219, 302
Craig, Larry 212, 221, 224, 226, 230, 250
Crime and Security Act 2001 56
Cuba 62

D

Debs, Eugene V. 109
DeLay, Tom 206
Dempsey, James X. 213
Dinh, Viet 80, 203
Domestic Security Enhancement Act of 2003 179, 180
double jeopardy 66, 67, 68
Durbin, Dick 212, 215, 221, 243, 244, 252

E

Emergency Detention Act 57, 110
enemy combatant 59, 60, 61, 63, 64, 65, 66, 68
Eshoo, Anna 204
Espionage Act 109, 114

F

FBI Awareness Program 99
Feingold, Russ 16, 17, 18, 100, 212, 213, 214, 215, 221, 222, 224, 225, 226, 232, 243, 250, 251,

252, 253, 254, 256, 269
Feinstein, Dianne 15, 212, 214, 252
First Amendment 9, 26, 32, 84, 94, 96, 132, 133, 136
Fitzgerald, Patrick 78
Flake, Jeff 207
Fourth Amendment 11, 94, 121, 213
Freedom to Read Act 203, 204, 207, 212
Freedom to Read Protection Act 99

G

Gallup, George 160
Gonzales, Alberto 201, 224, 245
Graves, Lisa 204
Greenpeace 83
Guantanamo Bay 55, 61, 62, 68, 69, 183, 253
Gun Owners of America 12, 91, 212

H

Hamdi, Yaser Esam 61
Hamdi v. Rumsfeld 61, 97
Hatch, Orrin 15, 16, 50, 187, 211
Homeland Security Act 58
Hoover, Edgar J. 110
House Judiciary Committee 14, 16, 17, 85, 204, 205, 231, 241, 247, 256
House Rules Committee 203

I

Illegal Immigration Reform and Immigrant Responsibility Act 58

J

Jackson, Robert 86
Jefferson, Thomas 117
Johnson v. Eisentrager 62

K

Kerry, John 77, 187, 188, 227
Korean War 60, 167
Kyl, Jon 214

L

Leahy, Patrick 15, 16, 41, 187, 222, 224, 226, 242, 253

M

McCain, John 214
McCarran-Walter Act of 1952 110
McCarran Act of 1950 110, 114
McCarthy, Joseph 207
Milligan, Ex Parte 65
Moore, Michael 39, 102
Moussaoui, Zarcarias 65, 66, 68

N

Netanyahu, Benjamin 86

O

O'Neill, Tip 34
Office of Intelligence Policy and Review 113
Olson, Barbara 102
Omnibus Crime Control and Safe Streets Act 112

P

Padilla v. Bush 63
Palmer Raids 67, 98, 109, 118
Pearl Harbor 87, 151, 167, 168
polling 82, 159, 160, 161, 162, 164, 167, 168, 169, 170, 172, 173

Q

Quirin, Ex Parte 60, 61

R

Rasul v. Bush 97
Revolutionary Armed Forces of Columbia 82
Ridge, Tom 118
Roberts, Pat 211, 212, 213
Rockefeller, Jay 212
Rohrabacher, Dna 206

Roosevelt, Franklin D. 57, 60, 76, 110, 167
Rumsfeld v. Padilla 97

S

Salazar, Ken 212, 221, 244
Sanders, Bernie 99, 203, 204
Science, State, Justice & Commerce Appropriations Act for FY 2006 204
Sedition Act of 1918 109, 114
Senate Intelligence Committee 107, 211
Sensenbrenner, Jim 187, 205, 206, 220, 231, 241, 242, 246, 247, 252, 256
sneak and peek 25, 91, 94, 201, 215, 221, 241, 251, 261
Soviet Union 86, 110
Specter, Arlen 211, 214, 215, 221, 222, 227, 242, 247
Subversive Activities Control Act 110
Sununu, John 221, 224, 226, 229, 230, 244, 250, 251
Sununu Compromise 250, 251, 252, 253, 256

T

Taft-Hartley Act 110
The League of Women Voters 207, 215
Torrio, Johnny 50
Truman, Harry 60, 76, 167

U

United States v. Truong Dinh Hung 113
USA Patriot Act Additional Reauthorizing Act of 2006 250
USA Patriot Improvement and Reauthorization Act of 2005 214, 251, 253, 254

V

Vietnam War 253
Visa Entry Reform Act 58

W

Walker Lindh, John 62, 82
Watergate 112
Wilson, Woodrow 109
World War I 109, 167
World War II 60, 62, 67, 110, 118

Made in the USA
Columbia, SC
02 April 2025